Women, Work and Achievement

The Endless Revolution

Bernard Carl Rosen

Professor of Sociology
Cornell University

MACMILLAN

First published 1989

Published by
THE MACMILLAN PRESS LTD
Houndmills, Basingstoke, Hampshire RG21 2XS
and London
Companies and representatives
throughout the world

Printed in Hong Kong

British Library Cataloguing-in-Publication Data
Rosen, Bernard Carl
  Women, work and achievement
  1. Women. Employment. Implications of psychosocial
  aspects of human sex differences.
  I. Title.
  331.4′01′9

ISBN 0–333–48868–7

ISBN 0–333–48869–5 pbk

SB 1886 /12.99 11 90

To my brother
Boris

Contents

List of Tables   viii

List of Charts and Figures   x

Preface   xi

1. The Waning of Sexual Inequality   1
2. Women in the Labour Force   19
3. Sex Differences in Early Achievement   35
4. The Social Context of Sex Role Socialisation   52
5. The Sex Role and Female Personality   82
6. The Chameleon Syndrome   109
7. Sex Differences in the Status Attainment Process   148
8. Domestic Roles and Occupational Choice   181
9. Conclusion   208

Appendix: People, Places, Procedures   217

Notes   227

Index   238

List of Tables

3.1   Mean IQ and Grades, by Sex and Country   41

3.2   Correlations of IQ and Grades with Educational and Occupational Expectations   45

3.3   Mean Activities and Awards Scores, by Sex and Country   48

4.1   Mean Perception of Parents Scores, by Sex and Country   68

4.2   Mean Evaluation Scores of Parental Work Role, by Sex and Country   74

4.3   Correlation of Adolescents' Educational and Occupational Expectations with Parental Indices, by Sex and Country   78

4.4   Adolescents' Educational and Occupational Expectations Regressed on Independence Index, Age and Social Status, by Sex and Country   80

5.1   Mean Self-assessment Scores, by Sex and Country   92

5.2   Correlation of Self-assessment Scores with Social Status, Independence Index, Academic Grades, Educational and Occupational Expectations, by Sex and Country   94

5.3   Mechanisms for Handling Anger, by Sex and Country   104

5.4   Correlation of Anger Index Scores with Social Status, Independence, Age, Academic Grades, and Educational and Occupational Expectations, by Sex and Country   106

6.1   Mean Acceptance of Sex Role Stereotypes, by Sex and Country   119

6.2   Mean Perception of Opposite Sex, by Sex and Country   124

6.3   Mean Sex Role Behaviour, by Sex and Country   127

6.4   Mean Chameleon Syndrome Score, by Sex in the United States and Britain   135

6.5   Mean Chameleon Syndrome Score, by Intensity of Parental Pressures towards Chameleonism in the United States and Britain   139

6.6 Mean Chameleon Syndrome Score, by the Type of
     Dating Relationship for 11th and 12th Grade
     Females in the United States and Britain   142
6.7 Mean Chameleon Syndrome Score, by Level of
     Domestic Orientation in the United States and
     Britain   144
7.1 Percentage of Type of Educational Expectation, by
     Sex and Country   156
7.2 Percentage of Level of Occupational Expectation, by
     Sex and Country   161
7.3 Coefficients of a Model of Status Expectations for
     11–12th Grade Females, Trivial Paths Deleted   166–7
7.4 Coefficients of a Model of Status Expectations for
     11–12th Grade Males, Trivial Paths Deleted   168–9
7.5 Direct, Indirect and Total Effects of Status
     Expectations, 11–12th Grade Females and Males   172–3
8.1 Means of Domestic Expectation Variables, by Sex
     and Country   194
8.2 Mean Sex Role Values and Sex Role Stereotypes, by
     Life-style Expectation for Females in Three
     Countries   196
8.3 Percentage Distribution of Occupational and
     Labour Force Participation Expectations, by Sex
     and Country   200
8.4 Discriminant Analysis for Sex-typicality of
     Occupational Expectation Groups, Females with
     Dual Role Expectations   205

List of Charts and Figures

CHARTS

4.1   Statements about Parents   67

6.1   The Chameleon Syndrome Index   133

FIGURE

7.1   A Causal Model of Status Expectations   165

Preface

This is a book about the impact of the industrial society and its techno-service sector on women, on their expectations, values, personality, and achievements in the labour force. It explores the changes that have occurred in the female sex role, in the personality of women and its origins in the family and peer group, in the quantity and quality of positions available to women in the paid labour force, and in the occupational achievement of women in Western industrial societies. But this book does more than describe what is happening; it attempts to explain why it is happening and what its effects are on women and society.

Inevitably, the book cuts against the grain of the times. It challenges the orthodox wisdom that industrialisation and modernity necessarily weakened the economic position of women and undermined their self-esteem and security, leaving them exposed to exploitation. Running through the book is a unifying theme: that the industrial society stresses individualism and achievement, which, far from damaging women, actually strengthens them; that the stress on individualism encourages egalitarianism and weakens the ideological underpinnings of sexual segregation in the workplace; that the stress on individual achievement changes the sex roles of society and alters the personalities of the women and men who perform them, producing as one of its effects a new woman whose achievements are exciting comment and admiration.

Most of the material examined in this book is drawn from my research on female and male adolescents in the United States, Britain and Italy, and on social change in Brazil. Adolescents are apt subjects for research on changes in sex roles, personality, and behaviour because at their stage in life change is especially noticeable and its origins in family, peer group, and the school still accessible to the researcher. But this is not just a book about adolescents in four countries. Rather, the adolescent is treated as a case in point, as an example of what is happening to sex roles and achievement in modern societies. In addition to my own data, I also draw upon material collected by researchers in other countries and disciplines.

To the best of my knowledge no other book has sought to do what this book has done. No other book contains the kind of cross-national interview and survey data presented here; no other book examines the relationships of sex roles and personality to occupational expectations and achievement within a context of changing industrial society; no other book links the psychological origins of female achievement to macro-social change. This is not to say that there are no other books on women and achievement. But these books are either surveys of existing research or collections of loosely related articles, often without theoretical coherence or significance. In contrast, this book presents the reader with an integrative theoretical perspective buttressed by empirical data specifically collected to test an overarching hypothesis. Moreover, this book is unlike others in that it employs a multi-disciplinary approach, which draws freely upon historical, anthropological, psychological, and sociological sources.

The data reported in this volume were collected over a period of twenty years in four countries and on three continents. Over the years many people and institutions advised and helped me in the collection and analysis of the data and put their resources and facilities at my disposal. My debt to them is enormous, far greater than I can acknowledge in this limited space, and though I can mention only a few of them here I have not forgotten the others. I shall always be grateful for their help.

In Brazil I was helped by Hebe Guimaraes Leme and Darcy da Silva. I shall always remember with pleasure the friendship they showed me during my years in Brazil. Among my American colleagues, I am particularly indebted to my graduate students, who helped design and administer the questionnaire in the United States. Principal among them were Carol Aneshensel, Barbara Richardson, Carol Ireson, David Bender, and Christine Russell. With one of these students, Carol Aneshensel, I published papers, portions of which are reported in this book; others used the data to obtain PhD degrees; all contributed generously of their imagination and energy to the research. In Britain I was substantially helped by Bruce Choppin, then at the Foundation for Educational Research in England and Wales, who vouched for my scholarly legitimacy when I approached various headmasters for permission to work in their schools, and who helped me find staff to administer the questionnaire. T. S. Robertson advised me on the class system in England and provided critical help in assigning students to various social strata. In Italy I was fortunate to work with Professors Dora Capozza and Anna Maria Manganelli Rattazzi of the University of Padua and Professor Alma Commucci Tajoli of the University of Verona. Their help was of the utmost importance in translating the questionnaire, gaining access to the schools, and collecting the data. I am deeply grateful to them for their help and friendship.

I want also to express my appreciation to the institutions that supported my work. At different times the National Institute of Mental Health, the National Science Foundation, and the Cornell Office of Sponsored Research provided funds to cover the heavy costs of conducting cross-national research. In Britain the Foundation for Educational Research in England and Wales, and in Italy, the Department of Psychology at the University of Padua, provided me with office space in which to work. Cornell University gave me leaves of absence to conduct research in Britain and Italy and generous amounts of computer time. I want to thank Ann Haas for cheerfully typing the various drafts of the manuscript. To all these people, and to the many field workers, school administrators, and students who participated in the research, I shall always be indebted. For without their help this book would literally not have been possible.

Bernard Carl Rosen
Ithaca, New York

1 The Waning of Sexual Inequality

Throughout the industrialised world women are entering the labour force in unprecedented numbers: a movement that began as a trickle in the last century has become a torrent. No longer content to stay at home, impatient with the ties that bind them to the kitchen and the nursery, women are exchanging the apron and baby carriage for the business suit and computer, and now seek new experiences and rewards in paid employment. But women have done more than merely join the labour force; they have changed it. To a degree unparalleled in history, women have achieved lucrative and important positions in government, in the skilled professions, and in science and business, irreversibly changing the sexual composition of the labour force. Today, women work in all sectors of the economy and compete with men, often successfully, for advancement in fields long dominated by males, a revolutionary break with the past that is changing women and society.

Fashionable opinion gives to the women's movement virtually all the credit for starting this revolution and keeping it going. First as isolated voices, then as inspirited small groups, and finally as a powerful organised social movement, women attacked the barriers erected through the centuries to deny them economic and social justice. As fighters and revolutionaries they have been remarkably successful. One by one the legal barriers to the movement of women into the labour market fell before the pressure of militant women, who then put in place affirmative action programmes designed to help women enter areas previously closed to them. True, the informal barriers, prejudice and many subtle forms of discrimination, have proved difficult to dismantle, but they too are under attack and must fall eventually, for who can doubt that women will succeed ultimately in their struggle for full and equal economic opportunity.

But women were not alone in this battle: they had powerful allies – industrialisation and its offspring, the techno-service economy – without whose collaboration the eventual success of women's struggle for economic equality would have been uncertain and perhaps impossible, because a strong animus against sexual equality pervades traditional

1

social circles. Fortunately, industrialisation engendered social and psychological changes that not only weakened the conventional resistance to sexual equality, it also created a voracious need for labour. To satisfy this need, the industrial society had to open its opportunity structure to women; it had to recognise that the entry of women into the labour market was both desirable and necessary.[1]

An industrial economy needs women: machines must be tended, letters typed, sales made, claims adjusted, personnel grievances handled, credits and debits entered into the computer, patients and clients serviced; and women have shown that they can do these things as well as men, often better, and usually far more cheaply. That much has long been apparent. More than a century ago industrialists recognised the advantages of hiring women, and with a canny eye to profit and labour peace invited women to work in their factories to weave cloth, make shoes, roll cigars, decorate hats, for they saw that women constituted a vast reservoir of eager, hard-working, docile, cheap labour. They were not mistaken. By the end of the nineteenth century, enough women had responded to these invitations to make them a significant part of the industrial labour force. And when, in the twentieth century, the service sector burgeoned, employers actively recruited more women, this time not merely because of their availability, but also because women were thought to possess personal qualities ideally suited to service work.

Industrialisation not only opens up new opportunities to women, it also alters the psycho-cultural forces that impede their entry and performance in the labour market. For industrialisation erodes the traditional attitudes and values that keep some women out of the labour force altogether, channel others into sex-segregated 'pink ghettos', and hamper the performance of virtually all females who venture into male domains. Industrialisation's emphasis on individualism, on personal worth rather than birth, and on achievement, affects the way society perceives women: the talents and dispositions they are thought to possess and the goals to which they are expected to aspire. In addition, the industrial society, a milieu friendly toward individualistic striving and tolerant of assertive independence, encourages women to pursue achievement without guilt and helps them fend off the hostile reactions of family, friends, and employers who seek to confine women to the home. As a result, women today find that the resistance to their pursuit of achievement has become fragile and rickety; the door to female advancement stands ajar and the guards blocking their way act half-heartedly, seemingly disarmed by ambivalence and doubt. Small wonder, then, that the number of women in the labour force has grown steadily as industrialisation progressed.

MYTH AND REALITY

But can this be true? Were not women workers replaced by industrial machines? Were they not repelled by horrendous factory conditions and exploitative employers, and discriminated against by hostile, male-dominated industrial labour unions? As a result, did not industrialisation in fact drive most women out of the labour force, and were they not kept out until after the Second World War, when changes in the economy and the resurgence of the Women's Movement made most of the barriers to the entry of women into the labour force totter and fall? Sad to relate (for the answer 'yes' to all these questions is dear to many hearts) the data do not confirm the notion that industrialisation expelled women from the labour force, buried them in the home, and robbed them of the satisfaction and self-respect that productive, remunerative work ordinarily brings. Although reliable data on female participation in the labour force in the early years of the Industrial Revolution are extremely scarce, such data as do exist, gleaned mostly from surveys of a few nascent industries in scattered mill and factory towns, show that by the second decade of the nineteenth century women had already become a significant component of the work force in Massachusetts, Manchester, and Milan. Thus in 1821 the Waltham, Massachusetts mills employed 4.5 times as many women as men; by 1860 women in the United States made up 53.4 percent of the workforce in the textile, 45 percent in the clothing, and 27.3 percent in the paper and printing industries.[2]

After 1870, when the United States census began collecting information on women in the labour force, it became clear that a significant number of women were working outside the home. And the number kept growing. In 1900, 20 percent of all females 14 years of age and older were working; by 1950 the percentage of females 16 years and older in the labour force had risen to 24 percent,[3] by 1986, 56 percent of females aged 16 and older, and 63 percent aged 18 to 34, were in the work force.[4]

These statistics clearly show that by the beginning of the twentieth century women had already established a visible and important presence on the work scene.

What are we to make of the argument that industrialisation segregated the sexes into different spheres of work, forcing men to leave home to work for pay and requiring women to remain at home, and that as a result a new ideology of domesticity arose which contributed to the expulsion of women from the labour force? This mid-nineteenth-century ideology, it is said, seduced women into staying at home by extolling the attributes we now consider traditionally feminine and by exhorting them to devote their lives to housewifery and motherhood.[5] Determined to protect motherhood and the family, throngs of writers, lecturers, and clergymen thundered against the idea of women working in factories, arguing that factory work coarsened women, endangered their health, and made them unfit to play their proper role as homemaker. Possibly this polemical outburst caused some women to avoid the labour market, but its appeal could not have been great, largely limited as it was to middle-class women, who at that time showed little interest in working outside the home – indeed there were then few positions they could have filled without losing status. Paid employment appealed mostly to lower class women, who desperately needed the money and to whom the ideology of domesticity, if they knew of it at all, must have seemed remote and impractical. And of course for blacks and other poor women the emulation of middle-class life-style, of which this ideology formed a part, was quite simply out of the question. Not until the affluent years following the Second World War did sizeable numbers of lower-class women have the option of remaining at home, but by then the pattern of women working full-time outside the home had become well established.

Of course, no one can deny that industrialisation made some female jobs redundant. But it created many more: witness the huge influx of women into the mechanised textile, garment, and shoe industries. Nor can we ignore the negative effects of long hours, low wages, and hostile male co-workers on female morale and health. No doubt bad working conditions forced some women, exhausted and dejected, to leave the labour market. But the departees were more than outnumbered by new arrivals: the women who went to work joyously, exulting in new freedoms and opportunities; the women who did so reluctantly, driven by need – money for a sick husband, for indigent parents, or for a brother's education. Still, whatever their reasons, as industrialisation spread, more and more women moved into the labour market.

Granted, the movement of women into the labour force ebbed and flowed. It ebbed when wretched working conditions made the work-place intolerable or when cheap immigrant labour and economic depression caused massive unemployment – but these conditions affected men as well as women. It flowed when economic upswing or war-induced prosperity created severe labour shortages; then employers wooed women with promises of good wages or appeals to patriotism, and invariably women responded. True, after the prosperity subsided, after the war ended, the majority of women returned to full-time homemaking. But some stayed at their workplace, swelling the ranks of gainfully employed females. The idea that industrialisation drove women from the labour market is a myth.

What is the source of this myth and why has it been so endlessly repeated in the literature on women? The original source, apparently, is an influential book by Frederick Engels entitled, *The Origins of the Family, Private Property and the State,* published in 1884. Engels argued that industrial capitalism excluded women from participation in social production and reduced their role and status to that of servants in their own home.[6] But he offered no evidence to support this thesis; his analysis is based principally on historical and ethnographic information about the ancient Greeks, Romans, Germans and Iroquois, none of whom had been touched by industrialisation. Moreover, he specifically excepts proletarian women, whose presence in the work force must have been abundantly obvious to him – his father, after all, was a wealthy textile manufacturer and the son had worked in one of the father's mills. Exclusion from social production applies, then, to middle-class women, whose role in the labour force had been little affected by industrialisation in Engels' day. Nonetheless, from that time to this, many writers, some filled with anti-capitalist bias, others infatuated with idealised pictures of women's condition in the pre-industrial village, have repeated the myth without bothering to check up on its accuracy and without troubling to provide evidence in its support.

But there are other reasons for the myth's persistence apart from sloppy or wishful thinking. To begin with, the myth is rooted in the irrational hatred many intellectuals feel toward industrialisation and modernisation. To intellectuals schooled in a hatred of modern society and taught to loathe industrialisation, the industrial city is a place of dark satanic factories whose smokestacks belch dirt into the grimy, almost unbreathable air, and whose effluents turn the rivers into putrid sludge. Industrialisation evokes in their minds frightful images of people forced from the land, crowded into ghastly city slums, proletarianised and exploited. The city, they say, is an impersonal place, rife with anomie and violence, where rootless people drift through fragmented and anonymous existences, where even pleasure is tawdry and sterile, for without traditional culture to sustain them their lives have been robbed of meaning. In sum, as many intellectuals see it, the city is nothing less than a disaster, a catastrophe that leaves many city-dwellers stunned, helpless and broken.[7]

This unhappy image of the industrial society has a long history. It could be found in the eighteenth century among the gentry of England and America, many of whom distrusted cities and detested industrialisation. Thomas Jefferson, for example, wrote that a yellow fever epidemic should not be considered a tragedy 'since it would discourage the growth of cities in our nation, and I view great cities as pestilence to the morals, the health, and the liberties of man.'[8] Nor were the poets and novelists and literary critics of later periods slow to echo these sentiments. Their aversion to technology and industrialisation was keen, shrill, deep, and articulate. For, as Norman Podhoretz put it 'what else were most of the canonized writers [of England and America] saying – from Blake to Dickens to D. H. Lawrence, from Cooper to Mark Twain to William Faulkner, from Carlyle to Ruskin to Eliot – if not that industrial civilization was a plague and a curse?'[9] Intellectuals today are still echoing these ancient complaints long after most of the distressful conditions that originally evoked them have disappeared.

REVOLUTION AND OPPORTUNITY

Its enemies recognised early that industrialisation was much more than just a new system of production; they could see that it was also a new system of social organisation and a body of related values that insidiously penetrated every sphere of life. Naturally enough, visible change in the productive system first attracted their attention because the changes in this area were truly revolutionary. Production moved from the cottage to the factory; inanimate sources of energy and advanced technology replaced human and animal muscle. For the first time, large numbers of workers laboured in formal, bureaucratic settings controlled by bosses and managers whose authority rested upon their possession of capital, technical skill, and administrative competence. Although these changes were enormously important, they were soon followed by others still more revolutionary. The division of labour became more complex and, because of technological advances, occupational specialisation increased rapidly. The middle class grew prodigiously in size and influence, and the working class became predominantly urban and industrial rather than rural and agricultural. Schools developed to educate the working class and universities grew to train the elite; the communication and transportation systems improved so that information and people circulated rapidly; the market system expanded and the economy took off.

Much has been written about the exploitation and misery caused by the Industrial Revolution, and no doubt to the unemployed and homeless the initial stage of revolution was a disaster. But for those fortunate enough to find a place in the new society – and their number was large – life improved. For example, between 1790 and 1810 money wages increased by 75 percent in Great Britain, and real wages increased by approximately 25 percent between 1800 and 1824, 40 percent from 1824 to 1850 and 77 percent between 1860 and 1900 – improvements in the general standard of living that occurred during a period of particularly wrenching economic and social change.[10] As a result of the Industrial Revolution, the opportunity structure of society opened itself to a horde of newcomers, men and women from all stations of life, people seeking work and advancement, and many had found both.

Many of the industrial society's detractors seem not to have noticed how much it has changed. Gone from most Western societies are many of their noisy and noisome factories; gone is much of the ugly industrial squalor that so offended the sensibilities of Blake, Wordsworth, and Coleridge; gone are the workhouses and the unprotected labour force; gone are the children working in mines and mills under horrendous conditions for pitiable pay. Where dirty smokestack industries once flourished, new sanitised factories now stand, regulated and closely watched by agents of the state to insure that adequate standards of safety and health are observed. Children now attend schools, not sweatshops; the hungry and jobless are cared for by the Welfare State, not left to fend for themselves in a cold and heartless world.

When the smokestack factories closed down, they left behind blighted 'rust belts', huge areas filled with decaying buildings and dying industries. But these are gradually being replaced by high technology factories equipped with automated and robotised machinery, and by service industries that minister to the needs of manufacturers and the general population. A techno-service economy silently emerged as a supplement to the manufacturing and agricultural sectors and soon became the major employer of women, who found in the techno-service sector a warm welcome and ambience in which they felt comfortable. Much of the growth in female employment since the Second World War reflects the enormous structural changes that accompanied the expansion of the techno-service sector in most Western societies. On the east and west coasts of the United States, south-central England and northern Italy, areas especially touched by the techno-service revolution, the lineal descendant of the first industrial revolution and the most recent stage of evolving industrialisation, women are finding eager bidders for their services and employment in a wide variety of jobs, some of which bring with them status, power and wealth.

But structural change will not automatically bring women into the market place or necessarily place them in positions suited to their interests, desires or abilities. Before a structurally created opportunity can attract claimants, it must first be perceived and valued. Without that perception, some women will act as though the barriers to their employment were still in place long after they have fallen, and timidly avoid certain fields for fear of rejection. These women crowd into traditional feminine occupations despite the poor wages, tenuous job security, and low prestige usually associated with stereotypical women's work. Nor will a structurally induced societal need invariably bring a favourable response. Sometimes jobs that desperately need filling go begging for lack of applicants because, despite the great need for their services, women find the work unappealing: the price of acquiring uncongenial skills seems excessive, the promised rewards appear not commensurate with the costs of leaving home, of working in dangerous or dirty surroundings, of jeopardising prized self-esteem. In short, in order for a favourable structural change to affect the behaviour of women they must recognise the change for what it is, they must want to take advantage of it, and they must acquire the attitudes and skills required to exploit the new opportunities society offers them.

For this to occur, two things must happen. First, the role of women in society must change. The traditional female sex role, which incapacitates women who enter the labour force, must be replaced with a new role that permits women to work outside the home, compete with men in the workplace, and pursue occupational achievement without unacceptable physical, psychological, and social costs. Without this change, without a new definition of womanhood, many women – unless driven by poverty – will prefer to stay home performing the tasks they have been socialised to regard as the only ones worthy of a woman's dedication. When necessity drives these women into the labour market, they tend to seek work congruent with their conception of the female role – work that appears feminine. To do otherwise would be to violate the most precious of their sentiments.

Second, women must change: they must acquire new personality traits and values; they must see themselves and their relationships to society, the family, and men in a new light; they must cease being traditional. For the traditional feminine traits – dependence, passivity, a willingness to subordinate oneself to the interests of husband and children – mesh clumsily with the needs of an industrial society. An industrial economy requires independent, competitive, ambitious, achievement-oriented workers in order for it to function smoothly and efficiently. To be sure, many women already possess these traits and await only the opportunity to employ them. But others have never been socialised to work in the competitive male-dominated sectors of the economy, and without the requisite industrial values, personality traits, and skills, they find the going difficult when they venture into non-traditional occupations. Traditional square pegs, they fit poorly into the industrial round hole.

THE INDUSTRIAL VALUE SHIFT

The massive movement of women into the labour force was more than simply a response to the perception of the new opportunities created by structural change; it was also a reaction to a modern value system brought into being by industrialisation – a value system that legitimated and applauded the entry of women into the labour force. For an opportunity must be valued before it will be seized, and as long as the value system gave housewifery and motherhood priority over paid employment outside the home, traditional women ignored the new jobs and stayed at home. Dire necessity might drive a woman into the labour market but her condition was considered pitiable; her husband and children, it was thought, must inevitably suffer from neglect. Comfortably-situated women who pursued careers away from home were considered selfish, insufficiently devoted to their families, and often became the targets of social obloquy. Charles R. Morris gives an example of how some middle-class women were treated even as recently as a generation ago when they went out to work. 'My Irish grandmother worked as a cleaning woman much of her married life, and no one regarded it as particularly remarkable. When my mother went to work in the 1950's, on the other hand, it was a subject of much comment ... the priest regularly sermonized on Sundays about the moral dangers to a family with a working mother. We all kept our heads down.'[11] Only an exceptionally strong-willed and determined woman could stand up to this kind of abuse. Consequently, as long as the prevailing value system inflicted unacceptably high psychological and social costs on working women, the average woman with family responsibilities chose not to take advantage of the new job opportunities. Social values had to change before she could comfortably take her place in the labour force.

But few social inventions resist change more adamantly than social values, particularly those attached to sex roles. Entrenched social interests and popular opinion usually support the existing value system and bitterly resist change. That industrialisation took generations to change the old values is not surprising; that it changed them as drastically as it did is remarkable, perhaps industrialisation's most astonishing accomplishment. Change came inevitably when industrialisation gave women jobs in factories, mills, stores and offices, jobs as demanding of energy and endurance and skill as those performed by men. Side by side with men, women operated machines in textile mills, endured sweatshop conditions in garment lofts, stood long hours to serve customers in departmental stores, handled clients' complaints, and closed deals in business offices. Not only did women perform their jobs as well as men, they often functioned better than men in situations requiring meticulous attention to detail, the ability to endure routine and repetition, or a sensitivity to the expectations of customers and clients. The traditional belief that women could not cope with the rough and tumble of the industrial world, that they lacked the endurance, aptitude, skill and motivation to compete successfully with men in the world of commerce and manufacturing sank in a sea of evidence that drowned opinions to the contrary. In advanced industrial societies today young people take the entry of women into the labour force for granted and hoot with derision at the notion that women cannot function adequately in work milieus away from home.

As the popular perception of women changed, a dramatic shift in values took place: individualism, egalitarianism, and achievement, values intrinsic to industrialisation and part of a larger complex called modernity, but heretofore restricted to males, became attached to the female sex role. Unlike the pre-industrial traditional society, which tends to value hierarchy and submission to the group, the industrial system, particularly in its Western capitalistic form, is inherently individualistic and meritocratic. Before the industrial machine all workers are equal; what matters is the quantity and quality of their work, not their race, sex, or other ascriptive ties. As Daniel Bell points out, individualism, the right 'to be responsible for oneself, to be free of ascriptive ties, to be able to fashion oneself into any image the heart desired' was at the heart of the nineteenth century's conception of liberty.[12] Under industrialisation's influence the individual, not the family, the guild, the tribe or clan, became the basic unit of society.

In its industrial form individualism championed the right of everyone to develop his or her talent; it maintains that ability can be found in the most unlikely places and that society has an obligation to turn talent into skill and put it to use. Although individualism first flourished as a philosophy of the market place, it quickly attracted adherents whose goals were political and whose target was not merely man as worker and employer but man as ruler, father, husband, playmate. And it was as a political as well as an economic value that individualism changed the shape of the relationship between males and females.

Individualism supported women's struggle against male dominance, championed their right to pursue their own best interests, and challenged the traditional male's assumption that his needs must take precedence over the female's. It called for a definition of sex roles that treated men and women as individuals and equals, thus depriving men of one of their principal cultural supports – the notion that males are inherently superior to females and that society functions better when women are submissive to men. On the contrary, individualism and its ideological handmaiden, sexual equality, asserted that society works best when men and women are equal.

From the beginning of the industrial era, women have argued that the denial of equality to women and the refusal of men to treat women as individuals separate from their families, not only damaged women, it also cheated society of the contributions educated and independent women could make to the common weal. Reformers quickly picked up this theme and echoed it throughout the nineteenth century in their campaigns for social change. During this period reformers established schools and colleges to train women in the liberal and practical arts, and lobbied vigorously to open the labour market to women. Education and achievement at work, they believed, would give women the chance to prove their right to equality. Today, women in the newly industrialising countries frequently justify their fight for equality by arguing that only as equals can women make their full contribution to the nation's development. 'We are not asking for liberation', said a leader of the National Women's Congress, Brazil's newly organised feminist movement, 'but participation in the development of our country.'[13] Their arguments did not go unheeded. Brazil, like many other industrialising countries eager for cheap labour and convinced that economic growth is impossible without altering the status of women, built schools to educate women, admitted them into the polling booth, and opened the doors of offices and factories to women seeking jobs.[14] Simple justice commended it; the industrial system, which could not function without women, required it; and women themselves, appealing to the individualistic–egalitarian ideology of industrialisation, demanded it.

The reformers who attacked sexual inequality under the banner of individualism, equality and achievement were simply affirming the rhetoric of the Industrial Revolution. From its beginning the industrial system valued individual achievement to a degree seldom, if ever, found in pre-industrial society, which even today tends to look askance at the achiever. To the pre-industrial mind the achiever is a trouble-maker, someone who excites envy, someone who seeks more than his fair share in a zero-sum world where one person's gain means another's loss, someone who steps out of ranks and upsets the established order. Achievement for the sake of the group may be acceptable, even laudable, but achievement for personal gain threatens the community. Consequently, the pre-industrial society curbs the individualistic striver and uses a panoply of sanctions – ridicule, envy, open hostility – to keep him in line, lest his enthusiasm cause mischief.

But, the reader may object, were not Periclean Athens, Renaissance Italy, and Elizabethan England places of extraordinary individual achievement? And did not incredible bursts of creativity occur there in the arts and sciences well before the advent of industrialisation? Of course, but the splendid achievements of those periods were primarily the work of a tiny elite, people of privileged birth or exceptional talent. Granted, a midwife's son became a philosopher, a glover's son a playwright, a notary's son a painter, but these were extraordinary men; not even the tight hierarchical systems of the times could suppress their magnificent genius. Ordinary people, even in those remarkable times, rarely entered the big games for money, prestige, and power; usually they stayed in their own circles and left the contests for glory to their betters. Then, as now in much of the pre-industrial world, people were expected to stay in their station in life, and those who did not, those who sought to enter a higher stratum through personal achievement, usually evoked the displeasure of the state, the reproaches of the established church, and the dangerous envy of their peers.

In contrast, industrial societies treat achievers generously, almost deferentially, and certainly with respect. They are sought out and encouraged and rewarded because the industrial system needs disciplined, energetic, achievement-oriented workers, women as well as men; workers to operate machines, to organise production, to distribute and sell the multitudinous products of its factories, mills, stores and offices. The industrial system in its capitalistic mode not only accepts individual achievement, it goes one step further – it considers achievement for profit quite respectable. In a capitalistic society achievers may proudly display the fruits of their labour without guilt or fear of public reproof. Even socialist industrial societies, despite an ideology that decries excessive individualism and that puts most economic production under state control, sooner or later discover the vital role individual achievement plays in production – witness the use in the Soviet Union and China of prizes, honours, vacations, and money as devices for motivating workers to increase production.

What society, other than an industrial one, worries about the waste of talent, systematically seeks out bright youngsters of every class, race, ethnic background, and sex, and plies them with scholarships, tempting them with visions of success in order to make achievers of them all, believing that society prospers when individual achievement is encouraged? What other society invites the little people as well as the big ones to enter the race for success? None, for not until the advent of industrialisation was the broad road to achievement opened to the populace; not until the triumph of industrialisation were women beckoned to enter the race for success.

As in any contest not everyone wins; nor is every race fair. Some contests are rigged, others place obstacles before contestants of despised religions, colours, or sex. Still there are many winners, because what sets the industrial society apart from other systems is the unprecedented number and variety of arenas in which people can compete and win, whether on the factory floor, in the executive suite, in the studio and laboratory, or out on the political hustings. And from these many competitions flow a stream of successes, large and small.

ISOMORPHISM AND THE NEW WOMAN

Social roles need appropriately trained performers to give them substance and meaning. Without actors, social roles are mere abstractions, disembodied rules and empty concepts without social consequences. But actors cannot simply be given a script, briefly rehearsed, and then turned loose on life's stage. Sex roles are much too important to be treated so casually because the inept performance of a sex role does more than create personal embarrassment, it seriously jeopardises relationships between the sexes and strains the social system. Consequently, every society exhorts its members to play their sex roles properly, reinforcing role expectations with powerful sanctions: approval and love for obedience to social norms, scorn and ridicule for mild infractions, rejection, ostracism, and prison for serious deviations.

But conformity to societal norms cannot be wholly coerced, no matter how attractive the rewards or damaging the punishments. Force alone usually elicits only grudging acceptance of social responsibilities and sloppy performance of social roles. On the other hand, conformity cannot be left to individual whim either because self-interest could easily lead to evasion of the rules when they prove irksome. In order to ensure that most people perform their social roles properly, including their sex roles, however burdensome or unfair they may be, society must make the individual want to play those roles. 'The demands of his social role', Erich Fromm and Michael Maccoby assert, must become second nature, i.e., a person must want to do what he has to do. Society must produce not only tools and machines but also the type of personality that employs energy voluntarily for the performance of social roles.'[15] This willing conformity to social norms occurs when the needs of society and those of the individual coincide, when, as Talcott Parsons put it, 'What is socially expected becomes individually needed.'[16]

Societal expectations reflect the needs of the social structure, most importantly its dominant mode of production, which in an industrial system requires that workers be disciplined, hard-working, self-reliant and achievement-oriented. Workers must be able to function in large, impersonal, bureaucratic organisations; they must carry out instructions without constant help or surveillance; they must value excellence in work and accept distinctions between workers based upon individual competence and productivity. In short, they must want to compete, to excel, to act independently and assertively; they must want to delay present gratifications in order to ensure future gains; they must prize punctuality and hard work, condemn sloth, and support the drive for success. Persons with these needs are the mainstays of the industrial system.

To make certain that workers possess the personality traits it values, the industrial society mobilises the energies of its most powerful socialisation agents – the family, the school, the workplace, the mass media – and puts them to work. Through exemplification, exhortation and the judicious use of the carrot and the stick, these agents seek to build into boys and girls the personality traits an industrial system considers desirable. In the home, in the schoolroom, in offices and factories, and in the mass media, they advertise the qualities the industrial society values in the citizenry. Parents and teachers proclaim the importance of hard work and achievement; the media celebrate the accomplishments of successful doctors, lawyers, politicians, and soldiers; corporate managers offer workers incentives for increased efficiency and production; and in the market place the give and take of economic exchange rewards the self-reliant, assertive, competitive, crafty buyer or seller. In all these spheres the industrial society sends it agents a message: teach children to value hard work and achievement, make them ambitious, competitive and independent – and their future is assured.

Alert and informed people in the audience get the message. Knowledgeable parents, ambitious for their child's success, have long sought to inculcate industrially valued traits in their sons. Now, recognising that the route to success through individual achievement is open to women, and eager to help their daughters succeed in a competitive world, they strive to imbue their female children with the personality traits an industrial society rewards. Girls as well as boys are urged to compete and to excel at work; girls as well as boys are encouraged to set their sights as high as their talents and circumstances permit. No longer do parents and teachers automatically channel girls into courses and programmes conventionally thought appropriate to females; no longer do they warn girls away from subjects deemed unfeminine – mechanical arts, mathematics, science, subjects which, incidentally, enhance the student's chances for admission into programmes leading to well-paying jobs. (If some girls still avoid these subjects it is less because they are advised against them than because they think them difficult and useless.) Nor do foremen and managers ordinarily shelter women from the hurly burly of the factory floor, the business office, or the market place, as most pre-industrial societies still do. For not only do modern industrial values argue against pampering women, the needs of an industrial system require efficiency at work from everyone without regard to the worker's gender. And so at home, in school, and in the workplace, women are encouraged to become independent, competitive and achievement-oriented, traits young people of both sexes must acquire if they are to succeed in a modern economy.

But more than exhortation and encouragement is at work changing women; the industrial society thrusts women into economic affairs to a degree rarely found in the pre-industrial world. At home not only do women keep accounts, purchase supplies, and decide how scarce resources shall be spent, at work they operate machines, make sales, manage businesses, and take part in the formation of economic policy. Shaping the daily life of others both within and outside the home, handling people, solving problems and making decisions, women acquire the knowledge and skills that enhance self-confidence, independence and competence, traits that serve them well on the job. This is not to say that every aspect of the traditional female personality goes by the board. Important parts of the old personality system remain in place and continue to be admired and rewarded. Thus verbal agility, vivacity and expressiveness, sensitivity and interpersonal skills, all parts of the traditional female personality system, are still considered feminine traits and earn exceptional rewards in the service industries, where the ability to understand and satisfy the customer's needs and wishes often constitute the job's quintessential requirement.

In the industrial world the traditional personality system, with its emphasis on obedience to authority, non-competitiveness and dependence, gives way to a new personality configuration – a new woman, self-reliant and independent, competitive and assertive, achievement-oriented, ambitious and determined to succeed, yet still possessing some of the old traits that mesh well with the rising service economy. It is this new woman who is rapidly moving into occupations long domininated by males.

RESEARCH ARGUMENT AND PLAN

In this book I shall argue that industrialisation and the techno-service economy have narrowed or eliminated many of the traditional differences between the sexes, between the way adolescent girls and boys perceive their sex roles, their parents, their peers of both sexes, and the opportunities awaiting them in a burgeoning economy. Less burdened today than in the past with self-denigrating stereotypes, less hampered by restrictive and over-protective parents, and more willing to be self-assertive and independent, adolescent girls are competing with boys in almost every sphere of activity – in academics, in aesthetics, in politics, and proving that where skill and motivation and hard work count they can do as well as boys, perhaps even better. As a result, the educational and occupational expectations of girls have risen to the point where the differences between the sexes are becoming negligible. No longer can it be said that most girls systematically rule out for themselves, long before entering the job market, the possibility of their advancement into the lucrative, prestigious fields of the labour force. No longer can boys expect to have these fields to themselves.

A change in expectations can have enormous consequences for the future of young people. Low expectations stifle achievement and extinguish serious hopes for occupational success; raise these expectations and the possibility arises that motivation, hard work and luck can do their bit to propel the aspirant along the road to high occupational attainment. High expectations mean that girls are raising their sights and aiming for high occupational targets, confident they can score as many bulls-eyes as boys. These girls are younger versions of the women who have moved so swiftly and vigorously in recent years into occupations once considered the exclusive domains of men.

But how to document the effects of industrialisation and the techno-service economy on the adolescent's peronality, relationships with parents and peers, and educational–occupational expectations? Where to turn for data on changing values, on new perceptions of sex roles, on feelings about changing domestic roles? To literary works, to historical documents, to journalistic reports? Perhaps. But these sources, though valuable for some purposes, provide an extremely fragile base upon which to build a solid argument about the impact of industrialisation on adolescent expectations and female achievement, especially when personality and other individual factors have played a large role in producing change.

To assess the impact of industrialisation on achievement and occupational attainment, I prefer to use the tools of modern social science. For despite their faults – and admittedly they are many – modern research methods usually generate better evidence about changes in sex roles, values and attitudes, perceptions and expectations, than can be found in impressionistic insights, journalistic reports and the literary chronicles of our times. Properly conducted, empirical research can provide evidence about what youngsters are thinking and doing, what their relationships with parents and peers are like, and what future they imagine awaits them. Interviews, surveys of large populations living in different nations, systematic observation and immersion in the cultures of the people being studied, all tools of modern social research, can give the researcher a sense of what is happening to people, how they are responding to change, and what the effects of those changes are.

Five research projects, conducted over a period of twenty years in four countries – the United States, Britain, Italy, and Brazil – provide the bulk of the data upon which this book is based. Data obtained from ethnographic reports of Southern Italy, and through personal observation and interviews in rural Brazil, give us a sense of what life is like in the pre-industrial community. These data are compared with information obtained from adolescents living in highly industrialised America, Britain and Northern Italy. In effect, this comparative study simulates a longitudinal research design, for I shall be arguing that the difference between traditional and modern adolescents in expectations and achievement reflect the changes in sex roles and personality that have been brought about by industrialisation. If this argument is correct, modern American, British and Italian adolescents, despite the differences in the histories and cultures of their countries, resemble each other far more than they do their traditional peers in the pre-industrial world. I used a variety of research techniques – questionnaires, personal interviews, observation of adolescents in natural settings. In addition, I lived and worked in all four countries and talked with adolescents, parents, and local experts on adolescence and family life in their respective countries. In all, about five and a half thousand adolescents, some of their parents, men and women from all walks of life, and a sub-sample of young women took part in the research. How they were selected, the nature of the communities in which they lived, and the methods used to study them are described in the Appendix.

In the following chapters, the reader will encounter a range of topics dealing with the effects of industrialisation and the techno-service economy on women and achievement. Chapter 2 examines some trends in the participation of women in the labour force and their distribution throughout the occupational structure. Chapter 3 looks at the controversial subject of sex differences in achievement; do they exist, in what areas, and why? Chapter 4 explores the nature and origins of sex role socialisation; Chapter 5 looks at the impact of industrialisation on personality; and Chapter 6 examines the perplexing survival of traditionalism among some contemporary girls, despite the efforts of industrial society to stamp out unsuitable personality traits. Chapter 7 looks at the antecedents of individual achievement and examines a path to status attainment, focusing particularly on the question of whether the path is the same for both sexes. Chapter 8 shows how anticipated domestic roles influence the occupational expectations of young people, especially females. Finally, Chapter 9 summarises the research findings and suggests how society can facilitate female achievement.

But before we look at the research data on the adolescents – their achievements and frustrations, their relationships with parents and peers, their perceptions and plans for the future – let us briefly examine the historical record of women in the labour force, focusing on the structural changes that have altered woman's place in society and workforce. These changes are in the true sense of the word revolutionary; the task of this book is to examine the effects of this revolution on women, work, and achievement.

2 Women in the Labour Force

All societies regulate the entry of women into the labour force. In some societies women are sequestered in familial environs and forbidden to have contact with strangers, a restriction that in effect excludes them from paid employment outside the home. Other societies permit women to work in non-familial settings provided the job is seen as an extension of their ordinary household functions – for example, preparing and serving food, caring for children, making, repairing, or cleaning domestic consumables. Only a relatively few societies let women choose work from a broad spectrum of occupations, and even these grow testy when women enter fields traditionally assigned to men. For all societies consider some work more fitting to one sex than to the other, though, of course, what is thought fitting differs from culture to culture.[1]

Pre-industrial cultures, past and present, tend to make sharp distinctions between men's work and women's work. Thus in late eighteenth- and early nineteenth-century Europe, so Scott and Tilly tell us, men and women not only 'performed different tasks, they occupied different space'.[2] On the farm men did most of the heavy work and handled finances: clearing and ploughing fields, buying tools and provisions, carting and selling crops. Of course women helped out at planting and harvesting time, but their principal assignment was domestic. Woman's work included spinning yarn and weaving cloth, making candles, cooking and preserving food, tending a garden, caring for small animals and children – all this and more kept a woman busy from morn to night. When she found the time and energy to earn money, it was usually at work much like her normal household duties: sewing gloves and garments, nursing the infants of strangers, selling vegetables and poultry at the local market.[3]

The sexual division of labour in the city was somewhat less rigid than in the countryside, but no less visible or significant. At home men and women worked interdependently at separate tasks, employing skills considered uniquely linked to their gender. For example, among Parisian launderers – laundering was typically a family affair with everyone pitching in – women did most of the soaping and ironing; and sometimes the wives of artisans and shopkeepers helped their husbands with the tailoring, shoemaking, and baking. Occasionally, a woman would set up a cafe in her home. There was, for instance, the Sheffield knifemaker's wife who prepared and sold a bottled fermented drink called 'pop' to the city's thirsty dwellers. Outside the home, urban women worked as servants, laundresses, seamstresses, barmaids and innkeepers. And when necessity drove them to it, some women would go from door to door selling meat pies, pastries, and similar perishable articles of food; still other women served as 'beasts of burden, hauling heavy loads many times a day'.[4]

In a world where the household was the centre of production and everyone's place was at home, the work women performed was essential to the family's survival. As a result, it has been argued, women in the past enjoyed high public esteem and exercised substantial power in family circles, advantages lost to women when industrialisation drove them out of the labour force, displaced many of their domestically made products with goods manufactured outside the home, and reduced the female role to trivial housewifery, robbing women of self-esteem and power.

But this picture of a lost golden era will not stand up under scrutiny: it is a myth. Edward Shorter, in a study of late eighteenth- and early nineteenth-century family life in Western Europe, could find no evidence of a golden era of female power. He reports that typically women were subordinate to men in families of every station of life, particularly among the peasantry.[5] William Stephens' extensive cross-cultural survey of pre-literate societies also found men generally dominant over women.[6] And my own examination of families in contemporary developing countries around the world, most of them just beginning to experience the effects of industrialisation, revealed that husbands tend to dominate their wives.[7] On the basis of the available data, it seems safe to conclude that most pre-industrial societies enforced male dominance: their cultures legitimated it and their sex roles necessarily revolved around it.

A caveat is in order here: we must be careful not to exaggerate the power of men over women in pre-industrial societies. Even in places and at times when popular attitudes and values supported the patriarchal ideal, women were often more assertive in the privacy of their homes than their public docility toward men would suggest was remotely posssible. Hidden from public view behind cottage walls, some women bossed their husbands around; other women were the mainstays of their families, holding jobs and earning money on which everyone depended for survival; and even peasant women sometimes took the initiative in all sorts of familial activities, despite the stereotype of rural women as tractable and passive puppets resigned to masculine domination. Still we must not forget, as Alice Kessler-Harris warns us, that 'domestic work fell low on any hierarchical scale. Despite the self-evident importance of the work done at home, the role of the wife was distinctly secondary to that of the husband.'[8] Not until the advent of industrialisation did the status of women begin to undergo significant and enduring improvement.

Industrialisation separated the workplace from the homeplace and thus changed for ever the way in which goods would be produced. Cottage industry, the dominant mode of production before the Industrial Revolution, gave way to the factory system. For only factories could house large, heavy, expensive machinery; only factories could fragment work into specialised jobs that required little strength, training or skill; only factories could organise and rationalise work in ways that increased production and profits; only factories could provide jobs for an expanding population increasingly displaced from the land and eager to find work. Many of those who sought work were women. The record shows that during the first quarter of the nineteenth century women began working in factories in significantly large numbers, first as members of family units and later as individuals, drawn to mills and workshops by the prospect of earning steady wages.

Who were these women? They were mostly the unmarried daughters of peasants, yeoman farmers, and urban workers, women who sought in factory work the means to help their families, to acquire a dowry, and to escape from domestic service. For although young women had been a part of the paid labour force prior to industrialisation, they had worked primarily as domestics: of the single women in the American labour force in 1840, 70 percent hired themselves out as servants.[9] Of course, industrialisation did not immediately end the dominance of domestic service in the hierarchy of jobs women performed. A generation later in 1866, across the sea in France, 69 percent of the women working outside of agriculture were employed as domestics.[10] And as late as 1911, 35 percent of the women in the English labour market were laundresses or servants; the 1911 census of Milan revealed a similar concentration of women in domestic service.[11]

But slowly the industrial system began to attract large numbers of women into its factories, mills, and workshops. The mills of Lancashire, the needle trades of Lyon and London, the glove factories and millinery shops of Paris and Rome, the garment lofts of New York, the shoe factories and textile mills of New England, all drew large numbers of women into their employ, until factory girls became a common sight on the floors of mills and in the streets of all manufacturing cities. In some New England mill towns women made up 65 percent of all the industrial workers and 90 percent of those working in millinery shops and textile mills.[12] By the end of the nineteenth century women had won an impressive share of the labour market, a share that has continued to grow up to the present time.

Consider the record in the United States. In 1870, the first year in which reliable data on working women were collected, women made up 14.1 percent of the labour force. Each decennial census thereafter reported a steady, though modest increase in the female component of the work force. Thus from 1880 to 1900 women's share of the labour market increased from 14.5 percent to 17.7 percent, a 1 or 2 percent increase per decade. As a result, by 1920 the percentage of women in the labour force had grown to 20.2 percent, and by 1940 women made up a quarter of the paid working population. After the Second World War the pace of growth quickened. From 1940 to the present, each decennial census revealed an increase of 4 to 6 percent in the female component of the labour force, so that by 1980, women's share of the labour force had grown to 42.4 percent; and by 1986, it had risen to 44 percent, a phenomenal rate of growth.[13]

STRUCTURAL CAUSES OF CHANGE

What caused this dramatic change in the participation of women in the labour force? Why after decades of slow growth did the numbers of women working outside the home suddenly explode? The most popular answer to this question, an answer sanctioned by conventional wisdom, is that feminist ideology and political action, after decades of effort, finally swept away many of the barriers that men had erected against women, allowing them at last to take their rightful place in the labour market. The Feminist Movement, the argument goes, advanced the cause of women's liberation by winning for women the right to vote and to control their own property. Without political power, women would never have been permitted to enter elite schools and occupations or to seek jobs in fields dominated by men.

And yet, contrary to popular opinion, the relationship between political rights and women's work has been difficult to establish. Consider the history of women in the British labour force. During the nineteenth century protracted political action brought women increased control over their property, admission into the universities (Oxford admitted them to full membership in 1919 and enfranchisement in 1918). The Sex Disqualification (Removal) Act of 1919 finally made it possible for women to enter many professions, including the Bar. Nevertheless, as Scott and Tilly point out, the overall participation of women in the labour force changed little as a result of these reforms: in 1861 about 25 percent of British women worked; in 1921 the figure was still 25 percent.[14] Nor are Scott and Tilly alone in their position. Lee Holcombe, after careful research into the status of women, concluded that feminist ideology accompanied and justified but did not cause the improvement in the work status of women.[15]

Ideology and political action should be given more credit for changing the work status of women than Scott and Tilly or Holcombe appear willing to grant. Most certainly the feminist emphasis on equality and achievement and the Women's Movement's mobilisation of female energy helped women move out of the home and into the labour force. Still, we must recognise – and it is no disparagement of the Women's Movement to do so – that the effect of feminist ideology and political agitation on the status of women stems in large part from feminism's historic connection with industrialisation. Modern feminism, I submit, is part of the industrialisation process. It is no coincidence that the Feminist Movement in the United States began at a time when industrialisation had just started to take off, or that the first American feminists' convention took place in a small manufacturing town, or that its founders came mainly from the industrial parts of the country. In short, industrialisation embodied technological, demographic, and socio-economic changes that made organised feminism possible. Moreover, by supporting feminism's values and goals it ensured the movement's eventual success. Without industrialisation feminism would have remained an unrealised ideal, a futile social movement of interest only to historians.

Nothing about the impact of industrialisation on women was simple. A confluence of factors, situational and structural, individual and psychological, have acted upon women for well over a century, with consequences that have been sometimes dramatic, occasionally harrowing, and often exciting, because they have made it possible for women to find in an expanding industrial economy opportunities never before available to them. Broadly speaking, these factors fall into three categories: (a) *technological,* machinery and the factory system, changes in how goods were produced and distributed; (b) *family structural,* changes in the organisation of the family, its size and functions, and the increased instability and divorce that accompanied industrialisation; (c) *social structural,* the development of organisations and laws designed to protect and advance women's interests; the growth of governmental bureaucracy, which required higher taxes to pay for it; and, most important, the rise of the techno-service economy. Interacting synergistically, these changes in technology, the family, and the social structure altered the condition of women in the workplace and in society.

Industrialisation first affected women through the impact of its technology on the conditions of work. Technology made work easier and less physically burdensome; equally important, it promoted equality between the sexes because technology's revolutionary innovation, the machine driven by an inanimate source of energy, drastically reduced the advantages that brawn, special training, and privileged position had long given to men. First water, then steam, and finally electric power, made it possible for women to operate machines that had once required great brute strength, the muscles of oxen, horses, and men, to turn and whirl efficiently – a fact mill owners discovered a century and a half ago when they found that women, assisted by water and steam power, could handle heavy looms as well as men. And today, power steering and power brakes enable women to drive commercial vehicles with relative ease. As a result, women are becoming a familiar sight on construction sites and in the cabs of buses, taxi-cabs and trucks.

In addition, in some areas technology eroded the edge that specialised skill and membership of closed organisations once gave men in their competition with women. Machines have made exotic or obsolete many of the skills men once spent years to learn: tinsmiths, coopers, saddlers, and similar artisans are in little demand today; the products they once laboriously fashioned by hand are now produced easily in factories, often on machines run by women. And the guilds and similar organisations, whose major function it once was to protect the skills and markets of its members, nearly always male, ceased to matter when apprenticeships in their defunct trades became meaningless. Not that men clubbing together in craft unions, social clubs, and service organisations have altogether ceased to discriminate against women – sexual equality still eludes us – but technology has made the advantages of membership of such groups, though still considerable, less important today than in the past.

As long as the uses of technology were restricted to manufacturing, the employment status of upper- and middle-class women was little affected by industrialisation. They had never been drawn to paid employment, certainly not in factories – noisy and dirty places, unfit environments for ladies – and the mechanisation of production did nothing to change their point of view: that the steam-driven spinning jenny had replaced the simple spinning wheel mattered little to them except perhaps in that it made thread less expensive. If upper- and middle-class women concerned themselves at all with the mechanisation of the workplace, it was to view with alarm the presumed evil effects of factories on the morals of young working girls or to complain that industrialists were seducing girls away from domestic service to better jobs in the mills, making the problem of finding and keeping servants exasperatingly difficult. And so, unlike lower-class women to whom the mechanised factory opened up a new world of opportunity, a world to which they flocked in large numbers, most upper and middle-class women at first resisted the lure of technology and stayed at home.

But the eventual introduction of technology into the home, the store, and the office changed all this. Labour-saving appliances made housework less exhausting and time-consuming, and privileged women found themselves with more leisure time than they had ever known before, more free time in fact than they knew what to do with. Some women spent more time in conventional upper and middle class leisure-time pursuits, giving parties and attending social affairs. Other women turned their energies to politics and charity, creating in the process the entirely new field of social work and its related occupations. Still others, their numbers small at first but growing rapidly in the early twentieth century, found jobs in stores, offices, hospitals, and schools, places that technology had made clean and quiet and safe, work that was sometimes intellectually challenging and socially beneficial – all qualities congruent with the popular image of work appropriate to ladies of their station. Soon the typewriter and the telephone (later the word processor and computer), the textbook and the thermometer became the familiar tools of middle-class women at work.

Technology was not the only, or even the most important, medium through which industrialisation affected women. More influential was the New Industrial Family – a smaller, more democratic, stripped-down version of its pre-industrial predecessor. Before industrialisation the family had easily absorbed a woman's time and energy, and most women who could afford to do so stayed at home, fully occupied with domestic chores and firmly convinced that family concerns took priority over all others, a sentiment society applauded. But when industrialisation stripped the family of many of its functions, when making clothes, preserving food, providing formal schooling and medical care, to name only a few of the functions performed by the pre-industrial family, became the responsibilities of extra-familial agencies, women had time for other things, including paid work outside the home. Equally important, industrialisation changed the structure of relationships within the family. On the positive side, husband–wife relationships became more open and democratic; women who wanted to work could overcome or override if necessary their husbands' objections. On the negative side, the marital bond became fragile and subject to dissolution through abandonment, separation, and divorce. As a result, thrown on their own resources, more women were forced to work to support themselves and their children. Fortunately, the advent of the New Industrial Family has meant that typically there are fewer children at home.

Everywhere in the West as nations underwent industrialisation fertility rates declined. To illustrate, the American birth rate dropped from 55 per thousand in the year 1800 to about 18 shortly before the Second World War. Following the war, the birth rate rose during the 'baby boom', only to collapse by the 1970s to its present point, a rate slightly below the replacement level. Other industrial nations went through a similar process, so that, by the late twentieth century, families with one or two children became commonplace, particularly in North America and Western Europe.[16] Now, we know that the love of children and the desire to nurture them are strong sentiments, strong enough to bind many women to the home. But what are women to do when there are no longer any children at home? What will occupy the time of mothers in their thirties when the need for their services dwindle, when their children are away at school or on their own in the big world? Still young, these women can anticipate another 30 or more years of active life, years they do not want to waste bemoaning the miseries of the empty nest. Not surprisingly, many women in mid-life turn to paid employment as an alternative source of stimulation, reward and purpose, as their growing numbers in the labour force attest.

Exactly how industrialisation promotes divorce is in dispute, but what cannot be denied is the close connection between the two, at least in the West. For over a century, the divorce rate in Western industrialised societies has been rising; in the United States it has more than doubled since 1960: if the rate continues, as pessimists believe it will, four out of ten marriages will end in divorce.[17] Few women can safely ignore these statistics; indeed, many older women and their children already know the costs of divorce from personal experience. Thrown on their own, unable to live on the income from meagre and unreliable alimony or child support, they must go to work or live on welfare. Many prefer work, if they can find it. Young women, often themselves the children of divorced parents, live with the knowledge that their marriage may not endure and wisely prepare for that possibility by acquiring marketable skills and work experience.

The entry of women into the labour force is not, of course, merely a defensive response to the threat of divorce or an act of desperation; on the contrary, many women enter the labour market gladly. But this was not always the case. Even in periods of national emergency it was not easy to get women into the work force. According to Walter Karp, 'There was nothing spontaneous about the unprecedented influx of women into the wartime shipyards and factories. Far from picking up rivet guns with joy, American women had to be exhorted, cajoled and browbeaten to take traditionally male jobs.'[18] Today, as in earlier stages of industrialisation, the fear of hunger and other imperious needs drive some reluctant women into the work force. Most often, however, in the modern industrial world it is appetite, not hunger, that shapes the decision of women to enter the labour force. Whetted by consumerism, the demanding child of the affluent society, appetite feeds upon itself, generating an ever greater need for goods and services: a larger TV console, a new microwave oven, a second car, a trip to Paris. The good life, an affluent standard of living once thought possible only for the few, now appears atainable and necessary to the many.

But as everyone knows, the good life (in its hedonistic sense) costs money. Unfortunately industrial capitalism, despite its enviable record of improving the general standard of living, occasionally starves the very appetites it excites. Periodically, the business cycle throws people out of work; inflation puts families on a financial treadmill that forces them to run ever faster just to stay in place; or taxes rise and private money flows into government coffers to meet public needs. Whatever the reason, for some people the money stops or one income proves inadequate to maintain the desired standard of living, and the wife must put on work clothes and find a job or keep the one she may have thought of relinquishing.[19]

THE RISE OF THE TECHNO-SERVICE ECONOMY

Though undoubtedly of great importance, the technological, demographic and family changes just examined do not fully explain the rapid movement of women into the labour force in recent decades. Many of these changes have been at work for generations, changes that made paid employment necessary for some women and inviting to others, changes that gradually enlarged the female component of the labour force. But the number of women in the labour force would have grown far less rapidly had not industrialisation given new impetus to the techno-service economy. For, more than anything else, it was the explosive growth of the service economy in the past twenty-five years that caused the dramatic increase in women's share of the work force.

A pygmy in the nineteenth century, the service sector today has grown into a giant looming over all other sectors of the economy. For example, in 1986 it produced 68 percent of America's gross national product, accounted for 25 percent of its exports, and employed 71 percent of its workers.[20] This shift toward service employment reflects a major restructuring of the American economy that took place in the decades following the Second World War. During this period, agriculture declined, manufacturing grew sluggishly, while the service sector exploded. Thus between 1929 and 1965 farm employment in the United States dropped by 5 million; today farmers make up slightly less than 3 percent of the labour force. The manufacturing sector, formerly the most robust part of the economy, increased by 10 million, whereas the service sector, heretofore the economy's least dynamic economic segment, grew by 20 million.[21]

During the 1960 to 1980 period, manufacturing jobs grew 1 percent annually, while service employment grew 3.2 percent a year, with 17 million out of a total of 19 million created in the 1970s alone. The years 1981 to 1986 saw a further explosion in service jobs – by some 10.4 million.[22] It is not that the manufacturing sector is disappearing; it remains a vital component of America's economy, producing in 1986 about 23 percent of the nation's gross national product. But the number of blue collar jobs continues to decline. Today manufacturing employs 1.8 million fewer blue collar workers than in 1979. As blue collar jobs shrink, jobs in medium-sized high-technology companies, and in the information and knowledge industries, expand. If the present trend continues, blue collar workers may well be surpassed in numbers by service-orientated professional, managerial, and technical workers by the end of this decade.[23] A similar shift from the manufacturing to the service sector is taking place throughout the industrialised world. For instance, the British service sector employed 39.7 percent of the labour force in 1901; by 1970 that number had grown to 50.3

percent. And, to cite another example, Italy, the least service-orientated member of the six original Common Market (EEC) countries, saw its service sector more than double in two generations, rising from 17.1 percent in 1901 to 38.4 percent in 1970. In 1986, although they made up one-third of the total work force, women constituted only one-quarter of Italians employed in goods-producing industries.[24]

This shift toward the service sector shows no signs of slackening in any Western industrial country. Social pressures will not permit it. Population trends and changing social policies increasingly pose problems that call more often for services than for goods, and vast bureaucracies in government and in the health and amenity industries develop to provide these services. The poor and disadvantaged, the sick and aged, the retired and footloose more often need the help of governmental clerks and social workers, therapists and physicians, travel agents and hotel keepers than of welders, millwrights, and machine operators. Nor is it only the individual consumer who needs services; the goods-producing industries are themselves major consumers of services. More and more, industry finds it needs external agents to handle real estate, insurance, and advertising problems; it needs lobbyists and public relations firms to protect its interests in the state houses and capitals; and it needs consultants to work on old problems and to introduce new ideas. Taken together the needs of industry and of the individual consumer have pushed the service sector to the forefront of the economy.

The relationship of the service economy to industrialisation and the status of service work is frequently misunderstood. Contrary to Daniel Bell's assertion, the service economy is not a post-industrial phenomenon.[25] Rather, the service economy is industrialisation's most recent stage of development and its leading edge of change. Industrialisation occurs as readily in a service as in goods-producing industry. 'The process of industrialization is underway in every branch of service activity', writes George Gilder, 'as plastic cards revolutionize the extension of credit, television transforms the productivity of the entertainer, word processors exalt the efficiency of secretaries, and beepers make firemen and doctors more immediately available.'[26] Nor is the service economy composed primarily of low-skilled, poorly paid, dead-end jobs, as its detractors maintain. Hamburger-flipping is a service occuption, but so is investment banking. 'Many of the service people work alone or have customer contact, and this requires judgement, responsibility, ingenuity', says Audrey Freedman.[27] And we know that the fastest job growth in the United States has been in the higher paying service industries. According to Beryl W. Sprinkel, Chairman of the President's Council of Economic Advisors, more than 60 percent of the increase in employment since 1982 has been in the highest paying occupations, most of them in the service sector. Only 12 percent of the increase has been in the lowest-paying, low-skill service occupations.[28]

As it grew, the service economy developed a symbiotic relationship with women based on mutual need and attraction. Labour-intensive, the producer of intangible goods in whose formation machines play a secondary role, the service sector needs women to fill jobs and to keep the cost of labour down. Had the available pool of workers been limited to males, the cost of labour in the rapidly growing service economy would have sky-rocketed. Even that hidebound institution, the commercial bank, has had to drop its barriers against anyone who is not a WASP male. Forced by deregulation to become competitive, and desperate for skilled, aggressive executives, the banks are tossing aside old prejudices and converting their managements into meritocracies. As Barry M. Allen, First Vice-President of the Bank of Boston, put it: 'We can't afford to keep out any talented person.'[29] Being a woman no longer means automatic exclusion from the ranks of management. Women, in turn, needing work and eager for change, found in the service economy a relatively friendly work environment, unhobbled by traditional animosities and prejudices against women among employees and labour unions wary of competition from women. Happily for them both, the service economy and women found in each other a solution to their needs.

But economic considerations alone do not explain the relatively benign reception given to women in the service economy: women were welcomed because they were thought well-suited to the demands of service work. Service work often requires interpersonal skills and a sensitivity to the needs of clients and customers. Thus waitresses, travel agents, physicians, teachers, social workers, sales people, to name only a few service occupations, typically meet the consumer of their services in face-to-face encounters whose successful outcome frequently depends as much on the worker's interpersonal skill as on specialised knowledge. Significantly, popular opinion attributes interpersonal skill, the ability to empathise with others and respond sensitively to their needs, more often to women than to men – a belief that works to the advantage of women. Alice Kessler-Harris argues that the massive movement of women into personnel work, a growing job category for women after 1910, reflected the employer's belief that adjusting job grievances and maintaining proper working standards were matters with which women were especially qualified to deal.[30]

Women returned the service economy's good opinion of them in full measure, for service work appealed to women in ways manufacturing never had. For one thing, service work seldom makes demands for physical strength that women cannot meet; a hand strong enough to handle a skillet can easily hold a sales pad, punch a typewriter, or carry a briefcase. For another thing, to some people service work connotes contributing to the welfare of others, a notion congenial to the conventional conception of the woman as helper – of her family, of her friends, and of the community. Unexpectedly, this aspect of the woman's role, long considered uniquely linked to the family, eased the passage of middle-class women into the labour force. Before the turn of the century, many middle-class women had gained valuable experience dealing with people as volunteer workers in numerous charities, acquiring in this way a proficiency in supervision that could later be translated into jobs as factory inspectors, visiting nurses, truant officers, and child-labour investigators, work to which few men were then attracted. In addition, service work sometimes permits part-time employment and usually allows relatively easy exit when domestic responsibilities require the women's presence at home, as well as re-entry when the familial situation eases, all factors of great importance to mothers with small children at home. But, perhaps most significant of all, service work is typically clean, respectable, proper work, something a genteel woman can do without jeopardising her status as a lady.

Responding to the character of work and the expanding opportunity structure, women poured into the labour market during the decades following the conclusion of the Second World War. Thus in 1950 about 34 percent of all American women 16 years of age and older were in the labour force; by 1986 that number had risen to 56 percent.[31] In Europe women were joining the labour force in large numbers. Thus by 1981 about 58 percent of British and 41 percent of Italian women aged 15 to 64, were working outside the home.[32] But sheer numbers alone do not tell the whole story. Equally interesting is the entry into the labour market of women who had previously been reluctant to accept paid employment – married women and mothers with small children. At the turn of the century the typical working woman was young and single; 48 percent of all single Americans worked outside the home, as compared with only 6 percent of all married women. By 1962, a third of all married women were working outside the home and by 1982 51 percent were working or looking for work.[33] The European statistics are on the whole very similar to the United States; 51 percent of working women in Italy were married and 67 percent in Great Britain.[34] That is not all: many of these women had children of pre-school or school age – a marked contrast with the past. Thus in 1948 only 10.8 percent of women with children under 6 years old worked outside the home; whereas in 1984 three out of five women with children under 3 and 52 percent with children under 6; since 1980 most of the increase in female employment has been among mothers with pre-school age children.[35] For the first time in American history young children at home no longer keep the majority of women out of the labour force.

In the United States women work at jobs in every industry group, including those once thought too exhausting or dangerous for women to perform. For instance, the Census Bureau lists female as well as male stevedores and boilermakers and about 3800 women work in mines under the same conditions men endure. But many women still gravitate toward jobs traditionally thought proper for their sex, most of which are in the service sector: about two-thirds of working women are employed in the service sector; only one in six holds down a job in a goods-producing industry.[36] How different it was a century ago. At that time, six of the ten leading occupations of working women were in the goods-producing sector; today only one of them, sewers and stitchers, can unequivocally be called goods producing; the remaining nine are in the service sector – secretaries, waitresses, nurses, cashiers, household cleaners and servants.[37]

Some service jobs once considered the exclusive property of men have become increasingly identified with women. Thus a majority of all claims adjusters and bill collectors are women; they also constitute 48 percent of all bartenders and 49 percent of bus drivers. These are not, as a rule, well-paying jobs; hence men lose little by letting women fill them. Indeed, many of the service jobs filled primarily by women are poorly paid: more than nine out of ten typists and secretaries, book-keepers and bank tellers, house cleaners and servants are female – none of these occupations are noted for their high salaries. Nor do elementary school teachers, social workers, and registered nurses, all female-dominated professions, command good pay.[38]

What about the jobs that really pay off in prestige, power, and money? It must be admitted that the movement of women into prestigious and lucrative fields of work has been relatively slow. Nonetheless, even in fields that have long resisted admitting women significant change is underway. 'We're penetrating professions we were not in before', said Lenora Cole Alexander, Director of the Federal

Women's Bureau.[39] She could have pointed to the rise of women engineers, from 1 percent in 1962 to 6 percent in 1982; to the fact that in 1984 women made up 14 percent of all lawyers, 20 percent of physicians, 25 percent of college teachers, and a majority of psychologists.[40]

Sceptics maintain that these numbers are less impressive than they appear. What the numbers do not reveal is the stubborn gap between the wages of men and women: at every educational level women earn less than men. Over all, the average earnings for American women who worked full-time were 70 percent of those for men in 1986, up from 62 percent in 1979, but still significantly below the earnings of males. No doubt a bias against women and the persistence of sexual segregation in some sectors of the labour force accounts for a part of the wage gap. The evidence is clear that working in an occupation with a high proportion of women has a negative influence on earnings. Data indicate that regardless of sex, people in female-dominated occupations have lower earnings than those in integrated or male-dominated occupations. But the work history also accounts for a part of the wage gap. The work history of men and women tends to differ in some significant ways: women are more than three times as likely as men to have had interruptions in their work history; they also tend to have less time on their current job then men; and among college graduates women are still less likely than men – though this discrepancy is rapidly narrowing – to specialise in high-paying fields. On the bright side, the disparity between the wages of women and men has declined among younger workers. In the 21 to 29 age group, women with no interruptions in their work history earn, on the average, 83 percent of what men earn.[41] And within the same job categories women and men earn essentially the same amounts. Janet Norwood, the Commissioner of Labor Statistics, says her agency found that pay discrepancies between women and men 'nearly disappeared when each occupation was broken down into its component levels based on skill and experience'.[42]

What is perhaps more important, the future, so far as new jobs are concerned, seems to belong to women. For the new jobs are primarily in the service sector and, as Jack Metzger, an expert on the growth of service industries, remarked, 'service jobs are mostly women's jobs'.[43] Apart from the twenty occupations traditionally held by women, all of them in the service economy and all expected to grow, the new positions being created, positions in computer science, in legal services, in health and education, and in government, increasingly attract women. The Bureau of Labor estimates that of the ten occupations that will add workers in the next decade, eight are considered female occupations. Between 1982 and 1995 women will account for about 65 percent of all new workers.[44]

That women will continue to move into the labour force seems more than likely; that they will take advantage of the new opportunities opening to them in the service economy cannot be doubted; and that some women will excel in their fields is certain – these facts most people now recognise. But what is not generally understood is that females have long competed with males and that in this competition females have often excelled, frequently surpassing the performance of their male counterparts. Competition between the sexes begins early in life and can be seen in the differential achievements of girls and boys in school, in extracurricular activities, and in community activities. In the next chapter we turn to an examination of sex differences in early achievement.

3 Sex Differences in Early Achievement

The rapid movement of women into the higher echelons of the American occupational structure surprised a lot of people, women as well as men. Who would have thought so many women would achieve so much in so short a time? Today, a woman advises a major motion picture company, another heads a successful Wall Street investment firm, still another manufacturers a brand of cosmetics sold throughout the world; and these are only a few of the stars that dot a constellation crowded with achieving women. More achievers are in the making, for the enrolment of women in American law, medical, engineering and busines schools has more than doubled in the last decade. Clearly, still more female luminaries loom on the horizon.

But why the surprise? Could it not have been foreseen that once the barriers to female occupational achievement had been dismantled, that once enlightened legislation had made discrimination against women illegal, that once employers were no longer able to deny advancement to employees merely because they were women, that once labour unions could no longer exclude women from their ranks – after these changes had taken place, was it not obvious that the pent-up needs, desires and abilities of women would erupt in an explosion of achievement and that women would then take their rightful place in every part of the occupational structure? Indeed, it is obvious if you believe that the explanation for women's status in the labour force can only be found in the operation of oppressive institutions that keep women down.

But not everyone shares this point of view. Though not ignorant of the negative effects of discrimination on female occupational aspirations and performance, some observers insist that personal factors also seriously affect performance in the workplace, factors such as experience, education, skill, aptitude, motivation, and intelligence, each an intangible form of human capital which influences the deal a woman can make for herself in the market place of labour. Human capital theorists believe that a general deficiency in personal resources hampers women's efforts to compete in a tight labour market.[1] For example, it has been said that women usually lack advanced training in mathemat-

35

ics and science, a serious deficiency in an increasingly technological world. Moreover, since their interests, aptitudes, and motivation centre on family affairs, women must necessarily immerse themselves in the kinds of routine domestic pursuits that deprive them of intellectual stimulation and blunt their native wit. People with this view of women were understandably surprised by the abundance of female occupational achievement in recent years.

Much condescension and not a little prejudice permeates the human capital argument: it has in fact been used as a justification for discrimination. But more than that, it betrays a profound ignorance of recent research findings on sex differences and an inexcusable inattention to what females are actually doing. In this chapter we shall look at the research on the interests, abilities and achievements of school-age boys and girls, since presumably the accumulation of human capital begins early. Evidence of sex differences in early achievement would tend to support the argument that even in childhood scantier personal resources of females restrict their achievement, a situation that grows worse as they mature. As we shall see, the data do not support the human capital thesis, but neither do they wholly refute it. The picture that emerges from the data is far richer and more complex than the apologists and interpreters of female achievement imagine.

SEX DIFFERENCES IN ACADEMIC ABILITIES

Nothing so vividly demonstrates the power of prejudice to blot out contrary evidence as the stubborn survival of the notion that men are brighter than women. This idea is ancient and hardy. Through the centuries Western societies have endlessly reiterated the myth of male intellectual superiority: biblical society commanded women to submit to men because their superior intellectual endowments made them the natural protectors and masters of women; medieval society enjoined women to recognise their mental limitations and urged them to turn their rich feminine talents to women's proper work, the loving care of husband and children; Victorian society warned women of the debilitating effect mental exertion would have on their ability to perform their more important familial role. The Biblical prophet, the Medieval priest, and the Victorian divine, each radically different from the others in a host of ways, all proclaimed the necessity and rightness of male superiority.

All the while women were running farms and estates, managing stores and inns, writing poems and novels, organising intellectually demanding salons and editing journals, indifferent to the general consensus that such activities were quite beyond the natural scope and talent of women. Achieving women could be found in the most unlikely places. In Brazil, a country whose Iberian culture had long affirmed the inferiority of women to men in every sphere except familial, numerous stories recounted the exploits of women who surpassed their menfolk in energy, courage, intelligence and good sense. Stories are told of housewives who took over the direction of vast estates when the husband died or proved incapable of handling family affairs, of matriarchs who kept armed retainers and executed their own justice, of female politicians who directed the affairs of entire regions, of Amazons who planned campaigns and fought against foreign invaders – stories, in short, of women whose lives belie the notion that women necessarily lack the character, intellect and wit to achieve eminence in their society.[2]

On occasion a flawed generalisation sanctioned by centuries of venerated authority may escape criticism, even when it ignores everyday experience. But inevitably daily experience wins out, and experience tells us that females are not less intelligent than males. Parents know this: they do not routinely find their daughters dumber than their sons; teachers know it also: they cannot escape noticing that girls do at least as well in class as boys; and finally, researchers know it best of all, for they have spent decades studying sex differences, documenting the ways in which the abilities, interests, and achievements of boys and girls differ. And in their research lie findings that must cause a major rethinking of the notion that the sexes differ sharply in their possession of human capital. We shall begin this rethinking by examining sex differences in a critical human resource: intelligence.

THE IQ CONTROVERSY

Achievement in a complex industrial world rests on intelligence. Brute strength may be enough to clear a field for cultivation, courage may carry the day on the battlefield, and good looks may conquer in the bedroom, but in the boardroom and classroom, in the laboratory and engineering shop, and in the studio and *atelier,* a reasonably good mind is the *conditio sine qua non* for achievement. Without intelligence to guide them organisations stumble from one bad decision to another; without intelligence to draw upon individuals draw wrong conclusions from experience and never hit upon novel solutions to their problems. Industrial societies know this and go to great lengths to identify bright people, train them, and pick their brains. In principle, it matters little to an industrial society whether the brains are cased in a male skull or female one; and in practice, it has become painfully apparent that no society can compete successfully in an international market dominated by technologically advanced industrial societies without using every ounce of brainpower it can muster, male or female.

In such circumstances it is important that intelligence be identified and measured accurately. This task, not surprisingly, was first undertaken in Western countries at the beginning of the twentieth century when the triumph of industrialisation had become obvious to everyone. Of course, countries varied, and still do, in the methodology they employed to assess intelligence. Some countries relied on the subjective judgements of teachers, on trusted assessments derived from long and intimate contact with the student; others used teacher's assessments buttressed with lengthy written or oral examinations; still others used a standardised test designed to determine the individual's IQ, or intelligence quotient. None of these approaches satisfies everyone, of course, in part because of deficiencies inherent in the methodology, and in part because it is not entirely clear what is being measured. Parenthetically, this multiplicity of measures has made comparison of intelligence across countries extremely difficult.

Nonetheless, researchers interested in sex differences seized upon the IQ test as a handy device for comparing boys and girls, and quickly began building a body of data about general intelligence. By the 1950s enough research had been done to warrant two extensive reviews of the literature on sex differences in intellectual abilities, one by Terman and Tyler, in 1954, and another by Anastasi four years later.[3]

These reviews were later updated by Maccoby in 1966 and again in 1974 by Maccoby and Jacklin.[4] Nothing in the research conducted since that time changes a conclusion abundantly clear from earlier studies, namely that males and females do not differ consistently in total intellectual ability. Some studies report higher IQ scores for girls, a few give the advantage to boys, most show no differences at all when well-balanced tests not standardised to minimise sex differences were used.

Sex differences have been found, however, in the scores of students on the verbal and quantitative components of most intellectual tests. Although up to about age 11 or so, no consistent differences in verbal ability appear between the sexes, in high school and through the college years girls tend to score higher on a variety of tests measuring verbal skills. Not only do girls do better in such routine skills as punctuation and spelling, they also outperform the boys in higher-level skills such as comprehension of a complex written text, quick understanding of complex relationships expressed in writing, and verbal creativity as measured by Guildford's test of divergent thinking.

In quantitative areas, the tables are turned: boys outperform the girls in mathematics and general numerical aptitude. The superiority of boys in quantitative matters appears in adolescence, an unexpected development because up to that time the girls were doing about as well as their male peers. But in adolescence the boys move ahead and stay there throughout the school years, even when the amount of training in mathematics that the girls and boys had received is controlled. This generalisation does not of course hold for every study nor for every place. A 1967 American study, for example, using thousands of cases, found no significant sex differences in quantitative ability, and a Swedish study reports only a trivial difference favouring boys.[5] Nonetheless, the preponderance of evidence points toward male superiority in mathematics. Witness the finding of the 1984 Second International Mathematics Study, This study, the largest such cross national analysis ever conducted, showed that whereas no significant sex difference exists in the mathematics scores of 8th grade students, among 12th graders the boys generally performed better than the girls.[6] But the verbal or quantitative advantages that one sex enjoys over the other cancel each other out when the sub-category scores are totalled; the result is an almost identical average IQ score for boys and girls.

SEX DIFFERENCES IN MENTAL ABILITY

As it happens, some of the evidence collected in the studies upon which this book is based, bear on the question of sex differences in intelligence. But before we look at the data, a brief statement about how they were collected may be helpful to the reader. (A more comprehensive description of sampling and data collection procedures appears in the Appendix.) The bulk of the data reported in this book were obtained from adolescents attending the junior and senior high schools of three American, seven British, and two Italian cities. Hour-long questionnaires were administered to the students in the classroom and completed forms obtained from 3049 American, 1060 British, and 1325 Italian students. Most of the data were in the form of answers to questions about aspirations and achievement, about perceptions of parents and peers, and about sex roles and plans for the future. In addition, in the United States, we had access to the students' academic files, which contained in a majority of cases a measurement of intelligence based on response to an IQ test which permitted us to compare the IQ scores of the sexes. From their files we obtained the IQ scores of 1183 girls and 1190 boys, all drawn from a larger sample of one-third of the population attending all the junior and senior high schools of three American cities. Unfortunately, we were unable to make cross-sex comparisons of the IQs of British and Italian students because schools in Britain and Italy do not routinely administer intelligence tests. Still, the data on the American students enabled us to test once again the hypothesis that one sex is more intelligent (as measured by a standardised test) than the other. The American data were taken from student performances on the California Test of Mental Maturity (CTMM), the total score on the Otis-Lennon Mental Ability Test (OLMAT), and the verbal and numerical sections of the Differential Aptitude Test (DAT), depending on the test scores available in the student's school district. Since the CTMM and the OLMAT already have a mean of 100 and a standard deviation of 16, we standardised the DAT with the same mean and standard deviation, using national norms so that the characteristics of the local sample would not be lost.

The mean scores of American male and female students are shown in Table 3.1, which also contains information about their grades, a topic that will be discussed below. As can be seen in this table, the average IQ scores of American males and females are very similar: the boys have a mean score of 108.9, the girls a score of 108.3; the difference between these scores is not statistically significant. This finding agrees with most research into the mental ability of females and males, that among students there is no significant difference in IQ between the sexes. In short, if the sexes differ in human capital, it is definitely not evident in their performance on standardised tests of intelligence.

Another way of assessing sex differences in mental ability is to look at how well boys and girls are doing in the classroom, for obviously academic grades reflect the teacher's assessment of the student's abilities and performance. Research on academic performance shows that females generally outperform males in school, at least as measured by the traditional grading system, beginning in the elementary grades and continuing in college, and that they have been doing so for a long time.[7] As far back as 1929, educational researchers reported finding

Table 3.1   *Mean IQ and Grades, by Sex and Country*

	IQ		Grades	
	Females	Males	Females	Males
United States	108.3 (1183)	108.9 (1190)	5.8* (1481)	5.1 (1468)
Britain	—	—	5.6 (195)	6.0 (224)
Italy	—	—	5.8 (653)	6.3 (640)

*$p < 0.05$

better grades for girls than for boys, a finding that kept cropping up in study after study. For example, Project Talent, a nationwide survey of high school seniors conducted in 1960, revealed that 51 percent of the girls reported grades of 'mostly A,s and B,s' as compared with 39 percent of the boys.[8]

This pattern persists in college. Although no comprehensive national study of grades in college exists, surveys in particular colleges show a decided relationship between sex and academic performance. To illustrate, a study at Berkeley in 1970 revealed that 46 percent of freshman women made first semester grades of 'B' or better, as compared with 39 percent of the men. For the seniors, the figures are almost identical: 45 percent of the women and 38 percent of the men had average grades in the spring semester of 'B' or better.[9] Examining these findings, which extend over a long period of time and cover various subjects, Maccoby and Jacklin concluded that the better grades of girls reflect 'some combination of greater effort, greater interest, and better work habits'.[10] Female resources, then, include not only an IQ equal to that of males but also encompass traits and acquired skills that should pay off in occupational as well as academic success.

To see if the girls in our study out-performed boys academically as much previous research suggested they would, even though the three countries in which they live are substantially different in culture and history, we examined the student's grade average. Students were asked to locate their grade average attained in the previous semester on an eight-point scale, ranging from eight, indicating mostly 'A's, to one, mostly failing grades. For the Americans a request for semester grade averages presented no insuperable problem: they knew their grades and could tell us if they wished. Unfortunately, self-reported grades sometimes suffer from error, deliberate or otherwise, and hence we sought to validate our measure of academic performance by comparing the students' responses with the school records. On checking into the academic records of 27 percent of American sample, we found a 0.77 correlation between the students' self-reports and their recorded grades, indicating that the self-report and the actual grade were not far apart, a positive testament to the memory and honesty of the student.

Obtaining data on school grades in Britain was considerably more difficult than in the United States. For one thing, British comprehensive schools do not grade students in the American manner; rather than giving numerical or letter grades, the teachers make written evaluations of each student's performance, somewhat subjective reports that do not readily lend themselves to reduction into a numeric or letter grade. Some schools, however, rank students academically within their form. When this occurred, we were able to group these rankings into eight categories, each category approximating an American letter grade. Unfortunately, many students were unsure of their form rank; consequently, the number of British students about whom cross-sex academic comparisons could be made was relatively small. The Italians presented no serious problem: the numerical system employed in the senior high schools (ranging from one, which equals 'poor', to eight, which equals 'excellent') could easily be translated into the American grading system. It is important to keep in mind, however, that differences in national curricular standards and grading systems make comparisons across countries extremely hazardous and generalisations from these data about the quality of academic performance in one country as compared to another are unwise. But this presents no problem for us. We do not wish to evaluate the quality of education across countries; rather we want to compare the grades of the sexes within country, and for this purpose the data are relatively satisfactory.

Table 3.1 shows the mean grades of upper division students in our samples separated by sex and nationality. The samples shown in this table are not strictly comparable either by age or year in school. The upper division American group contains high school juniors and seniors, whereas the British and Italian samples include, in addition to juniors and seniors, some students from the sixth form (Britain) or 13th year (Italy). The English and Italian groups, therefore, are slightly older and more advanced academically than the Americans. We chose older students because it seemed probable that they had begun to think about the future, possibly making plans for a life beyond secondary school and perhaps even focusing on an occupation. In these circumstances academic performance takes on special meaning, for it may affect the educational and occupational decisions the student must soon make, graduation being not far away. Moreover, by the junior or senior year of high school, many of the academically inadequate or unmotivated students have left school, leaving behind a relatively select group of academically screened adolescents from whose number will emerge most of their nation's achievers.

As can be seen in Table 3.1, the academic performance of males and females differs very little: on the average, the girls and boys in these samples receive about the same grades, mostly 'B's, a scattering of 'C's, and some 'A's. In the United States the mean grade for girls is slightly higher (5.8) than the grade for boys (5.1), a finding that agrees with the evidence reported in many other samples. In Britain and Italy boys do somewhat better on the average than girls: thus the mean grade of British boys is 6.0; girls, 5.6; the mean grade for Italian boys is 6.3; girls, 5.8. National differences in grades by sex reflect the structures and sex compositions of their schools and labour forces. More females than males in the United States attend college; the reverse is true in Britain and Italy; also more women in America participate in the labour force than in Britain or Italy.[11] In general, the openness of the American social structure encourages girls to seek high grades as a way of easing their way into advanced schools and better jobs. Probably as the opportunity structure becomes more open in Britain and Italy, which is presently happening, the differences between the sexes in academic performance will decline. But even under present conditions, the academic performance of the sexes in all three countries are not greatly different from each other.

These findings rebut the argument that females lack the intellectual resources and motivation to compete successfully against males in an area defined as appropriate for cross-sex competition – academics in school. And this is precisely our point: the school in an industrial society has become an acceptable place in which males and females can compete, and the reason for this is not hard to find. An industrial society encourages competition in school between the sexes because it needs an achievement-orientated, efficient work force, men and women with disciplined work habits, with the trained intelligence to carry out instructions, and with the motivation to compete against standards of excellence. Where better to start this training than in the school? Where better to start making it clear that society no longer considers female gender an impediment to competitive success in the workplace? With its sexually integrated student body, its increasingly sexually non-differentiated curriculum, and its emphasis on achievement, the school has become an important training ground for female achievers, as it long had been for males. Why, then, should anyone be surprised when girls get good grades in school? Why should anyone be puzzled when they transfer their talent for achievement from the school to the occupational world?

As a reward, good grades in school bring smiles and approbation from teachers, hugs and kisses from parents, and money and scholarships from society. But delicious as these external rewards are, the internal gains that come with success are perhaps more important. Good grades increase self-confidence and self-esteem, they reinforce useful skills and habits of work, they help create a perception of the world as a friendly and supportive place, and they become part of a history of accomplishment that can lift the individual out of the muck of mediocrity on to the high ground of success. But perhaps most critical of all for occupational achievement, good grades affect the student's educational and occupational aspirations. How well one presently performs in school affects how well one expects to perform in the future. These expectations shape the decision to continue in school beyond the secondary level, influence the choice of college and curriculum, and thus play a vital part in the creation of occupational achievement. Not surprisingly, therefore, researchers have concluded that academic ability and performance are primary sources of variation in occupational attainment.[12]

The impact of mental ability and academic performance on the expectations of adolescents in this study were examined by relating their IQ scores and grades to their educational and occupational expectations. Educational expectations were measured by their responses to the question: 'How far do you *actually* expect to go in school?' We phrased the question this way in order to encourage responses that not only tap educational aspirations but also include an appraisal of how realistic such hopes are. The responses could range along a continuum from (1) don't expect to graduate high school, (2) graduate high school, (3) technical or business training after high school, (4) graduate from four-year college (5) graduate from a professional or graduate school after college. Though slight modifications had to be made in this series to fit the educational systems of Britain and Italy, the idea of a continuum of increasing educational expectations fits the systems of all three countries reasonably well.

A measure of occupational expectation was constructed from the student's responses to this question: 'What job do you think you will end up having when you are your parents' age?' Worded this way, the question encourages answers that express expectations linked to an adult stage in the life course rather than fantasies associated with youth. The student's response was coded into one of six categories corresponding to categories in occupational indices that have been developed by researchers in the United States, Britain, and Italy, as described in the Appendix. The categories ranged in status from the manual trades, to skilled technical or clerical jobs, to managerial, business, administrative, or professional work, with each occupational category given a weight of ascending importance from 1, the lowest, to 6, the highest. Again, as in the case of educational expectations, the indices vary somewhat from country to country, but all contain the idea of occupations falling along a continuum of prestige.[13]

The effect of mental ability and academic performance on the educational and occupational expectations of American, British, and Italian adolescents can be seen in Table 3.2, which shows the correlations of IQ and school grades with occupational expectation scores. Turning first to the American students, the data show that IQ and grades are positively correlated with the expectation variable, though in three out of four comparisons the correlations are greater with mental ability than with grades and greater for males than for females. Since no IQ data exist for the British and Italian adolescents, only grades could be correlated with expectations, but in their cases, as with their American counterparts, grades are positively correlated with educational and occupational expectations. Generally, the correlations in all three countries are higher for males than for females; the correlations are also higher for educational than for occupational expectations,

Table 3.2 Correlation of IQ and Grades with Educational and Occupational Expectations

| | Educational Expectations | | Occupational Expectations | |
	Females	Males	Females	Males
United States				
IQ	0.34** (270)	0.43** (248)	0.31** (270)	0.50** (248)
Grades	0.38** (444)	0.36** (461)	0.28** (353)	0.37** (346)
Britain				
Grades	0.30* (44)	0.34* (68)	0.20 (33)	0.26* (64)
Italy				
Grades	0.12* (234)	0.15* (231)	0.02 (147)	0.10 (168)

*$p < 0.05$
**$p < 0.01$

suggesting that teenagers of both sexes see a closer relationship between grades and continued schooling than between grades and occupational choice. And on the whole, the correlations are higher for the Americans than for the British, and higher for the British than for the Italians. These national and sex differences will be examined in more detail in a later chapter.

The data clearly indicate that achievement in an academic milieu affects the expectations of girls and as well as boys. No longer is academic achievement merely an ornament, a badge of accomplishment to be laid aside when a girl ends her formal schooling and begins the workaday activity of family life. Girls, like boys, carry with them well into adult life the effects of academic endeavour: achievement shapes a girl's image of herself and of her ability to solve complex and abstruse problems; it influences her willingness to tackle the demanding requirements of college work; it gives direction to occupational choice and defines the boundaries and limits of occupational achievement. Though by itself academic achievement guarantees nothing, yet coupled with hard work and motivation, it can set a youngster on the path to success in the world of work, a world increasingly open to women as it has long been to men.

SEX DIFFERENCES IN NON-ACADEMIC ACHIEVEMENT

A talent for achievement, a taste for competition, and a nimbleness at problem-solving can be expressed in ways other than through academic performance, as anyone proficient in sports or active in clubs or skilled in the creative arts knows. Some boys blessed with good eye and hand coordination get a sense of achievement by smashing a ball far across a field, to the enthusiastic applause of watchers and team-mates; some girls pirouette elegantly across a dance floor, stunning their envious friends and winning dance contests. Many and varied are the arenas in which early achievement can occur; the schoolroom is only one of them and for many youngsters not necessarily the most important. Indeed, achievement daily takes place in areas only peripherally related to the schoolroom, as in sports and its ancillary activities, cheerleading and team management; or outside school as in community enterprises such as service clubs and religious groups; or in largely pleasure-giving, creative activities such as talent shows, plays, musicals – all have become areas in which achievement occurs. Consequently, in a modern industrial society rich in complexity and blessed with resources, ambitious and determined youngsters can readily find the chance to show how well they can do. As a result, achievement has become plentiful, even commonplace, though of course not everyone is an achiever.

Achievement is seldom its own reward; nor does it have to be. Modern society values achievement and showers young achievers with signs of its regard: gold medals or blue ribbons for success in a variety of competitions, ranging from sports to pie-making to animal husbandry to poetry-writing. And when it comes to competing for these awards neither sex can any longer be said to enjoy an overwhelming advantage over the other. True enough, in any competition where height or weight or muscle count heavily, men tend to have an advantage over women, and hence such competitions are usually intrasexual. But increasingly both sexes compete in the same contest, vying for the same awards and prizes, jousting for the same positions of honour and power. After all, girls as well as boys can belt out a song in a musical or emote in a drama; girls as well as boys can organise a group and raise funds for a good cause; girls as well as boys can hold office in a club or political group. As a consequence, the resource-building, ego-lifting, and mind-expanding effects of achievement can be felt perhaps as often today by females as well as by males.

The industrial society wants it this way. As we have already noted, the industrial society needs large numbers of achieving women, and when better to start their training in achievement, when better to begin encouraging competition through rewards for success than in the early years. Perhaps some readers will find this argument perplexing and unconvincing. For is it not true that society so confines girls, so limits their physical movement, so robs them of the opportunity to acquire marketable skills that it, in effect, denies them an equal chance to become achievers? No, not so; or at least, not any more. However accurate this charge may have been in the past, it is no longer true. The modern industrial world invites achievement from almost everyone, and it makes it attractive to women, enticing them to take part in the same activities that have long permitted men to develop and display their excellence.

Some idea of how much the situation of women has changed and how powerful the appeal of achievement is to females in industrial societies can be seen in the responses of the adolescents in the study to questions about their participation in a broad spectrum of activities. They were asked, first, to tell us how often in the last 12 months they had taken part in performing activities (musical groups, talent shows, plays, etc.); in sport activities; in school-related club activities, such as a debating team, student government, the school newspaper; and in community activities such as fund raising, service clubs, religious groups, and the like. Then, they were asked whether during those 12 months they had won any awards, held any office, or received any special recognition in any of these areas. The answers to the question about amount of participation could range on a four point continuum from 'none' (weight of 1), to 'some' (2), to 'many' (3), to 'very many' (weight of 4). To the question on winning awards or holding office, the responses ranged from 'never' (1), 'sometimes' (2), 'often' (3), 'very often' (4). From these weighted responses we derived a score for each individual: the higher the score, the more active the adolescent has been and the more offices or awards he or she had won during the previous twelve months.

Table 3.3 shows the mean scores of males and females in the United States, Britain and Italy for each activity area. What strikes the eye when scaning the table is the great similarity between male and female score in most areas. True, the boys tend to be slightly more active and win more awards in sports, whereas the girls shine more in the performing arts, sex differences the conventional mind would find

Table 3.3   *Mean Activities and Awards Scores, by Sex and Country*

| | United States | | Britain | | Italy | |
	Females	Males	Females	Males	Females	Males
Activities						
Performing	1.8**	1.5	1.6	1.5	1.6*	1.4
Sports	2.1**	2.3	2.0**	2.3	2.3*	2.6
Clubs	1.6**	1.3	1.4	1.5	1.7	1.7
Community	1.8**	1.5	1.7	1.8	1.7	1.7
Awards and Offices						
Performing	1.9**	1.5	1.6**	1.5	1.5	1.4
School	1.4	1.4	1.4*	1.6	1.3*	1.5
Sports	1.4**	1.7	1.4**	1.6	1.4**	1.9
Creative	1.3**	1.4	1.2	1.3	1.4	1.6
Clubs	1.5**	1.3	1.2**	1.3	1.3	1.4

Ns for United States   *Ns for Britain*   *Ns for Italy*
Females: > 1482 < 1502 Females: >486 < 496   Females: > 655 < 669
Males: > 1508 < 1525   Males: 535 < 546   Males: > 632 < 658

*p <0.05
**p <0.001

entirely explicable. But the differences between the sexes are extremely small, never more then four-tenths of a point. In the other areas, there are virtually no differences between the sexes: girls participate in community activities, win awards, and hold office about as often as boys.

Anyone familiar with the aims and efforts of women's groups may think the similarity of male and female scores simply unsurprising. After all have not these groups, and others sympathetic with their aims, made the participation of females in every sphere of activity one of their most salient goals? Have they not argued that girls ought to be permitted to take part in any activity open to boys, and that restricting anyone to those areas traditionally thought proper to one's gender is morally wrong? And have not women's groups been extraordinarily successful in using their political muscle to wrest concessions from tradition-bound institutions and organisations? If so, why should the similarity between the activity scores of girls and boys surprise anyone?

But it is not that simple. Political power waxes and wanes, and women's groups, like other political movements, have had their ups and downs, sometimes rising sharply in power and influence, and at other times sinking into near oblivion. Between the great wars and well into the 60s of this century, feminism in America slumbered. In Britain feminism became relatively quiescent after the end of the First World War, when it won for women the right to vote; and in Italy, it never attained much influence at all, attracting few adherents outside of the big cities of the North, though alliances with labour unions and political parties did win for women substantial victories in their battles to strike down discriminatory practices in the labour market. Still, until very recently the women's movement in America never gained broad acceptance in the general population, and remains in Britain and Italy an organisation of middle-class, educated females whose numbers and influence were never great enough to radically change the orientations of young people in the schools and in community affairs.[14]

Nor will political action explain another interesting facet of the data: namely, the surprising similarity of scores across countries. For despite differences in the histories and cultures of their countries, differences that might make it difficult for these youngsters to understand each other, the American, British, and Italian students are remarkably alike in the degree of their participation and achievement in school and community affairs: the differences between the national groups are never more than a fraction of a point. This is not to say that no differences exist between adolescents in the three countries. British social scientists maintain that British adolescents are less likely to be joiners than their American peers, and that the school or church is less likely to be a focus of club activity in Britain than in the United States.[15] In contrast, the Church is a place of much youth activity in Italy, particularly in those regions where religion still exercises considerable influence in community affairs.[16] Nevertheless, the data in Table 3.3 do not reveal significant differences between the national groups. Knowing a student's nationality or sex helps very little in making an accurate prediction about what activities a girl or boy will take part in, how often, and with what success. For what most visibly separates these students from one another, mainly their sex and nationality, is less important than what they have in common: they all live in highly industrialised regions and countries.

Only a force as powerful as industrialisation could override the inhibiting effects of traditional culture on female activity and achievement, for, make no mistake, traditional culture is by no means dead. For example, even today many people in Italy frown upon any activity that might distract a woman from what they consider her primary role in life, that of wife and mother, and try to limit her mobility and the scope of her endeavour. Not that tradition would keep women in purdah, far from it; but tradition discourages women from working outside the home after marriage, and seeks to restrict their movement when unaccompanied by responsible elders; and traditional people worry when nubile young women and girls associate with strangers, particularly those of the opposite sex. And yet our data show that most of the Italian girls in the two industrial northern cities included in this study are not stay-at-homes: they take part in community and school activities, and they assume positions of leadership in clubs about as often as Italian boys. They can do so because both sexes move in a society where the power of traditional culture has become attenuated. Modern industrial norms, much more than traditional rules, govern the behaviour of the young people in our samples, and modernity permits, indeed requires, females to take part in non-familial activities and encourages them to be achievers.

To say that industrialisation has made girls as active and successful as boys begs an important question: how did industrialisation manage to achieve this remarkable result? For formidable barriers had to be overcome before sexual equality in the work and play that youngsters take part in could be achieved. Industrial society had to persuade people to discard old values and tradition-sanctioned relationships, and replace them with new ideas, practices and responsibilities. In short, people had to be induced to give up old sex roles and adopt new ones. How girls and boys are socialised into the new sex roles acceptable and necessary to an industrial society is the topic of the next chapter.

4 The Social Context of Sex Role Socialisation

'When a child is born parents first look at its genitals. If it's a boy they spoil it, if it's a girl they discipline it.' So spoke a Brazilian physician who, in describing the way parents rear children in rural Brazil, expressly pointed up the early age at which sex role socialisation begins in a pre-industrial community. For pre-industrial parents know that gender critically affects a child in almost every arena of activity: in the home when relating to parents and siblings, at school when responding to teachers and other persons of authority, on the playground when interacting with peers. And on becoming an adult, the child's gender will fix its status in the family and community, dictate or limit the work it will perform, and shape the way it will relate to people of either sex. Hence conscientious parents, and even others not as dutiful, early on teach their children the attitudes and values, and the skills and competencies it will need to function as a male or female throughout the course of life.

Traditional parents accept the sexual division of labour as part of the natural order of things, and with the effects of sex culture on work powerfully apparent to everyone, they make proper gender socialisation an important part of childrearing. To be sure, parents are not the only agents of socialisation in a child's life; peers, teachers, and others also participate in sex role socialisation and may on occasion win out in the competition for the child's attention. Still and all, no agent plays typically a greater part in the social development of children than the parent, for although socialisation does not end with the family, it begins there for most people.

Usually, the child makes its first contact with the social world in the family, when it is still unformed and plastic, vulnerable and defenceless, and hence especially susceptible to social influences. It is in the family that the child first experiences the joys of acceptance and affection, learns the meaning of authority and control, and develops a sense of identification with other human beings. It is in the family that the child first encounters the values, norms and behaviour patterns of the general society, mediated through parents who transmit culture and help maintain socially acceptable behaviour. And it is in the family that the child first learns about sex roles. The sex role embodies an important segment of social values, rules, and behaviour patterns, whose influence the child can observe in the daily actions of parents and other adults.

All theories of sex role socialisation give to the family a major part in the learning process, though the importance assigned to the parental role varies with the theory.[1] Social learning theory sees the parent as an important reinforcer of behaviour (albeit only one of several) and the giver of rewards and punishments contingent on the child's fulfilment of sex role expectations. Cognitive and developmental theories ascribe to parents the major responsibility for giving the child a personal sense of gender identity and teaching related concepts of masculinity and feminity. Once gender identity is acquired, usually by about age three, the child goes on to select an appropriate sex role model, ordinarily the parent of the same sex, and from that time on sex role socialisation increasingly becomes an autonomous process. Psycho-analytic theory puts the parent at the dynamic centre of the learning process. As this theory understands it, sex role socialisation begins with the establishent of a strong emotional bond (identification) with parents. Later, after numerous vicissitudes and confusions that vary with age and gender, the child singles out the parent of the same sex for special attention, internalises that parent's values and expectations, and models himself or herself on that parent, learning in the process an appropriate sex role. Only dogmatic partisans for one theory or another insist on making these theories and their derivatives – e.g. operant conditioning theory, information processing and scheme theories, biological and other developmental theories – mutually exclusive. Most theorists see something of value in all these theories, and all recognise the singular part parents play in sex role socialisation.

Theorists have good reason for stressing the parent's part in the sex role learning process. For they recognise that parents are not simply passive instruments of cultural transmission, not merely uncritical transmitters of whatever messages the society cares to send; rather, they understand that parents try to screen out noxious ideas and misinformation as best they can, letting in only those ideas, values and goals with which they agree, though the filtering process is never perfect and some objectionable matter inevitably flows through. In addition, some parents are skilful creators of needs and wishes, shapers of attitudes and feelings, builders of hopes, plans and goals, mostly drawn from their own world view and experience, and in so doing they help create the rich variety of personalities that enriches social life. Notwithstanding this variety, however, every society also abounds in uniformities that stem from the childrearing practices common to people who fill similar positions in the social structure and who share the same culture. It is a measure of industrialisation's enormous power that it produces new uniformities in the midst of great social change. Among the most important of these uniformities is the sex role.

INDUSTRIALISATION AND SOCIALISATION

Pre-industrial parents train their children to perform sex roles in a world very different from the one industrial people inhabit.[2] Traditional parents in the villages and small towns of a pre-industrial society try to prepare the child to take its place in a world where submission to authority at every level – the family, the school, the workplace – is the linchpin that holds the system together, a world that fills most positions by ascription, with little leeway for individual initiative and with little tolerance for deviation from conventional practices and norms.

Work that is related to sex roles forms an important part of the child's ascriptive world, whose rules he must learn to obey without hesitation. Consequently, parents in pre-industrial, agrarian societies introduce their children very early into the existing sexually segregated world of work, partially initiating them in this way into the meaning of their sex role. By age eight or nine, sometimes earlier, boys accompany their fathers into the field, helping in the planting and harvesting of crops, and doing whatever chores their physical strength and time permit. Little girls learn their work-related sex roles even earlier than boys; by age five or six they have begun helping their mothers with household chores and may begin caring for younger siblings while they are still children themselves.

In this way, at home and in the field, at the work bench and in the shop, and by a process characterised more by observation and imitation than by direct instruction, children acquire the skills and practices, the values and attitudes, the feelings and motives that society expects males and females to possess. In most pre-industrial societies, children learn that men work outside the home, at tasks that require, permit and even applaud independence, achievement, and assertiveness; women work in or near the home, caring for others, performing tasks that require and reward nurturance and self-denial. And in time these work-related traits become part of the personalities of children, eventually affecting the way they perform their roles as a men or women.

In the traditional world most parents believe themselves perfectly competent to prepare their children for adult life. Their own biographies, they believe, exemplify the future awaiting the child; their roles are the roles the child will play as an adult; their skills are the ones he or she must learn in order to survive; their values are the ones the community supports and will continue to applaud for the foreseeable future. And so, believing the future to be relatively clear and predictable, traditional parents see no reason not to guide children toward conventional goals and no reason not to use established procedures to get them there. But this state of affairs, which depends largely on the society remaining agrarian and stable, comes to an end with the growth of industrialisation.

Industrialisation shatters the traditional patterns of interaction between parents and their children. It makes the relationship between parent and child more open and demonstrative; it increases the status of the child by removing the father from the centre of the familial stage and putting the child into the spotlight of attention and concern; it alters the parents' personalities and actions, making them more optimistic and competent; it enlarges the resources at the parents' disposal, thus enabling them to improve the child's social and psychological well-being. In brief, industrialisation changes what parents can do to and for a child – how they respond to the child's cries for help, appeals for affection, and assertions of independence. These changes reflect the parents' experience in the ambience of an industrial society, an ambience that encourages achievement and independence.

Parents in an industrial society must prepare their children for an unknown future; almost nothing can be assumed about tomorrow except that it will be different from today. Ideas that had developed slowly and painfully over generations become outmoded with mind-numbing rapidity. New ideologies sweep old cherished ideas into the dustbin of outworn philosophies. Deeply prized values and habits that gave meaning and stability to one generation are derided by the next as irrelevant, old-fashioned, comical; and generations are no longer measured in decades but in years – often only a few years separates one generation from the next. In these circumstances, a strong commitment to traditional ideas and a devotion to established methods and goals can be suicidal. And so, to help their children survive and prosper in a swiftly-changing society, modern parents must focus on the future and try to anticipate it; they must be flexible and ready to jettison the past if it gets in the way.

When society intrudes into family affairs; when it instructs parents to promote independence and achievement in their children, even though doing so will make the parents' lives more difficult; when it encourages parents to show affection toward their offspring long after they have ceased being docile and adorable babies; when it frowns upon strict discipline lest the child's psyche be bruised – and the industrial society does all these things – then it has brought into being a new set of parental roles. These roles have a social purpose: they promote independence and achievement. For, in the realm of work, an industrial society treasures independence and achievement in its citizenry and seeks, through manipulating the socialisation process, to promote these qualities in children, believing that as adults they will bring to their jobs the motivation and discipline upon which an industrial economy depends.

Industrial society restrains the traditional family's penchant for placing the entire burden of childrearing on the mother's shoulders. In an industrial society women come to expect their husband's help in taking care of children. No longer are men excused from feeding, bathing and changing the baby; no longer can they avoid the tedious task of entertaining small children; in short, no longer are men exempt from almost all socialisation chores until the child is old enough to join them at work. Modern men must pitch in and help. For with women increasingly being recruited into the labour force to work in factories and stores and offices where children cannot accompany them, and with fewer surrogate caretakers at home, men must accept more responsibility for the rearing of small children, even of girls, a sex whose training previous generations of fathers had watched from afar as interested but puzzled observers, since the development of womanhood was thought to be a mystery quite beyond the ken of ordinary men. That many fathers today become involved in childrearing reluctantly, that in most cases their part is far smaller than the mother's cannot be denied, but that their involvement has increased with industrialisation is incontrovertible.

As it changes parental roles, industrialisation also transforms the people who perform them. Not only do the mass media in an industrial society teach parents new ways of rearing children, not only does industrial work give parents the income to improve their childrens' lives – more nutritious food, ampler shelter, better education, more interesting ways to spend leisure time – but also the industrial society, when its exacting demands are met successfully, can give parents a sense of personal efficacy and a feeling of optimism that encourage them to guide their children toward more ambitious goals than they themselves had ever aspired to. And wanting a bright future for their children, knowledgeable parents try to inculate in their progeny the attributes they feel most likely to assure survival and success in an industrial society – independence and achievement. They recognise the important part that a penchant for competition, a predilection to strive for high goals, and a capacity for self-direction play in the struggle for success in a modern economy.

THE EROSION OF PARENTAL AUTHORITY

The modern society's strong orientation towards the future drastically alters parent–child relationships by conferring special status on children, who are seen as more in touch with the present and better able to adapt to the future than their parents. Describing the painful condition of hapless parents living in a rapidly changing, future-oriented world, Philip Slater writes, 'They must face the irrelevance of their knowledge and skills for the world in which their children will mature . . . parents cannot define the parameters of the future for their children – cannot even establish the terms of possible change or a range of alternative outcomes. They are, therefore, useless and obsolete in a way that rarely befell parents of any previous century.'[3] Moreover, even when parents recognise what is is their children need to know in order to cope with a changing industrial world, they may lack the ability to transmit this knowledge. Only the exceptionally competent and lucky parent can accurately predict and skilfully prepare the child for the future.

But when parents become confused and uncertain as how best to prepare the child for the future, when they suspect their own skills and knowledge are no asset to the child – worse, perhaps a liability – then a serious erosion of parental authority sets in. Baffled by a world they have helped to make but do not understand, and bewildered by social change, parents lose confidence in themselves and become unsure of their ability to guide a child through life's uncharted waters safely into port. Consequently, parental prestige and power deteriorate and the relative position of the child improves. In a future-oriented family the child becomes the central figure in the drama of family life, a far cry from the traditional scene in which children play only supporting roles or wait quietly in the wings while the parents perform all the major parts and receive most of society's attention and rewards.

THE EXPERIENTAL CHASM

The erosion of parental authority and power has its origins in several related aspects of industrialisation. The first is rapid technological change, a condition which often produces personal disorientation and confusion, a state of mind not exactly conducive to convincing, rational displays of authority. Technological change disorients the conventional mind because it tends to occur in quantum jumps, not in small incremental steps. Suddenly, machines enable people to traverse in hours distances that once took days or weeks to cover; suddenly, machines force people to work in places and at times and in ways totally alien to their previous experience or inclination. Not surprisingly, not everyone finds these changes either pleasant or comprehensible, despite the machine's vaunted claims to efficiency and productivity, and its undoubted contribution to the material welfare of most people.

But technological change does more than disconcert the mind; it can also create a gulf between the generations, an experiential chasm that separates a child reared in an advanced technological age from a parent brought up in less complicated times. For what can a father who once kept the company's accounts with the aid of a simple calculator say about book-keeping to a son who tackles a similar problem with a computer? What can a stay-at-home mother whose view of the world stems from limited personal observation say to a business-world daughter whose everyday experiences give her a varied, far-ranging, constantly changing picture of life? Not much that is mutually intelligible. And this experiential chasm insidiously undermines parental authority: 'Such a chasm serves to invalidate parental authority and the pertinence of parental wisdom, for parents have not experienced what is of central importance to the child, or at least have not experienced it in the same way, at the same time of life.'[4] Having grown up in different worlds and daily moving in separate circles, parents and children in rapidly changing societies may drift apart until the generation gap becomes a canyon.

Industrialisation also diminishes parental authority by restricting the parents' freedom to shape and control their children. In the industrial city the police, the courts, and the children's bureaux may come between parent and child and attempt to regulate parental behaviour, moving when necessary against parents who use undue force to extract obedience from their children. Such intervention, no matter how well-intended, inevitably reduces the authority of parents over children.

Finally and more subtly, an industrial society weakens parental authority by placing before children non-parental models whose attitudes, values and behaviour may run counter to those of their parents. In the school, children may encounter teachers whose views are substantially at variance with those advocated by their parents. Or, as often happens, children may come upon, in magazines and newspapers or on television, that ubiquitous modern figure, the expert, whose prestige in advanced technological societies is enormous and whose advice sometimes nullifies parental teachings. To be sure, experts are not always resented or resisted, since many parents turn voluntarily to the expert for guidance, willingly substituting someone else's judgement for their own, a tactic that makes it difficult for the parent to maintain a posture of omniscient authority. Whatever their point of entry into the family, non-familial models generate torrents of counter-ideas and visions that rudely erode the foundation on which traditional parental authority rests.

But knowledgeable parents can build bridges across an experiential chasm. Granted that industrialisation produces a rift between the child who embraces change and the parent who resists it; still, it does not follow that industrialisation will make all parents want to fight change. Some parents, in fact, eagerly embrace new ideas because they know that for good or ill change is inevitable. Moreover, industrialisation can give parents the motivation and skill to reduce the gap between themselves and their children or the wisdom to keep it from developing in the first place.

Parents can minimise the possibility of a gap developing between themselves and their children by adopting the values of the changing world and actively preparing their children to take their places in it. To do this effectively they must identify the qualities society will reward and examine their children carefully for signs of these valued characteristics, nuturing them when found and inculcating them when absent.

What are these qualities? Some are difficult to identify, for the future is murky to even the most prescient parent. But others are quite clear because, repeatedly in the mass media, in the schoolroom, in offices and factories, and in the marketplace, the industrial society proclaims to all who will listen the qualities it cherishes in its citizenry. In the school, children's readers reiterate the importance of hard work, independence and achievement. In the mass media, soap operas and other serialised stories celebrate the victories of the successful lawyer, physician, actor, politician, soldier. In the factory, management solicits suggestions to improve efficiency and offers incentives for increased production. In the marketplace, the give and take of economic exchange rewards the competitive, assertive seller or buyer.

In all of these spheres, the industrial society identifies the qualities it would like its inhabitants to have. Teach your children, the society says, to value hard work and achievement, make them ambitious and independent and competitive, and their future is assured. Persistence, hard work, careful planning, the slow accumulation of knowledge, skill, a certain gusto for competition, a willingness to be independent, a tendency to be optimistic – all these qualities pay off in industrial societies, and parents who recognise them strive to inculcate them in their progeny.

Because they value independence and achievement, knowledgeable parents accept their unpleasant as well as positive effects. They know that promoting independence in children will encourage a degree of self-assertiveness that can be annoying but, recognising the value of this trait for the child's future success, they accept it and step gingerly lest they crush the child's efforts to be independent. And understanding the importance of achievement, parents respond enthusiastically to any signs of skill and unusual accomplishment in the child, nourishing these phenomena with approval and material rewards.

Modern parents, and perhaps some who are not modern but would like their children to be, view the experiential chasm not as a calamity but as a natural and salutary development, an inevitable accompaniment of technological progress and a sign that their children are adjusting well to social change. Rather than bemoan the experiential distance between themselves and their offspring, sensible parents want the child to enjoy the new world it is entering. And as conscientious socialisers, they try to prepare the child for the challenges awaiting the young would-be achiever in a rapidly changing world. To do this, parents must first free themselves of some old-fashioned ideas, including the traditional definition of sex roles.

Not everyone, of course, welcomes change in sex roles. To some parents, the idea of abandoning the traditional sex role seems unnecessary, foolish and dangerous. Unnecessary because, as they see it, men have always been socialised to be independent and achievement-oriented. Ambition and work, self-reliance and independence have always paid off for some men, even in pre-industrial societies; hence, these qualities need only be encouraged in the industrial society to produce the desired effect – success. No change is required here. But inducing achievement and independence in women? The traditionalist demurs. Giving women independence, encouraging them to make their own decisions, letting them choose occupations that would put them in close and unsupervised contact with men seems the height of folly. For encouraging women to strive for success in paid employment would only distract them from their obligations to the family, with dangerous consequences to themselves and to society. Something must be done, of course, to insure that males are achievement-oriented and independent, but promoting these qualities in females is another matter entirely.

And yet the industrial society needs women in the labour force and will have them, whatever traditionalists think; moreover, it needs independent, achievement-oriented women. And so, willy-nilly, parents must learn to give their daughters more freedom, must permit self-reliance and independence, must encourage assertiveness and achievement outside the narrow boundaries of domestic culture, notwithstanding the anxiety and fear these unaccustomed attributes engender in the hearts of parents. By supporting their daughters' efforts to experiment with new lifestyles, by rewarding them when they strike out in new directions and seek new careers, even though the choices seem bizarre and the possibilities for failure alarming, parents bridge the experiential chasm and effectively change the female sex role.

THE MAKING OF A NEW SEX ROLE

The training of boys and girls into a new sex role congruent with the needs of the industrial-service economy is already far advanced. For decades now, parents in the industrial West have understood the importance of preparing their children, girls as well as boys, to be ambitious and independent. Acting upon that understanding, they had reared, by the 1970s, a generation of youngsters who perceive their parents as encouraging independence and achievement and as tolerant and supportive of actions outside the traditional mould, particularly when they work to the child's occupational advantage.

Perhaps parents who insist, as many do, that they treat their sons and daughters alike, that they make only trivial distinctions between the sexes in dress and deportment, will find our conclusion unremarkable. And yet on this matter no unanimity exists in the scientific community:

researchers are deeply divided on the issue of whether parents treat boys and girls differently. Some researchers report early, persistent, and significant differences in the socialisation of boys and girls; others find few, if any, important differences in the way parents socialise the sexes. Who is one to believe?

Let us look at the data. First, it must be recognised that both sides can marshal data in support of their positions, using as evidence the many studies of sex differences conducted during the past two generations by educators, psychologists and sociologists. Since a case-by-case examination of these studies would be wearisome and excessively time-consuming, we will turn instead to several reviews of the research literature, which fortunately have done much of the work for us.

One such review, a 1974 book by Maccoby and Jacklin, examined dozens of studies and concluded few differences exist in the way parents treat boys and girls.[5] Both sexes receive about the same amount of parental attention, warmth, restriction and achievement pressure; neither sex is more likely to get its dependency behaviour reinforced; and aggression directed at the parent is generally frowned upon, whether that aggression comes from a girl or a boy. Both sexes receive about the same amount of punishment, although boys are on the receiving end of physical chastisement somewhat more frequently than girls. There are, however, a few interesting cross-sex differences. Fathers appear somewhat more tolerant of aggression from their daughters than from their sons, whereas mothers are more accepting of challenges from sons than daughters. Fathers are more supportive of dependency in daughters, mothers more in sons, and as a rule, parents are more restrictive with children of their own sex than of the opposite sex. But on the whole, the authors concluded, there are few consistent, significant differences in the way parents socialise boys and girls.

Challenges to this conclusion were not long in coming. In a review of the Maccoby–Jacklin work, Janet Block, and later Althea Huston, noted a number of problems in the studies under review.[6] They pointed to the fact that most of the studies reviewed by Maccoby and Jacklin involved pre-school children (many of them from middle-class families), a potentially serious problem because differences in the socialisation of the sexes may increase with age as sex role related expectations and behaviour become more salient to parents. Also, most of the studies focused on mother-child relationships, although it was apparent from the data that fathers are more likely than mothers to treat the sexes differently and to emphasise the importance of proper sex role behaviour. Finally, the behaviours assessed were mostly those related to the personality aspects of sex-typing, such as dependence, aggression and achievement; almost no attention was paid to the differential socialisation of girls and boys with respect to activities and interests. Yet activities and interests, as for example the choice of toys, games and hobbies, are among the earliest manifestations of sex-typing, and such choices can have powerful consequences for the future behaviour of adult men and women; witness the nuturance that some females are said to transfer from the early treatment of dolls to the much later relationships with their own children, clients and patients.

Sampling and related design flaws do not exhaust the problems detected in earlier studies; the conclusions drawn from these studies also came under attack. Reviews of the research literature since 1973, one by Marini and Brinton in 1984, the other by Huston in 1985, report greater differences between the socialisation of girls and boys than was picked up by Maccoby and Jacklin.[7] Experimental and observational studies conducted since 1973 tend to support the conclusion that from infancy onward boys and girls are encouraged to take part in different types of play activities. Parents, particularly fathers, respond positively to sex-stereotyped gross motor behaviour: running, jumping, rough play are all right for boys; drawing, painting, cutting patterns, playing with dolls are best for girls. And toys tend to be highly sex-typed almost everywhere. A British study of parents choosing presents for their children found that no one bought a scientific toy for a girl: chemistry sets are fine for boys, not for girls; no one bought a doll for a boy.[8] Another study of toy advertisements in British mail catalogues revealed them to be rife with sex stereotypes: boys are routinely shown as engineers, artists, hunters, carpenters, scientists, commandos and the like; girls as teachers, nurses, secretaries, designers, and mothers. Though the researcher scrupulously notes that some catalogues – the Habitat catalogue is singled out for mention – are quite careful to avoid gender-typing, she concludes nonetheless that the sex-typing of toys is widespread and probably predisposes children to take part in gender-specific play.[9]

Some researchers are finding stronger evidence than hitherto reported that parental socialisation practices do in fact vary with the sex of the child. Block, explicitly taking issue with Maccoby and Jacklin, examined several European and American samples and found that males more often than females were taught to compete, to suppress tears and feelings, and to conform to social expectations. Girls, she reports, receive more warmth and affection than boys, and are more frequently the open objects of parental concern and worry. Thus the

Newsons' longitudinal study of British boys and girls emphasises the supervision and surveillance ('chaperonage') that parents impose on girls, especially the restrictive rules and practices that limit what they may do, where they may go and with whom, and how freely they may visit public places alone.[10] On the other hand, after summarising a large body of research, Althea Huston concludes that the evidence on the socialisation of boys and girls is ambiguous: thus some studies report that girls are more likely than boys to be socialised to be timid and dependent, affectionate and demonstrative, passive and non-competitive, while other studies report no significant differences between the way parents treat the sexes. Faced with this muddle of contradictory conclusions (are girls and boys reared differently, or not?), a writer might be forgiven if he threw up his hands and called for more research – the familiar dodge of the bewildered scholar – and dropped the whole matter. But the situation is not as bad as it seems: the contradictions in the data may be more apparent than real.

There are several reasons for this sanguine conclusion. First, the difference between the way girls and boys are reared, when they are found, are seldom large. Certainly these differences are far smaller than in pre-industrial societies. Consider the practice of chaperonage. The Newsons were struck by the amount of surveillance girls endure in contemporary Nottingham. But such supervision pales into insignificance when compared with the control females must put up with in many rural communities. 'Even today', says Rudolph Bell of Nissorini, a Sicilian village, 'single women of any age avoid being seen in public in the sole company of an unrelated male.'[11] Second, as already noted, many researchers of sex role socialisation obtained their data from small, atypical samples. Admittedly, considerations of time and money severely limit the size and representativeness of most research in the social sciences, and unfortunately the study of sex role socialisation is no exception. Thus, although large representative samples and the longitudinal observation of parent–child interaction are highly desirable in any study of child socialisation few researchers can afford the cost in time and money that the lengthy, intensive study of a large sample would involve. Researchers must often settle for a smaller, and possibly more unrepresentative, sample than they would like, even though the price paid for this compromise can be high. Third, many of the newer studies suffer from some of the same flaws that beset earlier studies: for example, an insufficient attention to the father's contribution to socialisation and a tendency to focus upon the pre-pubescent child. Adolescents still attract far less attention in studies of sex role socialisation than this critical stage in human development deserves.

Finally, not enough is known about how children perceive and experience their parents' hopes, expectations and childrearing practices. And yet, the child's perception of what is happening is a critical factor in the socialisation process for, as David Ausubell and others have argued, parental behaviour towards the child, though an actual event, affects the child largely to the extent and in the form that it is perceived.[12] And yet, as any clinician knows, perceptual distortion occurs in most human relationships, not least in the family and, as a result, a reserved, *laissez-faire* father may be perceived as cold and indifferent; a warm, protective mother as oppressive and interfering; responsible, controlling parents as unreasonable and harsh. In short, no matter how reasonably and responsibly the parent may be acting, the child may distort and misjudge parental intentions and actions, with consequences the parent neither anticipates nor wants. For this reason, it is vital that we know how the child perceives parental expectations and behaviour, even though (or, perhaps, especially because) the child seriously distorts what the parent is doing.

HOW ADOLESCENTS SEE THEIR PARENTS

The studies reported in this volume were also affected by limitations of time and energy and money. Ideally, the samples could have been larger, the representativeness of the data better, and the research design longitudinal. Still, the cross-sectional survey has its merits. In our case it enabled us to obtain data from 5434 adolescents, boys and girls from twelve cities and three countries, an unusual sample for a study of sex role socialisation and achievement. This study also has the advantage of focusing upon adolescents, an age group especially affected by sex role expectations and norms. Furthermore, we took seriously the need to assess the youngster's perception of what parents want and do. Lastly, the father is not neglected; data about the father's input into the socialisation process, as perceived by the adolescent, make up an important part of this study.

PERCEPTION OF PARENTAL BEHAVIOUR AND EXPECTATIONS

Paradoxically, getting at the adolescent's perception of the parent proved both easy and difficult: easy because all adolescents have opinions about their parents and with proper encouragement will tell you what those opinions are; difficult because perceptions seldom fall into the clear, neatly delineated categories that researchers like. Children hold diffuse, multifaceted, emotionally-charged, defensive images of their parents, images filled with contradictions, and pulling out of this complex bundle the information needed to test a research hypothesis is never easy.

Fortunately, our needs were relatively modest and hence attainable. Not needing to know everything about parental socialisation practices, we could focus on a small number of parental expectations and behaviours, specifically those tied to sex role socialisation and related to occupational achievement in an industrial society. We wanted to know whether parents differentially socialise boys and girls to be achievement-oriented, independent and assertive – qualities important to occupational achievement in an industrial economy. Put in the language of perception, we wanted to know whether girls are less likely than boys to perceive parental emphasis on achievement; whether they perceive more parental restrictiveness, more parental concern about assertiveness, and less parental tolerance of behaviour that deviates somewhat from this sex role norm. The answers to these questions, if our hypothesis about the impact of industrial life on parental behaviour is correct, must be no: the differences between the sexes in the way they perceive their parents are necessarily small. To test this hypothesis, we put the following question to the students in our school surveys: 'Are the following things more like your father, more like your mother, like both equally, like neither?' The question took the form of fourteen statements about parental behaviour and expectations to which the respondent could react by selecting the response, 'more like my father', 'more like my mother', 'like both equally', or 'like neither'. Obviously, these statements assess parental behaviour and expectations indirectly; a frontal attack, we felt, would tend to arouse defensive responses laden with the bias of social acceptability. The statements, shown in Chart 4.1, are grouped in three categories: achievement, independence and support, and a concern with interpersonal relations.

The three statements in the achievement category touch upon matters of realistic concern to adolescents, areas of present and future performance that are readily understandable to them: school grades, the perception of parental satisfaction with those grades, and talk with parents about the job a student will hold when schooling ends. As regards the first category, achievement, I believe that parents who monitor grades, who express happiness when the grades fall short of expectations, and who show an interest in their progeny's future work,

Chart 4.1   Statements About Parents

'Are the following things more like your father, more like your mother, like both equally, like neither?'

Achievement
1. Acts unhappy when you get worse grades than you should have.
2. Says you can do a better job than you are doing.
3. Talks about the kind of job you will have when you're out of school.

Support-Independence
4. Gives you the feeling you can talk to them honestly.
5. Won't let you solve your problems for yourself.
6. Treats you as though you're younger than you really are.
7. Would stand up for you if you wanted to do something not usually allowed to someone of your sex.
8. Encourages you to keep working at something when you are ready to give up.
9. Encourages you to think that you can have a job that isn't usually held by someone of your sex.
10. Stands by you when others discourage you from doing something different.

Peer Relationships
11. Tells you that people won't like you if you show them you're mad at them.
12. Seems unhappy when you don't have lots of friends.
13. Thinks it's better to keep your opinions to youself than argue with someone.
14. Worries that you'll get married and settle down too soon.

---

can logically be said to be putting pressure on the adolescent to achieve. Although the seven items in the second category, independence-support, are quite heterogeneous, they collectively assess the adolescent's perception of parental restrictiveness and concern, and the willingness of parents to grant the child some latitude in sex role performance. A parent who evokes feelings of trust, who grants the child the freedom to make his or her own decision when personal problems arise, and who tolerates or encourages the adolescent's efforts to strike out in novel directions can be said to be supportive and independence-granting. The third category contains four statements that assess the adolescent's sense of parental anxiety about the adolescent's relationships with peers; statements about parental worries that the child lacks friends, and cautionary comments about assertiveness and its presumed alienating effects on friends and peers.

Traditional parents see little point in training their daughters to be self-assertive, individualistic achievers. As we have noted, the world in which traditional women live out their lives is familial, not occupational; and in the family's close-knit, emotionally-charged, intimate milieu success for women depends far more on interpersonal skills and sensitivity than on competitiveness and achievement. If achievement and self-assertiveness are prized at all – neither trait evokes much enthusiasm in traditional societies – they are stressed in the training of men, whose lives centre on work and war, the traditional pursuits of men. But, as we have said, this difference in sex role socialisation declines in industrial societies, which value achievement and independence in almost everyone, women as well as men, at least so far as work is concerned.

In order to facilitate the analysis of the data, the response to each statement in Table 4.1 (numbered as in Chart 4.1 and abbreviated) were recoded so that a response 'like both equally' was scored 2, a response

Table 4.1   Mean Perception of Parents Scores, by Sex and Country

	United States		Britain		Italy	
	Female	Male	Female	Male	Female	Male
Achievement						
1. Unhappy about grades	1.35*	1.48	1.08	1.17	0.91*	1.11
2. Says can do better	1.26*	1.35	0.93	1.06	1.27*	1.40
3. Talks about job	1.11	1.16	1.29	1.22	1.42	1.36
Independence						
4. Can talk honestly	1.09*	1.23	1.22*	1.35	1.19*	1.31
5. Won't let solve probs.	0.40	0.50	0.44	0.54	0.45	0.65
6. Treats you younger	0.71	0.67	0.59	0.51	0.80	0.65
7. Stands up for you	0.92*	0.76	1.26*	0.80	0.78*	0.57
8. Encourages keep working	1.39	1.41	1.25	1.30	1.27	1.29
9. Encourages have job	0.61	0.28	0.64*	0.32	0.45*	0.26
10. Stand by do different	1.25	1.63	1.30	1.22	1.37	1.30
Peer Relationships						
11. Tells people won't like	0.45*	0.72	0.55	0.66	0.80	0.87
12. Seems unhappy	0.60	0.66	0.70	0.71	1.02	0.94
13. Thinks keep opinions	0.85	0.92	0.78	0.84	0.26	0.38
14. Worries get married	0.62*	0.42	0.66	0.49	0.78	0.73

Ns for United States	*Ns for Britain*	*Ns for Italy*
Females: 1396	Females: 431	Females: 605
Males: 1396	Males: 437	Males: 577

*$p < 0.01$

'more like my father', or 'more like my mother', was scored 1, and 'like neither' was scored zero. The assumption underlying this scoring is that an adolescent who responds 'like both' is receiving more pressure than one who choses only one parent, while the response 'neither' reflects no perceived parental pressure at all. The numbers in Table 4.1 are mean scores, cross-tabulated by sex and country; they indicate the amount of attention or pressure adolescents perceive their parents putting on three important areas of socialisation. The higher the mean score, the more pressure adolescents perceive their parents are exerting on them.

Anyone wedded to the notion that parents exert more pressure for achievement and independence on boys than on girls must find the numbers in Table 4.1 something of a shock. Where are the clear and meaningful differences between the sexes in achievement training, differences that conventional opinion would lead one to expect? True, in the area of school performance, boys in all three countries perceive slightly more attention from their parents than do the girls, perhaps because boys on the average perform less well in school than girls. But parents talk as much or more to their daughters as to their sons about future jobs. In any event, despite their statistical significance, due to the large size of the sample, the differences between the sexes in perceived parental concern about achievement are negligible.

Only slightly larger are the differences between countries, although here again the data do not support popular impressions about differences between national cultures. For example, parents in the United States (the achievement-oriented nation par excellence, or so it is thought) do not put more pressure on children to do well in school than do parents in Italy, where life is thought to be less competitive. On the other hand, American parents appear more unhappy about their children's grades than do British or Italian parents; and British and Italian parents talk more to their children, girls and boys alike, about future jobs than do parents in America, possibly because unemployment rates are higher in Britain and Italy than in the United States. Still, it is best not to make too much of these national differences; like the sex differences, most national differences in perceived emphasis on achievement are quite small.

The data on independence training and support also produced their share of surprises. For instance, although girls are often said to receive less freedom than boys, this is not the way the girls, on the average, see it. Granted, girls are somewhat more likely than boys to say they feel their parents baby them and interfere when they try to solve problems on their own, though the differences between the sexes are small. Still, girls are more likely than boys to feel free to make choices not traditionally allowed to their sex, including the option to choose an occupation customarily filled by members of the opposite sex. This finding is not entirely surprising, for some parents (fathers especially) grow anxious and even intolerant when sons consistently display behaviour associated with the opposite sex, as for example when a boy plays with dolls, uses make-up, or generally shows a lack of interest in sports or other activities traditionally thought to be masculine.[13] Girls, on the other hand, may experiment with masculine life-styles without necessarily evoking parental displeasure. Although, in our study, both boys and girls tend to find their parents generally supportive, people they can talk honestly to, boys are somewhat more likely than girls to think their parents approachable, another unexpected finding since it has been reported that parents talk more to female than to male children. But the reader should remember that with the exception of the item assessing parental reactions to a choice of a non-traditional job, the differences between the sexes are small in all three countries.

Lastly, the prevailing notion that parents put more pressure on girls than on boys to make friends, to inhibit assertiveness, and to suppress anger, finds no confirmation in the perceptions of these adolescents. If anything, boys are slightly more likely than girls to report parental concern about peer relationships and assertiveness: for example, boys perceive more pressure than girls from their fathers to keep opinions to oneself and to avoid showing anger. But the differences between the sexes within each country are trivial, and national differences are also small, except that the Italians are somewhat more likely than their Anglo-American peers to stress the importance of making and keeping friends; also the Italians seem to feel little or no pressure from their parents to hold their tongues when disagreements with peers arise.

Who is putting pressure on the teenager? No one in many cases. In five of the items one-half or more of the adolescents chose the response, 'neither parent'. On the other hand, many of the adolescents chose the response, 'both parents'. It was in fact the response chosen by one-quarter to one-half of the adolescents in seven of the thirteen items. But when the respondent chose a parent, the mother was selected far more frequently than the father. Only in the case of one item ('talks about the kind of job you will have when you are out of school') does the father figure more prominently than the mother. On the whole, our data agree with a finding well-established in the socialisation literature, namely that mothers are generally more involved in childrearing than fathers, a fact confirmed by the adolescents' perceptions.

LEARNING SEX ROLES THROUGH ROLE MODELLING

Children learn sex roles in part through role modelling, through a conscious or unconscious imitation of siblings, peers and adults, and among these adults few enter a child's life more fully than parents. Parents fill the child's day with their gestures, talk and movements, constantly bombarding the child with expectations and hopes, advice and warnings, scoldings, admonitions and love. At first the child sees only discrete, fragmented segments of parental behaviour: a smile, a scowl, a helping hand, an expectation that something must be done or avoided. But in time parental mood and behaviour coalesce into a coherent pattern that contains both idiosyncratic and general elements, a pattern derived from the parent's personality, situation, station in life, and sex. Eventually, the child recognises, though at first only dimly, that parental behaviour adheres to the parent's sex and to the relationships of the parents to one another. When that happens the child is well on its way to learning a sex role and a sex role relationship.

Children have powerful motives for modelling their parents. As exemplars of the adult world, as possessors of prestige and power far in excess of what a child enjoys, as givers of rewards and punishments, parents are the natural objects of a child's envy, affection and fear. Parents enjoy things a child learns to prize: staying up as late as one wishes, watching television until the wee hours of the night, saying 'to hell with spinach' without fear of rebuke. Parents are people with valuable competencies and resources: they make things and hold down jobs; they drive cars and spend money. Even though the child can do none of these things, even though she has few if any material resources of her own, she can vicariously enjoy these advantages through identifying with her parents. But perhaps more importantly, the child needs nurturance and thus comes to value parental affection and to fear parental rejection. By giving or withholding love, by dispensing reprimands and punishment, parents motivate the child to want to be like her parents and to win parental approval through acquiescence and imitation. In effect, a child imitating a parent is saying: love me because I am obedient, and because I behave and think much as you do.

This happy condition for parents does not endure for long. In time most children come to see their parents somewhat more realistically. They recognise that their parents are imperfect human beings: the heroic father may have feet of clay, the beautiful mother an ungainly walk. To some adolescents any imperfection in a parent seems tragical or comical, and altogether unacceptable. These adolescents find fault with the music their parents enjoy, the cars they drive, the food they eat, the attitudes and values they hold, the very lives their parents have so painfully put together. To the harried parent, these criticisms seem like total rejection.

But often there is less here than meets the eye. Usually, most critical, seemingly rebellious adolescents are simply asserting their independence, trying to put some distance between themselves and their previously omnipotent parents. With some help from their parents, much effort, and a lot of luck, most adolescents succeed in wrenching themselves free of parental dominance, but even so, they do not completely unlearn the attitudes, the values, and the behaviour patterns so laboriously acquired in childhood; they do not necessarily reject their parents as models, and though they may not be fully aware of lingering parental influence on their behaviour, they will continue to act in some degree as though their parents were examplars of how men and women should think and behave.

In the normal course of events, though seldom without the painful vicissitudes that make the identification process tricky, children come to identify with the parent of the same sex, girls choosing their mothers or some other adult female, boys choosing their fathers or a father surrogate. But this process is far less simple than it sounds. For one thing the sexes are seldom equal in prestige and power, because men frequently enjoy more freedom and wealth than do women, and hence it is possible that children of both sexes will model themselves after the powerful father. This should present no hazard for the boy, but it can be a problem for both the girl and society. Society depends upon getting a girl to identify with her mother as one way of teaching her the female sex role; without identification the role may be learned inadequately or not al all. Furthermore, a girl who identifies with her father may become confused about her identity and ambivalent about her sex role. Fortunately, the mother's greater accessibility to her children and nurturance may vitiate the father's appeal to her daughter and make identification with the mother easier.

Also mothers are beginning to pose their own status as a countervailing force to the appeal of the father's status and income. As we know, many mothers work at paid jobs in the labour force, some earning a sizeable income and enjoying the status that prestigious and lucrative work provides. They can, therefore, project to their daughters (and sons) images of resourceful, energetic, achieving people with whom their children can identify. For these reasons some researchers, for example Hoffman and Miller, among others, have suggested that the daughters of women in the paid labour force are more likely than the daughters of women who work only at home to want to be like their mothers.[14] More than that, the fact that her mother works, it is said, makes the daughter more achievement-oriented, raises her educational and occupational aspirations, orients her towards a career in the labour force, and discourages her from wanting to stay at home as a full-time housewife and mother.

To determine which parent serves as a model for the adolescent, we asked the respondents the following four-part question: 'How would you feel if, in the future, you found yourself doing: (a) what your mother now does outside the home, (b) what your mother now does at home, (c) what your father now does outside the home, (d) what your father now does at home?' The adolescent could choose one of the four responses: 'not like it at all', 'like it a little', 'like it some', 'like it a lot'. The adolescents' responses were then cross-tabulated by sex and country.

Followers of classical identification and role modelling theory will probably find our findings reassuring: girls tend to say they prefer their mothers' work, in and outside the home, over what their fathers are doing; on the other hand, boys prefer their fathers' role. Thus 36 percent of the American girls said they would like it 'some', 19 percent 'a lot', if they ended up doing what their mothers were doing in the home – positive though tepid support for the housewife's role. Substantially fewer boys found their mothers' work at home attractive: 14 percent of the boys answered, 'some', 7 percent 'a lot', when asked whether they would be pleased if they ended up doing what their mothers were doing at home. Mothers' work outside the home produced similar sex differences: 34 percent of the American girls and 20 percent of the American boys felt they would like it 'some' if they ended up doing what their mothers were doing outside the home; 16 percent of the girls thought they would like it 'a lot' as compared with 8 percent of the boys. Similar sex differences in the evaluation of the mothers' work exists in other countries. For example, 69 percent of the Italian boys stated that they would 'not like it at all' if they ended up doing what their mothers were doing in the home; 30 percent of the girls gave the same response. A statistical analysis of the association between sex and the perception of the mothers' work showed it to be highly significant in all countries: chi-squares ranged between 16.2 and 509.9; probability statements were between the 0.002 and the 0.0001 levels.

Fathers received much the same treatment as mothers in that sex strongly colours the child's evaluation of the fathers' work. Thus 40 percent of the American and Italian girls, and 49 percent of the British girls, said that they would 'not like it at all' if they ended up doing what their fathers were doing. The boys were less negative: only 18 percent of the American, 22 percent of the British and 20 percent of the Italian boys were hostile to the sort of work their fathers were doing. On the other hand, most boys were not exactly enthusiastic about their fathers' work: only 28 percent of the American, 26 percent of the British, and 21 percent of the Italian boys, said they would 'like it a lot' if their fathers' work became their own. But girls are even less drawn to the kind of work their fathers do. Only between 11 and 15 percent of the girls in the three countries said they would 'like it a lot' if their own work were the same as that of their fathers.

Table 4.2 presents the relationship between the adolescent's sex and preference for the parental work world. The data are shown in mean scores, a more tidy method for presenting the findings than afforded by the scattering of percentages presented in the preceding table. The adolescents' responses were scored on a scale of 1 to 4, with 1 presenting rejection of the parental work role ('not like it at all'), 2 'like it a little', 3 'like it some', and 4 great approval ('like it a lot'). Thus the higher the mean score the greater the adolescent's approval of the parent's work role. Scores were summed and cross-tabulated with the respondent's nationality and sex. As can be seen in Table 4.2, the data confirm our conclusion that girls tend to view their mothers' work role,

Table 4.2   Mean Evaluation Scores of Parental Work Role, by Sex and Country

	United States		Britain		Italy	
	Female	Male	Female	Male	Female	Male
Degree of liking what mother does						
Outside the home	2.42*	1.87	2.21*	1.75	1.96*	1.68
Inside the home	2.55*	1.70	2.41	1.66	1.92*	1.34
Degree of liking what father does						
Outside the home	2.13*	2.74	1.92*	2.62	2.03*	2.57
Inside the home	2.23*	2.59	2.03*	2.57	1.87*	2.15

Ns for United States	*Ns for Britain*	*Ns for Italy*
Females: > 1334 < 1479	Females: > 430 < 483	Females: > 319 < 631
Males: > 1367 < 1428	Males: > 468 < 508	Males: > 300 < 592

*$p < 0.01$

in and out of the home, more favourably than do the boys; while the boys incline more towards their fathers' work role.

What about the hypothesis that girls identify more readily with working mothers than with those who stay at home? To test this suggestion we compared the responses of girls whose mothers worked outside the home with those whose mothers were primarily housewives. The data do not support the hypothesis. Whether the mother works outside the home or not seems to make little difference to the girls. For example, 57 percent of the American girls with or without working mothers said they would like it 'some' or 'a lot' if they ended up doing what their mothers did inside the home. About 50 percent of the girls with working mothers said they would like the work their mothers were doing outside the home; but then the girls whose mothers were full-time housewives also gave the same answer, although it is not clear what outside work they had in mind. The British and Italian girls do not differ significantly from their American peers in this important respect; whether the mother works or not seems to have no effect on their evaluation of the mother's role. At this point of the analysis it seemed that the hypthesis must be rejected.

But, as it turned out, we were asking the wrong question. It turned out that what affects the girl's willingness to model the parental role is not whether the mother works but rather the status of the work she is doing. A correlation analysis revealed that the status of the mother's job is positively correlated with the satisfaction a girl says she would feel it she ended up doing the kind of work her mother does outside the home. The product-movement correlation is highest for the Italian girls, 0.24; somewhat lower for the American girls, 0.21; and lowest, 0.19, for the British girls; all the correlations are statistically significant at the 0.0001 level. Girls tend also to be attracted to the jobs of their high-status fathers; the correlations between the status of the father's job and the girl's anticipated satisfaction with doing that kind of work are 0.20 for the Americans and 0.16 for the British (both correlations are significant at the 0.001 level), and 0.10 (significance level is 0.01) for the Italian girls. In sum, the data show that work status tends to be a significant factor in the girl's willingness to model either parent's work role.

Not so in the case of the boys: gender, not status, seems to be the critical factor for males. The mother's work tends to hold no appeal to their sons, irrespective of its status. In none of the three countries is the correlation between the status of the mother's job and the boy's predilection for modelling the mother statistically significant. The boys, it would seem, are shying away from the idea of doing the kind of work a woman does. On the other hand, in the United States and Britain, the status of a father's job is a significant factor in its appeal to boys. Not surprisingly, American and British boys tend to prefer a father's job when its status is high. Italian boys simply prefer their father's work over their mother's without regard to the status of the job.

SEX ROLE SOCIALISATION AND EXPECTATION LEVELS

Knowing how parents rear their children and with whom the child identifies, useful as this information may be, does not answer all our questions. We also want to know whether parental pressure on the adolescent to be indepedent and achievement-oriented, and the tee-nager's choice of a parental role model, affect the adolescent's educa-tional–occupational expectations. Are parental expectations in the area of educational–occupational achievement having an effect? Do adoles-cents who model themselves after their mothers (or their fathers) have different aspirations from those who do not? At the centre of this query is the key question: does socialisation as it is experienced and reported by adolescents affect their ambition and achievement? Let us first examine the effects of role modelling.

Role modelling, as measured in this study, has no effect on adoles-cent expectations and achievement. A correlation analysis revealed no significant relationship between how the adolescents feel about their parents' work, in or out of the house, and their educational–occupational expectations and achievement. Whether the parent's status is high or low, whether the parent is a mother or a father, whether the adolescent is a male or female – none of these makes any difference. In all three countries the correlations between role model-ling and the achievement-related variables are trivial. Perhaps a more subtle, intensive, penetrating measure of role modelling might have uncovered a link between modelling and adolescent achievement expectations and behaviour. We cannot say, but it is clear from these data that the causal nexus between role modelling and a child's expectations and achievement is more subtle and complex than com-monly believed.

An analysis of the effects of perceived parental expectations and behaviour on the adolescent's educational–occupational expectations proved informative. This analysis proceeded in the following way. First we intercorrelated the items shown in Chart 4.1; this revealed small positive correlations among the items within each category. We then summed the adolescents' responses to the items within a category to form three Likert-type Perception of Parent Indices: the higher the adolescent's index score the more he or she perceives a parent as being concerned with achievement and peer relationships, and supportive of independence. Unfortunately, only the index of independence attained an acceptable level of iter-item reliability (Alpha 0.61). Although the achievement and peer relations indices are not statistically reliable, they are included in a portion of the following analysis in the hope that something useful can be learned from them, but the reader is advised to consider the findings generated by these two indices as only exploratory and suggestive.

As we have already pointed out, an interest in achievement, a sensitivity to peer relationships, and the capacity to act independently, are all congruent with the needs of an industrial society that is dependent upon a plentiful supply of achievement-oriented, interpersonally skilled, independent workers. Since people with these personal attributes have a reasonably good chance of moving into the lucrative and prestigious sectors of the economy, knowledgeable parents, recognising the utility of these attributes, will seek to instil them into their progeny in the hope of ensuring their child's occupational success. Therefore, it seems reasonable to argue that adolescents who perceive their parents as stressing achievement, good peer relationships, and independence will have already begun the climb up the status ladder by raising their educational and occupational expectations to the levels appropriate to someone who seeks the rewards of occupational achievement.

If this argument is sound, the indices of parental expectations and behaviour should be positively correlated with the adolescents' educational and occupational expectations: the more the parents are perceived as promoting achievement, interpersonal skills, and independence, the higher the adolescent's educational–occupational expectations. This hypothesis was put to the test (only the older adolescents, whose expectations were presumably more reality-bound, are included in this test) by correlating the parental indices with the adolescent's educational–occupational expectations. Unfortunately, as can be seen in Table 4.3, the data only partially support the hypothesis. Of the three indices, only the independence index correlates positively with adolescent educational–occupational expectations. The achievement and peer relations indices are not significantly related to expectation levels for the boys and girls in any of the three countries. This is both disappoint-

Table 4.3   Correlation of Adolescents' Educational and Occupational Expectations with Parental Indices, by Sex and Country

| | Perception of Parent Indices | | | | | |
| | Achievement | | Independence | | Peer Relationships | |
	Female	Male	Female	Male	Female	Male
United States						
Educational	0.00	0.02	0.26*	0.15*	−0.08	0.00
Occupational	−0.03	0.04	0.17*	0.13*	0.00	−0.01
Britain						
Educational	0.05	0.07	0.00	0.00	0.00	−0.05
Occupational	0.12	0.04	0.14	−0.11	0.01	−0.02
Italy						
Educational	−0.11	0.13	0.19*	0.11	−0.08	0.00
Occupational	0.03	0.14	0.25*	0.28*	0.04	−0.09

Ns for United States	*Ns for Britain*	*Ns for Italy*
Females: > 387 < 425	Females: > 129 < 158	Females: > 137 < 221
Males: > 318 < 441	Males: > 118 < 189	Males: > 160 < 217

*$p < 0.01$

ing and surprising. The connection between perceived parental stress on achievement and interpersonal relationships and the adolescent's educational–occupational expectation seems logical enough. Why then do the data not support the theory?

The answer lies, I believe, in the highly subjective nature of the adoiescents' responses. In order to understand the connection between parental behaviour and the adolescent's expectations we must take into account the adolescent's interpretation of that behaviour: we must know what the adolescent thinks the parent wants and is doing. Regrettably, the data do not provide this information; still, we can make some reasonable guesses. First, it is quite possible that some adolescents view the concern of their parents as nothing more than nagging, endless complaints about school performance and constant urgings to get better grades, perhaps because often the targets of these complaints are not the good students, but those who are not doing well at all. In any case, parental exhortations often appear futile or counterproductive: for instance, the correlation between the achievement index score and grades is negative for the American girls (-0.18, $p < 0.001$) and statistically insignificant for all the other groups.

Perhaps parental concern about achievement and good peer relations, however well-intended it may be, is experienced by the adolescent as just another form of parental control, more evidence of adult interference with their lives, and hence unacceptable. Unacceptable control often elicits resentment and an angry wish to get back at the controller by doing exactly the opposite of what is expected, by doing less well in school than the parent wants. To further complicate matters, exhortation, over-solicitous attention, and excessive control may produce anxiety in the object of all this concern. One way of handling anxiety is to lower self-expectations. It is possible that some over-anxious adolescents have lowered their educational–occupational sights as a way of coping with the tensions aroused by the pressures they perceive the parent is placing upon them to achieve good grades and to maintain good relationships with peers.

Independence training should have the opposite effect. Parents who encourage their children's efforts to do things on their own, who support some experimentation with non-conventional sex role behaviour, and who generate feelings of trust and understanding, are encouraging their children to be independent and autonomous. And through adventuresome, autonomous, successful behaviour, in the context of a supportive family milieu, the child gains self-confidence and self-esteem, a capacity to behave independently, and a willingness to take chances. Certainly, setting high educational and occupational goals for oneself involves taking chances, since the possibility of disappointment and failure increases as aspirations rise. Nonetheless, the autonomous adolescent, trained to think and act independently, will risk failure more willingly than the adolescent who has had fewer opportunities to acquire the self-confidence that successful self-reliant mastery brings.

Support for this argument can be found in the data shown in Table 4.3, in which the adolescents' educational–occupational expectations are correlated with their scores on the independence index. These correlations are significantly positive for the American and Italian samples: the more the adolescent perceives his or her parents as encouraging independence, the higher their educational–occupational expectations. Thus the correlations for the American girls are 0.26 and 0.17; American boys 0.15 and 0.13; Italian girls 0.19 and 0.25; Italian boys 0.11 and 0.28; with the exception of the Italian boys, all the correlations are statistically significant at the 0.01 level or better. Why the low correlations for the British sample? We cannot be certain, but it is possible that in an emotionally cool, non-demonstrative family system such as the British system is said to be, the parents' hands-off, *laissez-faire* attitude may strike the child as more an indication of indifference or inattention than as a sign of positive support for independence. In this circumstance, independence training may have no positive effects on status expectations.

But the effect of independence training on status expectations is complicated by the co-influences of age and social class. Thus, in all three countries, and especially among the males, higher-status adolescents tend to perceive more independence training and to have significantly higher educational–occupational expectations than the lower-status adolescents. And to complicate matters even further, the adolescent's age sometimes has a positive and at other times a negative relationship to educational–occupational expectations. In order to disentangle the effects of social status, age, and independence training on adolescent expectations, we regressed social status, age and independence training on the adolescent's educational–occupational expectations. The results of these regressions appear in Table 4.4, which shows the effects of each independent variable on the adolescent's expectations. To simplify the presentation, only standardised beta coefficients are shown in this table; they are very similar to the unstandardised coefficients and the trends are the same.

We can see that even when the effects of status and age are controlled, independence training continues to have a significant

Table 4.4 *Adolescents' Educational and Occupational Expectations Regressed on Independence Index, Age and Social Status, by Sex and Country, Standardised Coefficients*

	United States		Britain		Italy	
	Female	Male	Female	Male	Female	Male
Educational						
Ind. index	0.21*	0.10	0.04	−0.01	0.21*	0.15
Age	−0.04	−0.09	0.39*	0.34*	−0.05	−0.09
Social status	0.30*	0.29*	0.28*	0.25	0.34*	0.35*
Occupational						
Ind. index	0.16*	0.07	0.04	−0.10	0.23*	0.24*
Age	−0.05	−0.12*	0.33	0.41*	0.02	−0.12
Social status	0.08	0.21*	0.18	0.45*	0.21*	0.37*
N =	320	268	100	100	105	105

*$p < 0.01$

positive effect on the educational–occupational expectations of American and Italian girls: regression coefficients range from 0.23 to 0.16; all are statistically significant at the 0.05 level or better. Not so for the British girls, however. Age and social status, not independence training, seem to be the important factors contributing to higher expectation levels among the British; thus regression coefficients of educational–occupational expectations on age are 0.39 and 0.33; on social status 0.28 and 0.18; all are statistically significant. Apparently status characteristics still carry significant weight in class-conscious Britain.

In contrast to the females, the males in the United States and Britain are generally unaffected by the sort of independence training examined here. Remember, our index of independence training includes statements about parental willingness to let the child deviate somewhat from the conventional sex role, a deviation Western cultures grant more readily to females than to males, and possibly for that reason boys tend not to perceive this sort of independence as a meaningful grant of autonomy – or perhaps they flinch from acting on it. Italian boys apparently feel differently; independence training has a significant positive effect on their occupational expectations, possibly because in the more controlling atmosphere of the Italian family any autonomy, even in the area of sex roles, has a liberating, horizon-widening effect that raises the expectation levels of boys as well as of girls.

To sum up: the evidence I presented in this chapter, data drawn from numerous studies conducted over the past three decades, and from the three-nation investigation of adolescents upon which this book is based, give little or no consistent support to the notion that boys and girls are socialised differently in three important areas related to occupational success in an industrial society: achievement, sensitivity to peer relationships, and independence. Whatever sex differences in sex role socialisation may have existed in the past – and continue to exist in many contemporary pre-industrial societies – the current trend in the industrial world is away from making sharp distinctions between the sexes in the training of boys and girls. Achievement, sensitivity to peer opinion, and independence are becoming as much a part of the female sex role as they have long been of the male. We have already seen one of the consequences of this: the parental grant of independence raises the educational and occupational expectations of girls. But there are other consequences of sex role socialisation worthy of our attention, as we will see in the next chapter which examines the personalities of males and females.

5 The Sex Role and Female Personality

Women have never lacked detractors and enemies. From medieval times to the present, a long line of misogynists has cautioned men against the whims, weaknesses, and wiles of women. To medieval priests and theologians woman was 'a domestic peril, a deadly fascination, a painted ill';[1] to Renaissance poets and playwrights woman was an insidious threat to male hegemony and peace of mind; to some modern legislators and moralists, woman is an unstable life-force whose potentially disruptive energies must be controlled and safely chanelled into domestic work at home. Without this control, her detractors maintain, woman's weak and emotional nature, her proclivity towards deception and manipulation, would threaten personal happiness and endanger the social order.

Women can handle their enemies; their friends pose a more difficult challenge. In the interest of rehabilitating women, in the hopes of promoting social equality and advancing the cause of women in the labour market, some friends of women have subscribed to an image of women that rivals the most damaging descriptions of women offered by women-haters of the past. As these friends see it, oppressive societies have made women timid and helpless, complacent and submissive, passive and dependent; male domination has turned women into gullible and vulnerable creatures, the crushed and exploited objects of male sexuality and aggression. This image excites the sympathy of all right-thinking people and arouses the anger of women themselves, who then cry out for reform and reparation. Make no mistake, this image is not just a political device, not just an echo of past derogations, for unlike the pejorative images of the past, the modern image of woman is thought to be based upon theory and research, upon facts not slurs. Ironically, neither the theory nor the facts are new: both stem from research on male–female relations in traditional non-industrial societies.

MALE DOMINANCE AND ITS EFFECTS

Researchers generally agree that men dominate women in most non-industrial societies and, as the Western record shows, have long done so. Thus in medieval Christendom, canon law and theological opinion were hostile to females and unfailingly supported the claims of men to hegemony over women; in countless sermons, pastors and priests admonished women to 'submit yourselves unto your husbands, as unto the Lord.' Nor was civil law, which permitted wife-beating, refused women admittance in court, and gave the husband full control over all property belonging to his wife at marriage, any less anti-woman.[2] But, with time, the condition of women improved; still, even as late as the nineteenth century, observers reported peasant women living under the control of men hardly less patriarchal than their ancestors. In France, for instance, a local physician described the peasant wife as almost totally powerless: 'Not only does she serve her husband at the table without herself seated, and speaks to him respectfully as though to a superior, but she is the chief servant even to her sons and the male field hands.'[3]

Although the heyday of the patriarch is over, his spiritual descendants can still be found in many peasant communities, where men remain privileged persons, still enjoying noteworthy power over women. Thus ethnographers write of the contemporary Brazilian rural husband in language not different from that applied to earlier men: 'He rules the household. He is the one who is served at meals, whose clothing is always cleaned and pressed, who goes out the most.'[4] Women, it is said, seldom object when men dominate the stage, hogging the limelight, and garnering the applause. For tradition dictates that women be submissive, quiet, unobtrusive: 'In parties, a woman keeps herself away from the crowd. She will only come out to the porch in order to serve coffee, bread, or punch, staying most of the time in the house or by its doors and windows to which she is allowed in order to fill the plates and serve the guests.'[5] Male dominance can take harsh forms in some traditional communities. In Tepotzlan, a town in central Mexico, the husband was the undisputed master of the household when Oscar Lewis studied it a generation ago. A harsh taskmaker, the traditional Tepotzlan husband would unhesitatingly beat his wife for offences that ranged from not having a good meal on time to suspicion of adultery.[6] Although villagers beat their wives if the occasion requires, they usually need not do so because powerful norms condone the husband's domination of his wife and undermine her will to fight back. And so it goes, in case after case, ethnographers tend to support William Stephen's conclusion that men exert significant control over women in most pre-industrial communities.[7]

But masculine power does not always go unchallenged. Even in places where popular attitudes and values support the patriarchal ideal, women are often more assertive in the privacy of their own homes than their public docility would suggest was remotely possible. Hidden from the public view behind cottage walls, some women dominate their husbands; others are the mainstays of their families, running small stores, holding jobs and earning money on which the family's survival depends. Even the full-time rural housewife with no outside income to use as a bargaining chip in the game of marital power, can often hold her own in competition with men. Consider the case of a wizened old woman, a Brazilian peasant interviewed while she was preparing dinner, who told the writer that she was 'chefe' in her own home. Her neighbours, she allowed, might be dominated by their husbands, though this was by no means always true, but not her. If her husband did not agree with her, she told him to leave, as he had more than once, because in her own domain, the house, she was boss. This woman, and many others like her, belie the notion that all pre-industrial women submit passively to men. If it is true that men tend to dominate women in most non-industrial societies, it is a dominance much tempered by female resistance. Consequently, we must conclude that the image of the passive, tractable, dependent peasant woman is partly fiction, a troubling spirit of rural culture, and one presumably easily exorcised by research.

DIMENSIONS OF FEMALE PERSONALITY

And yet, paradoxically, despite disconfirming research, this spirit survives in contemporary industrial society as part of the traditional sex role, still influencing how people see the world and what they expect of their children. When parents view the world through the prism of the traditional sex role, when they believe that girls are inherently weak and dependent, they will tend to perceive these qualities in their daughters. Thinking their daughters vulnerable and helpless, parents restrict a girl's movemets and prevent her from exploring the environment. Believing girls to be inherently weak and dependent, parents become over-protective and try to shield their daughters from situations considered too difficult for the fragile feminine temperament to handle.

Expecting the social structure to severely limit a girl's occupational opportunities and believing this limitation proper, parents set modest goals for their daughters and warn them against excessive competitiveness and achievement. Such restrictive, anxious, protective socialisation makes a girl feel impotent and fearful. As a result, she will tend to hide her anger, avoid displays of hostility, denigrate herself and other females, and shun competitive achievement. In effect, parental expectations produce the characteristics originally imagined as intrinsically feminine, the traits and behaviour that form part of the traditional female sex role. Sadly, a friend of women, as Jean Lipmen-Blumen most certainly is, concludes that women frequently become the pathetic creatures the traditional image of women describes them to be: weak, helpless, dependent, passive, self-deprecating.[8]

But as we have seen in the previous chapter, the evidence that girls are socialised differently from boys in an industial society is ambiguous and contradictory; most often research has found no (or at least, small) differnces in the socialisation of boys and girls. And for good reason; an industrial society has little use for passive, dependent, submissive, non-competitive, achievement-avoiding women; these qualities adhere to a role developed in a agrarian society not congruent with the needs of an industrial society. An industrial society needs out-going, adventuresome, confident, independent, achievement-oriented workers – female as well as male – and it works to produce them through its agents: the family the school, the peer group, the media, the voluntary association, and the work setting. Through the media, the industrial society extols the virtues of independence and achievement. Through the family, the school, and the peer group, it seeks to inculcate in women qualities of independence, competitiveness, and ambition, using the socialisation mechanisms of role modelling, direct instruction, and reinforcement to produce the desired results. Through the voluntary association and the workplace, it gives women the chance to break out of the home's cloying seclusion, to mingle with the people whose ideas challenge the traditional conception of women, to acquire skills at organisation and leadership, and to earn the self-esteem that comes with good performance at a money-paying job.

If this argument is correct, then current research should find few if any differences between the personalities of males and females: specifically, the data should show that men and women are equally independent, self-assured, and ambitious. But here again, as so often happens with research on sex differences, the data are contradictory and weak, and firm conclusions are hard to arrive at. A brief look at the research on such aspects of personality as aggressiveness, dependency, nurturance and affiliativeness, emotionality, achievement motivation, and self-concept, explains why this is so. Consider the comprehensive review of the literature on sex differences by Maccoby and Jacklin.[9] These psychologists examined dozens of studies, compared numerous findings on sex differences with respect to a variety of traits and behaviours, and concluded that sex differences in personality were generally small or non-existent. True, there is some evidence that boys are more physically active and aggressive than girls, but little evidence exists that girls are more timid, compliant, anxious, and nurturant than boys; moreover, there is no firm evidence, the reviewers asserted, for believing that the sexes differ in sociability, conformity, dependency, achievement motivation, and self-esteem.

But other researchers do not accept many of these conclusions. For instance. Block criticised Maccoby and Jacklin for excluding many relevant sources, for ignoring evidence pointing to significant sex differences, and for focusing on research with pre-school children – important sex differences may only appear gradually with age. She then expressed puzzlement as to why Maccoby and Jacklin contradicted the conclusions of earlier reviewers, including Maccoby herself. Previous reviews, she pointed out, had all agreed that females, on average, when compared with males, had higher scores on school grades, suggestibility, anxiety level, fears, social and affiliative interests, and fear of failure; and that males, on the average, had higher scores than females on aggressiveness, field independence, realistic assessment of own performance, and difficulty in controlling impulses.[10] What could have possibly changed in so short a time to cause recent reviewers to set aside the conclusions of earlier researchers? In short, why is there now disagreement where near consensus had once prevailed?

The answer lies partly in the tendency of some researchers to overemphasise sex differences, and others to de-emphasise them; partly in the reviewers' treatment of personality as an aggregate of equally important variables, all at the same level; and partly in the indifference of most researchers to the linkages between personality, sex roles, and the social structure. As for the tendency of researchers to respond differently to the data, a close look at the research reveals the pointlessness of this tendentiousness. Even when sex differences occur, they are typically miniscule. And yet differences that barely attain statistical significance – essentially a statement about sampling error – are often transformed through some semantic magic into conclusions about basic personality differences between males and females. Some of these personality traits are at or near the core of personality, an area hidden to individuals and extremely difficult to measure, others at the periphery, and hence more accessible to introspection and research. Now, all traits at or near the core of personality are important, but not equally so. Aggressiveness and self-concept are core variables, both hugely affect individual aspirations and achievement, and both are found on every reviewer's list. But aggressiveness, for all its drama and salience, does not have the pervasive impact on behaviour that self-concept does; nevertheless, both usually receive the same attention in reviews of sex differences in personality. Unfortunately, this obsession with core personality, to the virtual exclusion of peripheral, distracts the researcher's attention from the vital impact that attitudes, values and perceptions have on human behaviour.

Most troubling of all, many researchers ignore the part social roles play as vehicles through which personality expresses itself. With exquisite skill and care, researchers isolate a trait, a predisposition, a need or motive, a pattern of behaviour, measure and manipulate it in highly ingenious ways, and yet in the end pay almost no attention to the social context in which the behaviour occurs. To these researchers, the relevant context is the personal interview situation, or a classroom specifically chosen for the administation of a paper and pencil test of personality, or a laboratory where subjects can be controlled, aroused and observed. The artificiality of such arrangements has been much commented upon, of course, but what escapes the attention of most commentators, what all too often fails to excite their curiosity, are the effects of social variables on personality, not only as the context in which behaviour happens, but also as the framework in which personality differences can be explained.

Consider the data on sex differences in aggression. Some biological reductionists, ignoring the social context altogether, see the greater aggressiveness of males as a result of the testosterone sloshing through their veins; psychologists posit the existence of a male need to be dominant; sociologists emphasise the greater willingness of society to accept, or even encourage, aggressiveness from males. That hormonal factors and psychological needs and social forces all influence aggression, that they might come together in the sex role, and that changes in sex roles and the economy might explain the findings on sex differences in aggression – none of this occurs to researchers who, content to follow a disciplinary track, singlemindedly continue to look for answers on one level of analysis. They look in vain. An understanding of sex differences – and similarities – in personality, including a predisposition toward aggression, can only be attained when researchers combine biological, psychological, and sociological variables in one integrated theoretical system.

That this system is a goal toward which we should be working seems evident; that it is, alas, an ideal still beyond our grasp is also true. We must, for the time being, settle for less. In this chapter we shall examine the impact of social variables, particularly sex roles, on personality and behaviour, eschewing biological factors, whose impact on personality is as yet little understood. Our focus will be on certain personality characteristics theoretically and empirically related to occupational achievement: self-assessment, the expression of anger, stereotypic thinking, perception of the opposite sex, and 'feminine' behaviour. Two of these personality characteristics, self-assessment and anger, form part of the core of personality; two occur at the periphery, one is cognitive, a form of stereotypic thinking, and the other, perceptual, a particular view of the opposite sex; the last is a self-report of behaviour that fits the traditional image of women.

By putting personality in a social context, by relating personality to sex roles and the changing economy, we hope to understand better why the personalities of the sexes once differed significantly and why these differences have declined. We shall argue that personality differences between the sexes, linked as they once were to distinctly different sex roles, declined or even disappeared as the sex roles necessarily changed to meet the evolving needs of an industrial society. Let us begin by looking at sex differences in self-assessment, a critical element in self-esteem, and a core personality trait that affects almost every aspect of behaviour.

AT THE CORE OF PERSONALITY: SELF-ESTEEM

Self-esteem is part of the psychological foundation on which the edifice of social behaviour rests. Damage that foundation, wound self-esteem, create doubts about personal worth, and the entire edifice shakes or topples. It is said that women suffer from the crippling effects of low or shaky self-esteem.[11] Challenges frighten them; they approach competition, particularly with men, with low expectations of success, and experience more anxiety about failure than men would in a similar situation, a timidity expressed in the tendency to avoid risky situations.

The idea that women are less self-confident than males is, of course, a stereotype; it originates, like most stereotypes of women, in the myth of the traditional peasant woman. This type of woman, it is said, suffers from low self-esteem: she denigrates herself and other women, she assumes men possess knowledge and skills she cannot hope to understand or acquire, she accepts her inferiority as part of the natural order of things. Reared in patriarchal homes, traditional females daily witnessed the subjugation of their mothers to male authority. Admonished to be obedient, they submit to male dominance without a fight, partly because resistance seems hopeless and partly because peasant culture endlessly reiterates the theme of female inferiority, until even the women themselves believe it. 'The men say', explained one woman in Cruz das Almas, a Brazilian village in the interior of a southern state, 'that women aren't worth anything ... All the men say that. And the women usually agree with them.'[12] Another woman confided to an interviewer, 'My sister always used to say a woman of gold isn't worth a man of clay.'[13] An attitude this self-defeating, a conception of one's sex this derogatory, inevitably develops in a society that disparages women, that severely curtails their freedom of action, and that frightens them with tales of exploitation and rape if they venture outside the safe confines of the family. For a restrictive and threatening ambience tends to make children timid and fearful, unsure of themselves, and troubled by doubts about their competence and value.

But this description of women, their social condition and state of mind, over-simplifies reality. For one thing, as we have already noted, male dominance seldom achieves the monolithic condition portrayed in over-simplistic descriptions of traditional societies. For another, and more importantly, traditional women base their self-esteem on criteria quite different from those employed by men. To traditional men in both agricultural and industrial societies, personal worth, leaving aside such ascriptive factors as lineage and class status, stems from valour displayed in combat, from excellence achieved in work, from honour attained among peers, from wealth and power gained through competition in the market place and political arena.

Traditional women use other criteria, other comparison groups, other frames of reference to assess themselves. To traditional women the relevant criteria for assessing self-worth are domestic skill at cooking, sewing, keeping house, finding and keeping a responsible, successful husband-provider, and rearing well-behaved children; the comparison groups are other women of similar station in life; the frame of reference is the family, nuclear and extended. Even the old woman referred to a few pages ago, who vehemently insisted that she was boss in her own home, gesticulating at the interviewer with a long, dangerous fork to make her point, even she would have most likely freely admitted that her husband excelled her in most activities conducted outside the home – as for example, working in the fields, trading in the market place, taking part in politics. These are things that men do, and it would not have troubled her in the least that her competence in these matters was inferior to that of her husband. But in the things that mattered to her, domestic things, family things, she would not have judged herself at all inferior to her husband.

Domestic activities and family affairs are highly valued in a traditional society. Work in these areas is usually assigned to women, and it is a matter of deep concern to the community that the work be performed adequately; it is also a matter of some pride to the family when the wife-mother demonstrates superior domestic skill. Perhaps to some contemporary sophisticated urbanites the ability to prepare savoury and healthy meals, to keep a husband and children dressed in clean clothes, to maintain an orderly, tidy home seems trivial, the work itself demeaning. But to the pre-industrial community domestic skills are anything but trivial. A competent homemaker sends a motivated husband into the workplace and healthy children into the school; and a woman diligent about maintaining ties with kinfolk helps keep the extended family strong and thus contributes to the cohesion of the community. For these contributions a traditional community gives much credit to women, and from this credit and from the praise of family and friends, they can build a solid self-esteem.

Industrial societies do not actively dis-prize domestic skills, but then neither do they give the homemaker's role the priority it once enjoyed. As we have repeatedly noted, industrial society expects women to work outside the home after marriage. In furtherance of this goal, it teaches them the skills needed for acceptable performance on the job, and carefully evaluates their performance in the paid labour force. As a consequence, inevitably, non-domestic skills became psychologically important to women, who then construct their self-esteem with many of the same building blocks men use: competence in sports and performance in school, leadership in groups, interpersonal skill with peers and others, creative endeavour, and accomplishment in work. Achievement has become the keystone around which women build self-esteem, as it long has been with men. But when achievement becomes the principal component of self-esteem, women suffer in comparison with men, since studies show that, compared to males, females have lower evaluations of their ability, their performance, and the likelihood of future success.[14]

This comparison begs an important question: achievement in what? If by achievement we mean the attainment of a satisfactory overall conception of self, then females differ hardly at all from males. Studies using standard personality tests have found no differences between males and females in generalised self-esteem.[15] When researchers used standard measures of self-esteem, it was found that females were high on nine studies, males on six, and there were no differences in twenty-four.[16] If, on the other hand, we mean by achievement the degree of competence attained in specific tasks or areas, a comparison between the sexes becomes extremely difficult because previous studies of self-esteem have rarely linked achievement and self-esteem to specific activities.

THE SELF-ESTEEM OF ADOLESCENTS IN THREE COUNTRIES

In this section we will examine how adolescent girls and boys assess their competence in a variety of areas: academic, organisational, interpersonal, recreational, and aesthetic. Given our theoretical perspective, we did not expect to find major differences between girls and boys in self-esteem. With the traditional division of labour disappearing, with women increasingly joining the labour force, with women competing with men and being judged by the same standards, with women and girls participating in organised activities of all sorts, including sports and civic affairs, the traditional view that women are inferior to men, and unsuited for the rough and tumble of competitive life has become an archaic notion that cannot be defended. Surely it has become evident that women can form organisations, become leaders, and run for political office; that women can manage businesses and become entrepreneurs; that women can write novels, paint pictures, and win prizes. Women daily sharpen their skills and wits in the market place and the bureaucratic maze, discovering in the process not only that they can do the work but also that they can compete successfully with men. As a result, their self-confidence rises. Thus the industrial society has produced exactly what it wants: self-confident women who work as well as men at any task set before them. Just as the image of the peasant woman as weak and self-deprecatory is a stereotype, so the image of contemporary woman as ridden with self-doubt and feelings of inferiority is ludicrous, a political slogan designed to earn sympathy for women and ease their position in the competitive struggle with men for power and income.

We put the following six-part question to the students in our sample: 'In general how good are you at the following things: (1) making or fixing things, (2) school work, (3) sports or athletics, (4) music, drama, or entertaining others, (5) organising or leading groups of friends, (6) understanding how other people feel?' To each activity, the student could make one of five responses: 'not good at all', 'fair', 'good', 'very good', and 'excellent'. In order to facilitate the analysis and presentation of the data we gave a weight of 1 to 'not at all good', a weight of 2 to 'fair', 3 to 'good', 4 to 'very good', and a weight of 5 to 'excellent'. Table 5.1 shows the mean scores of boys and girls in the United States, Britain, and Italy.

The differences between the sexes in self-assessment shown in Table 5.1 are small, never as much as one point, usually less than half a point; the statistical significance is due mainly to large sample size. But when sex differences occur, they tend to do so along stereotypic lines. Thus boys in all three countries have a higher opinion than girls of their own skill in making and fixing things and in sports, areas in which boys are generally considered more competent than girls. On the other hand, girls have higher self-assessment scores in the performing arts, in music,

Table 5.1   Mean Self-Assessment Scores, by Sex and Country

	United States		Britain		Italy	
	Female	Male	Female	Male	Female	Male
Making or fixing things	2.95*	3.21	2.51*	2.99	2.01*	2.58
School work	2.96*	2.80	2.62*	2.91	2.45	2.44
Music, drama, entertaining	2.51*	2.12	2.15**	1.98	2.14	2.07
Organising or leading peers	2.60	2.53	2.16**	2.33	2.20	2.21
Understanding peers	3.69*	3.14	3.22*	2.68	3.11*	2.87

Ns for United States	Ns for Britain	Ns for Italy
Female: > 1495 < 1507	Female: > 485 < 496	Female: > 654 < 666
Male: > 1535 < 1541	Male: > 524 < 536	Male: > 640 < 653

*p <0.01
**p <0.05

drama and entertaining; and the American girls have higher scores at organising and leading peers, areas requiring expressive or empathetic skills at which girls are thought to excel. Regarding academic ability the girls have a very slight edge over the boys in the United States and Italy, but the reverse is true in Britain.

National differences, too, are generally small. On average the scores are highest in the United States, somewhat lower in Britain and lowest in Italy, but too much should not be made of this ranking. Like sex differences, national differences are small and reflect cultural factors. For example, British and Italian schools generally provide fewer opportunities than American schools for students to engage in extra-curricular activities, arenas in which students can test their skills and talents in the performing arts, in organisation building and leadership, and in sports. It is perhaps for this reason that the British and Italian adolescents have lower scores than Americans in these areas.

Our interest in self-esteem stems not so much from a belief that a good opinion of oneself, when realistically based, is a happy state of mind to which both sexes are entitled, as from the recognition that self-esteem has consequences for achievement in the workplace, which is after all the primary concern of this volume. Timid, anxious workers, plagued by self-doubt and convinced of their inferiority, generally do poorly in a competitive world. Such workers avoid risks, seek out routine and unchallenging tasks, and set their sights low in order to reduce the chance of failure: they are not likely to go far. If in fact self-esteem were lower in women than men, then the future of women in the labour force would be bleak, the possibility of eliminating the differences between the sexes in occupational attainment would evaporate, and economic equality between the sexes would be impossible except through legislative fiat. If, in addition, children were reared in such a way as to make sex differences in self-esteem inevitable, then the economic future of women would be grim indeed.

This gloomy vision derives from the data in Table 5.2 which shows self-esteem correlated with social status, independence training, academic grades, educational expectations, and occupational expectations. The measure of self-esteem in this table is a summary index composed of the students' responses to questions about their abilities in the six areas described above. Before composing the index we correlated the students' responses, each sex and country treated separately; the resulting matrices showed individual self-assessments positively correlated, indicating a general tendency towards similar, though, of course, not identical judgements about one's skill across diverse areas. It

Table 5.2	*Correlation of Self-assessment Scores with Social Status, Independence Index, Academic Grades, Educational and Occupational Expectations, by Sex and Country*

	United States Female Male		Britain Female Male		Italy Female Male	
Social status	0.21	0.17	0.18	0.09	0.20	0.18
Ind. index	0.19	0.13	0.14	0.09	0.16	0.13
Academic grades	0.31	0.29	0.17	0.17	0.15	0.18
Educational expectations	0.35	0.37	0.24	0.22	0.29	0.28
Occupational expectations	0.20	0.24	0.21	0.19	0.31	0.19

Ns for United States	Ns for Britain	Ns for Italy
Female: > 1157 < 1457	Female: > 182 < 449	Female: > 434 < 637
Male: > 1287 < 1451	Male: > 198 < 472	Male: 442 < 614

All correlations significant to the 0.05 level or more.

appears, then, that people who think well of themselves in one area tend to have positive opinions about themselves in other areas as well. Similarly, people who have a poor opinion about themselves in one area tend toward negative judgements in others. In effect, the index is a general measure of self-esteem linked to individual ability, skill, and achievement, across a broad range of activities.

The roots of self-esteem are in family circumstances, in parent–child relationships, and in personal experience with success and failure in daily life. Children who have been reared in secure surroundings, who have been given autonomy and independence, who have been urged to test their skill competing with standards of excellence, and who have succeeded more often than failed – these children stand a good chance of developing positive feelings of self-esteem. The correlations in Table 5.2 tend to bear out this conclusion. Thus self-esteem is positively related to social class: the higher the social class and hence the more prestigious and economically favourable the family situation, the higher the adolescent's self-assessment index score, a relationship found among males and females in all these countries. Not that riches assure self-confidence, not that poverty necessarily leads to low self-esteem and failure – too many stories of rags-to-riches millionaires, too many examples of poor Dick Wittingtons becoming mayors of their cities, say otherwise. But money spares the child the degradation and humiliation that poverty frequently brings; money increases family security and stability, and lends the family prestige that the child also shares; money makes possible the novel experiences that enlarge a child's horizons, experiences gained through special schooling, travel and participation in costly clubs and sports. In short, money smooths life's way; it give success an edge over failure, and encourages the development of positive self-esteem. No doubt there are exceptions to this generalisation – money, we are told, cannot buy happiness, and not all rich people feel good about themselves – but in one's early years, money can be a useful element in the building of self-esteem.

Self-esteem is also positively related to independence training. Girls and boys in all three countries with high autonomy-independence index scores tend to have higher self-esteem than those with low independence scores. Probably, independence plays a far greater role in the development of self-esteem than the size of the correlation coefficients in Table 5.2 would suggest. Independence means much more to a child than being free of external controls and doing as one pleases, much more than being free to explore the environment: it means the opportunity to master problems on one's own without parental interference; it means the chance to discover and improve one's skills, upon which depends personal achievements, a sense of mastery and self-worth in an industrial society. Over-protective and over-controlling parents, however well-meaning, cheat a child of the experiences that produce self-confidence and high self-esteem. Hovering over the child, trying to protect it from life's disappointments, and keeping it from solving problems on its own, the over-controlling parent willy-nilly envelopes the child in a blanket of restrictions, warnings, advice, and anxiety that smothers the development of self-confidence and self-esteem.

Achievement in industrial societies importantly affects self-esteem. As a rule achievers enjoy more self-esteem than non-achievers, winners more than losers. Since academic performance, as measured by grades, is a form of achievement, the positive relationship between grades and self-esteem seen in Table 5.2 is not surprising: as grades increase, the self-esteem scores of males and females in all three countries tend also to rise. We are not, of course, arguing that achievement is the only basis for self-esteem; no doubt integrity, generosity, and the capacity to give and receive love, among other valued traits, can and should enter into self-esteem. Nevertheless, individual achievement stands at the core of self-esteem in industrial societies. And the more competitive the society, the greater the impact of achievement on self-esteem, which may explain why the correlations of grades with the self-esteem index in highly competitive America (girls, 0.31, boys, 0.29) exceed those in Britain (girls, 0.17, boys, 0.17) and Italy (girls, 0.15, boys, 0.18).

Finally, and most importantly for our thesis, the data show a significant relationship between self-esteem and educational–occupational expectational levels: the higher the self-assessment index score, the further the student expects to go in school and the higher the status of the job he expects to have, a relationship that holds for boys as well as girls in all three countries. For example, the correlation coefficients of self-assessment with educational expectations is 0.35 for American girls and 0.37 for American boys; the correlations with occupational expectations are 0.20 for American girls and 0.24 for the boys. Only in one case, the Italians, is there any marked difference between the sexes. In this case, the correlations take the same direction, both are positive, but the relationship is stronger for females (0.31) than for males (.019). Perhaps in Italy it takes more self-esteem to raise a girl's expectation level than it does a boy's.

What are the implications of these data for female achievement in the future? On the whole, not bad at all, since nothing in the data on self-esteem and its correlates dooms women to eternal economic inferiority. For females do not, as a group come from families of lesser status than men, neither in our sample nor in the nation at large. Females do not, as a general rule, perform less well than males in school; in fact girls do better than boys in some subjects, while boys exceed girls in others. Nor do girls receive less independence training at home than boys, at least not so far as our study and most other studies show. And finally, girls do not have lower self-esteem than boys. The sexes differ mainly, if at all, in the areas in which they excel and from which self-esteem is primarily derived. Therefore, if the sexes still differ in occupational expectations and achievement, as some observers maintain they do, this cannot be ascribed to differences in self-esteem.

THE USES OF ANGER

Every society makes use of human aggressiveness. Some societies channel this volatile, dangerous emotion and the energy it releases into warfare, putting men in combat and encouraging women to egg them on. Other societies find it safer to funnel aggression into sports and other socially approved individual and group rivalries. Still others, recognising its potentially disruptive role in everday life, clamp severe controls on aggression, limiting its expression to fantasy, gossip, myth-making and sex.

The industrial society puts aggressiveness to work in the economic world. Aggressive youths are urged to make their fortunes in the market place, to compete as entrepreneurs and managers, and to make their mark as professionals and performers, as foremen and techni-cians, as salespeople and factory workers. No blame is attached to aggressiveness in the workplace. Not only may the achiever who plays by the rules aggressively accumulate wealth and fame without fear of public reproach, he or she may in fact become a popular idol and exemplar of the rewards that hard work, skill, and a zest for the competitive fray bring. Thus by defining some forms of aggression as ambition and competition at work and extolling their virtues, the industrial society clothes aggression in socially approved habiliments; and by seeking out workers so garbed and by rewarding them for good work, the industrial society harnesses the explosive force behind aggression, turns it into productive channels and produces wealth. Other societies, because they are ambivalent or hostile to aggression, fritter away this valuable human resource in games, gossip, and bloodletting.

Competition permeates industrial economies, more so perhaps in capitalist than in socialist societies, though even collectivistic countries have discovered the value of the market economy as a way of motivating workers to meet production quotas, and are slowly chang-ing their system in order to harness the productive energy inherent in competition. Of late, authorities in socialist China and the Soviet Union have taken to exhorting workers to greater effort by promising special rewards to the aggressive striver and by emphasising the nation's need to compete with the capitalists they once threatened to bury. The old, tired slogans about socialist solidarity are being replaced with a new rhetoric that stresses the acceptability of wealth acquired through individual achievement and that reminds everyone of the need for a more vigourous and competitive economy to meet the rising expectations of the people for a better standard of living.

As a result, the language of commerce and industry has become laden with the vocabulary of competition, aggression and warfare. Most capitalist companies and some socialist communes at some time or another plan aggressive production and sales campaigns; they marshal resources, invade the markets and territories of competitors, do daily battle for customers, and celebrate unabashedly their victories over defeated rivals. To help in these campaigns they recruit aggressive and competitive young people and let it be known when jobs open that the shy and the withdrawn, the timid and the passive need not apply. Who wants a shy salesman? Who needs a passive production manager? What can a timid and self-absorbed worker do in a modern enterprise that is oriented towards the production and sale of goods and services in a competitive world market? Such people may eventually find places for themselves in an industrial system, but theirs are seldom the best-paying jobs.

In the popular mind the emotion most commonly linked to aggresion is anger, for anger often foreshadows aggression. Frustrated or humiliated, made to feel dissatisfied or inferior in some way, and pricked therefore to anger, we strike out at the cause of our discomfort. This reaction may take open physical form, as perhaps a punch on the nose; or it may be expressed verbally, as in angry shouts, screams, sarcasms, and other forms of abuse; or it may assume a more subtle and covert guise, as when the aggrieved party seeks revenge by quietly spreading malicious gossip about the aggressor. And, of course, some people do not show their anger at all: they suppress it entirely. Knowing that any overt display of anger would be futile or dangerous, they keep their feelings to themselves and consider quiet submission to aggression the better part of valour; or they may seek to win over the aggressor through soft words and favours, hoping in this way to avert future aggression. In short, expressed anger may take many forms. What that form will be depends on a complex mixture of factors, among the most important of which is the attitude of society toward aggression and its expression.

Because they greatly value social cohesion, traditional societies dislike personal aggressiveness and severely control the display of anger, for they recognise the power of anger to disrupt social relationships. Consequently, they closely regulate this dangerous emotion, dictating towards whom it may be shown, under what circumstances, and in what manner. As a rule, traditional societies closely tie the right to express anger to the aggressor's social status, which is usually ascriptive. Anger should be directed down, never up; it should flow from old to young, from superiors to inferiors, from men to women; it should only be expressed privately, never publicly, unless one wishes to humiliate the other person, always a dangerous thing to do. And anger should only be expressed in careful language and controlled gestures: losing one's temper often means losing the game. The Brazilian peasant husband who, in the presence of strangers shouted at his wife when she expressed an opinion with which he did not agree, 'Keep still! You are a donkey. You don't know anything,' broke most of these rules.[17] The anthropologist who observed this incident reported that the wife subsided into silence without protest, but no doubt she felt anger, and no doubt at a later time she made her husband pay for his rude outburst.

Industrial societies tolerate the open display of anger from more people and in more circumstances than most traditional societies would ever dream of permitting. This tolerance stems in large part from the fact that anger, like aggression, has its uses. In the workplace, anger underscores the urgency of an order, moving to action a worker who had been overly slow to respond to softer instructions, and thus gives special meaning to a reprimand that would have been ineffective had it been delivered in neutral tones. In effect, expressed anger may correct a situation that would spiral out of control if left uncorrected. Not that a free-wheeling industrial society encourages people to express anger unrestrainedly and without reason (the notion of a workplace infested with promiscuously angry people is too awful to contemplate), but judiciously applied anger can have some wonderfully healthy effects, both for the giver, who in venting a strong emotion rids himself of spleen, and for the receiver, who is energised to take the corrective action that saves his job. Even the Japanese, who still retain their traditional distaste for public displays of emotion, are learning the value of anger, particularly when they must deal with alien workforces in their factories abroad, and have begun to teach their young managers how to give vent to calculated anger when circumstances call for it. This is not easy for the Japanese, but it is something they will have to learn, for anger has its uses.

SEX DIFFERENCES IN THE EXPRESSION OF ANGER

Women are said to have more difficulty than men in being aggressive and expressing anger, a difference between the sexes that shows up quite early in life. Thus, most of the studies reviewed by Oetzel, by Maccoby and Jacklin, and by Block, found boys to be more aggressive than girls. This difference not only appears in childhood, it is also found in a variety of cultures, which suggests a possible link between aggression and as yet unclassified biological factors, perhaps testosterone or some other male hormone.[18] But most sociologists do not feel the need to look to biology for an explanation of sex differences in aggression. Thus Lipmen-Blumen, though she does not deny to biology any role at all in the development of aggressiveness and the arousal of anger, mainly blames sex role socialisation for the existence of sex differences in aggressiveness. She argues that society trains males, even as small boys, to be aggressive, and expects them to react openly with anger and hostility when others aggress against them.[19]

In the industrial West, the occupational world is a competitive arena in which success is measured in terms of the money and prestige and power one accumulates; it is a world in which males are expected to fight to gain these valued commodities using forceful measures against rivals when the situation calls for it. Training for success in this struggle begins early. Boys are encouraged to explore their environment and to seek out challenges by engaging in novel tasks; they are warned against showing fear in the face of danger, admonished to defend themselves when attacked, and advised to use counter-force if necessary. A boy who fails to meet these demands when attacked will have his courage called into question and his masculinity ridiculed; no boy likes to be called a sissy. Consequently, boys who pass the test of masuclinity tend to grow up aggressive and competitive, toughened against displays of weakness, seasoned warriors in the ceaseless struggle to get ahead.

The socialisation of girls, it is said, even in modern societies, is altogether different. From the outset girls are treated more protectively than boys, handled more gently, kept closer to home, not permitted to play rough and tumble games, and cautioned against being assertive and aggressive. In effect, they are taught, Lipmen-Blumen maintains, to be weak and fearful. These qualities, which would unman a boy, have different consequences for girls, since timidity in girls meets with much less reproach than it does in boys, and crying evokes less ridicule. A girl may act frightened when threatened, may burst into tears when frustrated, without either response jeopardising her femininity so far as society is concerned. But she must not be aggressive or competitive. Aggressiveness, she is told, is unfeminine and competitiveness will cost her the companionship of her friends. And since girls are taught that making and keeping friends, that developing and maintaining relationships with others, are enormously important, they tend to avoid any competition (except for men) the winning of which will cause them to lose a friend. 'Little girls', Lipmen-Blumen asserts, 'taught to value relationships above winning, often forgo the winner's crown in the name of friendship or love.'[20] But to many women the loss of the victor's crown is a small price to pay to safeguard the queen of emotions – love.

Female emotionality figures prominently in any discussion of the differences between the sexes. According to a cultural stereotype found in many societies and given expression in numerous novels and movies, women are more emotional than men. Women are thought to be more sensitive, anxious, and moody than men; they are said to be more manic, joyful and happy, more easily depressed, more irritable and sad, and often all of these things in quick succession within a short period of time. Some women, in fact, boast of their sensitivity and emotionality, brag of being, as the saying goes, in touch with their feelings, and proudly contrast themselves with men, who must learn to restrain and hide their feelings, almost to the point of being unaware of them. Yet, paradoxically, despite their emotionality, women are discouraged from showing anger in personal disputes. Though it may be acceptable to express anger in support of social causes, directing it against individuals for purely private purposes is frowned upon and girls are taught early to control hostility and to fear men whose training encourages them to react angrily against any challenge to their interests. The effect of traditional female sex role socialisation, with its litany of warnings against self-assertion, is to make women non-competitive, fearful, dependent and passive, traits that could severely hinder women in their struggle for success in the industrial labour market.

In addition, the traditional society deprives women of the opportunity to take part in group sports and other organised activities, opportunities that men take for granted, and hence women tend not to learn certain skills that are necessary for success in an industrial economy, which emphasises cooperation in organisational spheres and competition in private ones. Made fearful and timid by their sex role socialisation, taught that competitiveness is unfeminine and winning dangerous, traditional women tend to avoid risky, entrepreneurial jobs in favour of safe service ones, even though social rewards are positively correlated with risk in the marketplace. Cautioned against being aggressive and required to hide their anger even when its expression would be justified, women tend not to learn the self-assertive skills that are needed to protect one's interests in the rough and tumble of a turbulent economy in a modern industrial society. In sum, intentionally or not, traditional sex role socialisation hobbles the efforts of women to achieve equality in the labour market.

This diptych of contrasts – the competitive, aggressive male on one panel, the submissive, passive female on the other – appeals to people who see men as exploiters and women as their helpless victims. It is after all, a picture that both arouses sympathy for the victim, explains her condition, and illustrates a conception of women that has gained widespread acceptance – the image of the helpless female. In the hands of writers, this image has become the stuff of drama; in the hands of reformers and polemicists it has become a tool, used to mobilise female resentment and to forge social change. And yet, not withstanding its appeal, there is no strong and consistent evidence of its validity. Like so many other popular notions about women, the conception of the female as essentially non-competitive and unaggressive is a stereotype, one that at best describes only a small fraction of the women in an industrial society.

Consider the statement that women are less aggressive than men. Leaving aside popular anecdotes and impressions, the evidence that can be marshalled in support of this statement is not impressive. It is true that much of the research literature suggests that males are more aggressive than females, but given the problems associated with much of the research in this area – the pre-school age of many of the subjects, the artificiality of the situations in which aggression is studied, and the difficulties inherent in measuring aggression – this conclusion is not entirely convincing, at least not to Tieger, who has argued that the data obtained from children under six do not support the conclusion that boys are more aggresive than girls.[21]

Diane Ruble is not convinced either. She points to data that show females more verbally aggressive than males, and she also remarks on studies of group reactions to a newcomer that show girls more 'indirectly' aggressive than boys. Also, situated variables may strongly affect the willingness of females to be aggressive. Thus, in some experimental studies of aggression, when the situation is modified to remove the normal constraints on female aggressiveness, the differences between the sexes disappear. For example, one study found that females were as aggressive as males when they were assured that their aggression would be kept private. In sum, Ruble concludes that while males may behave more aggressively than females, though this is not entirely certain, it is probable that females do not differ much from males in their motivation or desire to act aggressively.[22] Remove the situational constraints placed on women and in all likelihood they will behave as aggressively as men.

A search for empirical evidence to support the conclusion that women are more likely than men to inhibit the expression of anger proved disappointing. Although the generalisation that females are more likely than males to inhibit the expression of anger is endlessly repeated in research reviews (Maccoby and Jacklin, for example, refer to women as 'being slower to anger' than men), little proof is offered in its support, and such proof as is offered derives mainly from the study of young children, often under seven years of age and sometimes as young as seven months.[23] Thus one study found that mothers report boys between $2\frac{1}{2}$ and 5 years old becoming angry twice as often as girls, and another study found that boys (aged 2), 'when left alone by their mothers in a strange room, were more likely than girls to beat or kick angrily upon the door through which the mother had departed.'[24] But no evidence is offered to show that this sex difference persists into adolescence or adulthood. Perhaps the difference grows larger with age, perhaps it becomes smaller or disappears entirely, or perhaps it even reverses itself. Could it be that adult males are more likely than females to inhibit the display of anger? Possibly, but no one knows for certain, given the inadequate research record on this question.

Fortunately, we can add to the research record on sex differences in the display of anger. We sought to learn how adolescents express anger and with what frequency by putting this seven-part question to them: 'When you are angry or upset with someone your own age, how often do you do the following: (1) talk quietly to them about it, (2) yell or argue with them about it, (3) hit or slap them, (4) cry, (5) get back at them in some other way, (6) keep it to yourself, (7) do something to make them like you? The respondent could chose among the following answers: never, seldom, sometimes, often. For parts 1, 4, 6, and 7 the response 'never' was given a weight of 1, 'seldom', a weight of 2, 'sometimes', a weight of 3, and 'often', a weight of 4. The response weights for the other parts were reversed. In effect, this weighting system means that the higher the adolescents' scores the more passive and inhibited her or his responses to an upsetting situation. The weighted responses of the students are shown as mean scores in Table 5.3.

The responses adolescents make to an upsetting situation can range from outright physical aggression, such as hitting or slapping the offending person; to verbal aggression, such as yelling or arguing; to indirect and perhaps hidden retribution by getting back at the other person in some covert way; to helplessness, as in crying; to plain and simple inhibition, keeping one's anger to oneself. Unlike traditional societies, the contemporary industrial society favours a direct approach to the problem of handling anger. Gone is that exemplar of self-control, the tight-lipped equable gentleman of an earlier era who never lost his temper and who hid his fury behind an urbane smiling façade. This response is now considered unhealthy. Burying anger, it is now thought, will only make matters worse, for it invites further offence

Table 5.3   Mechanisms for Handling Anger, by Sex and Country

	United States		Britain		Italy	
	Female	Male	Female	Male	Female	Male
Talk quietly	2.68**	2.24	2.38**	2.12	2.94	2.83
Yell or argue	2.61**	2.41	2.54**	2.36	2.95**	2.36
Hit or slap	3.71*	2.17	2.60*	2.04	2.85**	2.51
Cry	1.86*	1.15	1.71*	1.21	1.59*	1.17
Get back in other ways	3.10*	2.76	2.99*	2.47	3.58*	2.45
Keep it to oneself	2.65	2.64	2.61	2.52	2.15	2.10
Make them like you	2.41	2.35	2.17	2.17	2.50	2.44

Ns for United States	*Ns for Britain*	*Ns for Italy*
Female: > 1500 < 1508	Female: > 495 < 500	Female: > 657 < 664
Male: > 1534 < 1542	Male: > 544 < 550	Male: > 644 < 651

* $p < 0.01$
** $p < 0.05$

and, what is worse, may cause neurosis and other psychological problems to develop. How much better it is to get strong feelings off one's chest, to clear the air by venting one's anger, and thus making the offender pay dearly so that a similar offence will not occur again. Such is the current wisdom. Since catharsis through venting anger has become the recommended remedy for relieving the discomfort caused by frustration and irritation, a remedy equally valid for males and females, what reason is there to believe that a strong difference between the sexes in their response to an upsetting situation still exists?

In fact as we can see in Table 5.3, the reactions of males and females to being upset are remarkably similar. Thus, in keeping perhaps with the admonition that suppressing anger is unhealthy, girls and boys do not differ much in their willingness to hide anger ('keeping it to oneself'); the mean scores of boys and girls are identical in America (girls, 2.6; boys, 2.6) and Italy (girls, 2.1; boys, 2.1), and very close to each other in Britain (girls, 2.6; boys, 2.5). Nor is one sex much more given than the other to placating an offender ('make them like me'): in Britain the mean scores of the sexes are identical, and they are very similar to each other in America and Italy. And the sexes do not differ greatly in their willingness to express anger verbally ('yell or argue'), or more subtly by 'getting back in some way' at the offender. This is not to say that the sexes do not at all differ in how they express anger, only that the differences are far smaller than traditional opinion would lead one to expect.

Nonetheless, some of the differences, though small, between the sexes merit attention. For instance, boys in all three countries are more likely than girls to hit or slap someone who made them angry, and girls are more likely to cry when upset; both responses fit the cultural stereotype that portrays females as more emotional and less physically aggressive than males. And girls appear slightly more willing than boys to smooth over clashes with others through quiet talk, again a sex difference that conforms to the stereotype of women. These findings point to the existence of traditional attitudes among some girls who, even in an industrial society, continue to handle anger in traditional ways.

The data do not, however, fit some well-known stereotypes of national character: the self-controlled Englishman, the aggressive American, and the talkative Italian. On the whole, by their own admission, British adolescents are not the most inhibited, nor the Italians the most talkative, nor the Americans the most aggressive. On the contrary, the Americans are more likely to inhibit physical anger than the British, and more likely to express their anger verbally than the Italians. Still, though these data disconfirm certain popular stereotypes of national character, it is important to remember that the mean differences between countries, like the differences between the sexes, are generally small. However much cultural attitudes toward the expression of anger may differ among these three countries, if in fact they still do, the mechanisms used by adolescents to express anger differ far less than is commonly believed.

In order to examine the possible origins and effects of these mechanisms, we constructed a summary index of the adolescents' responses to the seven-part question on how they handle anger. Their responses to each part of the question were first intercorrelated, each sex and country separately; then, since the correlation coefficients between responses were positive, we felt justified in summarising them, constructing in this way a single index score for each individual that indicated how he or she reacted when upset and angry. The responses were weighted in the manner described earlier, so that the higher the score the more the adolescent inhibited the expression of anger, the more likely he or she avoided aggressive responses to frustration and offence, the more likely he or she tried to smooth things over through quiet talk and placation. These anger scores were then correlated with the adolescent's social status, age, perceived degree of independence training, academic grades, and educational–occupational expectations.

The correlations in Table 5.4 provide a glimpse of the social context in which the mechanisms for handling anger probably develop. In the United States and Britain, social status, age, and independence training affect how adolescents express their anger: the higher their status, the older their age, the more independence training they have received, the more likely they were to express aggression and to express anger in subtle and non-provocative ways. Thus the anger index score correlates positively with status, age, and independence training for American girls (0.08, 0.21, and 0.10 respectively); for British females the correlations are 0.15, 0.31, and 0.13, all slightly larger than the American coefficients. The correlations for the males are similar to those of the females in both countries.

These findings fit nicely with what is known about the relationship of child socialisation to social class.[25] Studies have long reported that middle-class parents are more likely than their lower-class counterparts to stress the need for the child to learn self-control and the importance of anticipating the consequences of impulsive action, and, in time, parental admonitions tend to take hold. Note that age is more highly correlated with the anger score than any other variable in the table. But parents must walk a thin line when they control and teach them the

Table 5.4   Correlation of Anger Index Scores with Social Status, Independence, Age, Academic Grades, and Educational and Occupational Expectations, by Sex and Country

| | United States | | Britain | | Italy | |
	Female	Male	Female	Male	Female	Male
Social status	0.08*	0.09*	0.15*	0.08	−0.04	−0.05
Age	0.21*	0.25*	0.31*	0.19*	0.01	0.05
Independence	0.10*	0.10*	0.13*	0.12*	0.04	0.05
Grades	0.17*	0.13*	0.01	−0.08	0.00	0.01
Educational expectations	0.18*	0.20*	0.25*	0.12*	−0.02	0.03
Occupational expectations	0.07*	0.18*	0.13*	0.18*	−0.09	0.03

Ns for United States   *Ns for Britain*   *Ns for Italy*
Females: > 1165 < 1491   Females: > 192 < 490   Females: > 431 < 634
Male: > 1003 < 1516   Male: > 214 < 537   Male: > 534 < 641
* *p* < 0.01

value of self-control. Too much control may make a child apathetic or rebellious, while too little control may allow the energy bound up in anger to be frittered away in self-indulgent aggression, energy that might better be put to work improving school grades and making plans for the future.

Reasonable, not over-strict, self-control of anger and temper helps academic performance and promotes planning for the future. The conclusion can be drawn from the modest positive correlations between the anger index score, academic grades, and educational–occupational expectations among American and British students. That self-control need not be felt as overly burdensome can be inferred from the positive correlation of the anger score with perceived independence training; that is to say, adolescents who tend to avoid angry reactions to irritation tend also to receive independence and support from their parents, which could make controlling one's temper seem less onerous. At any rate, adolescents who control their anger tend to have higher grades than those who do not (American girls, $r = 0.17$; boys, $r = 0.13$), though this relationship does not apply in Britain or Italy. Better academic performance, at least in the United States, may explain why educational expectations also rise with degree of anger-control (United States, girls 0.18, boys, 0.20; Britain, girls, 0.25, boys, 0.12). And with higher self-control, the student's occupational expectations also rise (United States, girls, 0.07, boys, 0.18; Britain, girls, 0.13, boys, 0.18).

The Italian data are a puzzle. None of the variables in Table 5.4 are significantly related to the anger index scores of Italian adolescents, and nothing in the data provides a clue as to why this should be so. Possibly the emotional climate of Italian culture and society so differs from that of the United States and Britain as to make both the expression of anger and its origins and effects markedly different; but what these differences are we cannot say. What makes this situation especially perplexing is the finding, seen in Table 5.3, that sex differences in the expression of anger are as small in Italy as they are in the other two countries. Industrialisation seems to affect the way sexes express anger in Italy, but an explanation of its origins and effects must be sought in variables other than those examined in Table 5.3.

In this chapter we examined the previous research literature for evidence of sex differences in two components of core personality – self-esteem and various mechanisms for handling anger. The findings on this subject, as reported in numerous studies, are ambiguous and contradictory, some researchers concluding that males enjoy higher self-esteem and find it easier to express anger than females, other researchers insist that no consistent differences in these areas exist between the sexes. Our data agree with the latter group. We could find little or no differences in self-esteem between girls and boys in the three countries; nor are the differnces between the sexes in their willingness to express anger especially noteworthy. To be sure, girls are somewhat more likely than boys to cry when upset and boys a bit more likely to resort to violence when angered but, on the whole, the differences between the sexes as regards to these two components of core personality are small and unremarkable.

Still, this leaves unanswered the question of whether the sexes differ with respect to certain peripheral aspects of personality, for example, their perception of the sexes and their willingness to accept sex role stereotypes. We will turn our attention to this question in the next chapter, for how adolescents perceive themselves and other members of their own and the opposite sex, and what ideas they carry in their heads about the basic nature of males and females, will seriously affect the educational and occupational goals they will set for themselves and their ability to attain them.

6 The Chameleon Syndrome

Dominant groups often treat the groups beneath them with condescension and contempt. Not content simply to curtail the access of outsiders to society's resources, not satisfied merely to keep the good jobs and high income for itself, the dominant group also heaps ridicule upon the unfortunate minority, calling it lazy, timid, stupid, lacking in creativity and achievement, hence basically inferior, and then uses these judgements to justify the discriminatory practices frequently directed against hapless minorities. Equally damaging, these judgements enter the general culture, whose values the dominant group usually defines, as indictments of the minority and as perceptions of its inferiority. Coalesced into stereotypes, they become powerful tools of social control.

Tragically, these hostile judgements, perceptions, and stereotypes often become part of the minority group's culture and inevitably enter the minds of many of its members. As a result, the accusations levelled against the minority group by its oppressors become charges the group directs against itself. Does the majority group consider us cowardly or slothful or dumb? Well then, this must be true and it helps explain our inferior position. Are we considered dependent and unresourceful, moody and flighty, drawn to frivolity and uninterested in work that requires personal commitment over long periods of time? This too must be true and justifies our exclusion from those sectors of the labour force that require high seriousness and dedication to the job. That such accusations are false, that they are based on stereotypes with origins in a vanished era, matters little once they have entered a group's culture and become part of its members' personalities. For after they have become firmly established in the mind, hostile stereotypes induce self-deprecation and self-hatred in minority group members, emotionally disabling them and severely handicapping efforts to improve their condition.

Of late, women have taken to describing themselves as a minority group, under-privileged and oppressed, denied equality of opportunity in the workplace, and paid less than men for the same work or for work of comparable worth. Men, some women claim, exploit women sexually and socially, treat them with condescension, and exclude them from certain clubs and associations where men, meeting together hugger-mugger, make profitable connections that advance their careers. Not all women see it this way, of course. Midge Decter, a writer and political activist, describes today's young, affluent, middle-class women as the most free, most vital and energetic – and the most economically and physically privileged – in history.[1] That these women proclaim themselves to be the victims of intolerable oppression perplexes Decter and may well puzzle future historians of our turbulent period.

But Decter and the militant feminists she is criticising both miss an important point. The objective condition of women, their economic and educational status, their ability to enter previously closed schools and occupations, their freedom to move in circles once forbidden to them, their prestige and income, may or may not be satisfactory, but this matters little as long as women feel inferior and unappreciated, vulnerable and victimised. For, what matters a good job to a woman if she believes that holding it will drive away male friends who have been made envious by her success? How can she feel content when she believes that competition with men will be thought unfeminine and that victory over men may earn her kudos from society but cost her love and marriage? How can she feel happy if she considers women intrinsically inferior to men, less competent, and less motivated to excel? And what must she think of herself if she finds women vain and dependent? In short, what if she has internalised the hostile judgements, perceptions, and stereotypes of women in the culture and turns them against herself? The result cannot be happy because the internalisation of hostile perceptions and stereotypes of one's group leads to anxiety, listlessness, and self-denigration.

Fortunately, as we have seen, at the core of personality where self-esteem resides, no significant damage seems to have occurred. Judging from the findings reported in the previous chapter, female self-esteem appears to be in good shape, neither better nor worse than that of the males. True, women tend to rate themselves below men in some areas, but in other areas they believe themselves to be superior to men. On balance, across a broad range of activities and skills, women assess themselves about as highly as men assess themselves, assessments which reflect objective reality, the fact that few significant differences exist between the sexes in latent ability and overt performance. But more than objective performance influences self-assessment. Also important are the assessments made by others, particularly by parents, whose appraisal of the child when it is young and plastic, when it has not yet acquired the experience needed to build an accurate self-image or the wisdom to separate hard fact from wishful thinking, makes an enduring mark on the child's personality.

During this crucial period, industrialisation works effectively to reduce the differences between the sexes in self-esteem. Working through the family and other institutions, the industrial society encourages parents to believe that both sexes possess equal talents and aptitudes, and that neither sex is entitled to enjoy an advantage over the other, or suffer a handicap, simply because of an accident of birth. The socialisation process in the home reflects this judgement. Surely no modern parent would deliberately seek to build into a daughter a sense of inferiority to males or try to damage her self-esteem so that she cannot work effectively outside the home. Consequently, the self-esteem of modern girls tends to be similar to that of boys; and self-esteem, once assimilated into the core of personality, resists change and influences future learning.

THE SOCIALISATION OF SEX ROLE STEREOTYPES

Peripheral personality components, perceptions and attitudes and opinions, develop later than those in the core, and hence reflect not only the influence of parents but also the inputs of peers, teachers, and the mass media of communication. These agents of socialisation pass on society's messages, encourage behaviour that agrees with society's norms and goals, and as faithful instruments of society confirm the values and judgements embodied in the general culture, which in an industrial society tends to de-emphasise the importance of sex differences in talents, motivations and abilities. In this respect the familial and extra-familial agents of socialisation are much alike; but they also differ in an important respect; the extra-familial agent tends to encounter a child at a time when its sensitivity to notions of masculinity and femininity is especially keen and when its tolerance for ignorance about sex role norms is minimal. The child desperately wants to know what gender implies, what is expected, what accepted and what proscribed, and often turns to parents, teachers, the media and, above all, to peers for instruction.

The peer group is a treasure-trove of truth and untruth about gender, a rich repository of culture into which children scrimmage for material with which to build their sexual identities. This building process usually begins at age 2 or 3 with the recognition of one's membership in a sexual category, which in the early years is only a label without sufficient content to make it socially and psychologically significant. But in time the child affixes this label to a package of sexually-linked beliefs and practices, already present in the culture, and which derive legitimation from the norms and sanctions of society. Ordinarily, society need not worry about the child's conformity to sex-role norms, for children rarely feel neutral about their gender and the beliefs associated with it: they not only like being a girl or a boy, they tend to evaluate their own sex much above the other. This tendency is strongly reinforced in highly sexually-differentiated pre-industrial societies, which divide most labour by sex, which place severe limits on the interaction between males and females, and which clearly declare one sex superior to the other. As a result, many evaluations of gender tend to be pejorative: the opposite sex is not only different, it is also inferior.

Traditional societies, whose social structures and cultures men usually dominate, often disparage women, except of course in the sexual and domestic domains to which women are thought to bring desirable resources and skills. But this does not prevent the culture from being permeated with hostile stereotypes of women nor keep men from denigrating women, even as they avail themselves of female resources   a curious case of men dis-prizing the vehicle of their pleasure and profit. These stereotypes, this image of the clever, devious, scheming, malicious, sexually hungry, omnipotent female (who, para-doxically, is believed to lack the wit and strength to defend herself) fills traditional men with fear and hostility, with wonder and confusion, and keeps them alert for the smallest signs of female assertiveness. When women behave assertively, when they threaten to win in any competition with men, some men flare up and strike back, while others sulk and withdraw; but whatever their response most men appear distressed at female victory. Not surprisingly, traditional girls are warned about the awful consequences of ignoring the sex role stereo-type of woman as witch and wanton, and of the dangers of recklessly competing with men.[2]

Children encounter sexual stereotypes in the family, first at their mother's knee while listening to stories of witches and warriors, later in the kitchen while absorbing gossip about relatives and neighbours, or in the field and shop while hearing father delate upon women, about their attractions, wiles and weaknesses. This learning process continues when the child joins a peer group, since a major attraction of belonging to a peer group is the chance to exchange information about sex. In the peer group, even in industrial societies, the comments about the opposite sex tend to take on a singularly unfriendly tone, one which emphasises sex differences and disparages the opposite sex. Significantly, this disparagement takes place in an atmosphere of deepening ignorance about the opposite sex since, well before the end of their first decade, perhaps as early as age 6 or 7, girls and boys tend to break up into same-sex groups, shunning each other's company and denying themselves the chance to get to know each other better. It is in this atmosphere of semi-isolation that sexual sub-cultures, rich in misinformation and prejudice, and rife with rumours about societal punishments for infractions of sex role norms, tend to develop, often with amazing speed. Immersed in this culture and influenced by its stereotypes and beliefs, boys perceive threats from girls where none exists, and girls grow apprehensive about retaliation from boys for actions that might in fact be viewed with indifference or possibly with favour. In fact, far from wishing boys harm, some girls – perhaps many – want to help and protect them; and some boys – perhaps many – like independent and self-assertive girls. But sexual stereotypes and misperceptions often prevent people from seeing others as they really are.

In industrial societies the schools and the academic culture slowly weaken the impact of sex role stereotypes on the adolescent's views of the opposite sex. Observing one another in the classroom and in various clubs and groups, adolescents cannot help but notice the discrepancy between the real and the imagined characteristics of the opposite sex. Willy-nilly, boys see that girls are not the shy, helpless, dependent, silly creatures that traditional male sub-culture makes them out to be. Girls take their work seriously and do well in school; girls accomplish difficult things without asking for help; girls stand up to aggressors, and assert themselves. And girls must see that boys are not the violent, insensitive, unfeeling, clumsy oafs that the female sub-culture makes them out to be. Boys can be shy and timid, caring and sensitive, assertive without being abusive and cruel. Slowly, sex role stereotypes and misperceptions melt away in the solvent of experience. Eventually, as they grow older and acquire more experience, most adolescents learn to think less stereotypically about themselves and the opposite sex.

Moreover, the school in an industrial society gives adolescents certain opportunities for self-discovery and development denied to youngsters in pre-industrial societies. Through working on school newspapers and magazines, through organising and leading recreational and political groups, through winning contests in public forums and on the gymnasium floor, girls discover needs and display talents the traditional society says that they do not possess. And boys, too, grow sharper and keener in the competitive milieu of the school where achievement in sports and academics brings recognition and the promise of future rewards – a sports scholarship, admission to a good college, and a head start in the race for success. These achievements affect not only the individual; they have social consequences as well because the achiever becomes an exemplar of what can be accomplished through hard work and ability and motivation, irrespective of gender.

The mass media pick up the theme of individual achievement, already made concrete in the school through test scores, grades, honours and awards, and emphasise it in news stories and television serials, dramatising in this way the irrelevance of gender for achievement. Readers encounter in newspaper stories women who have won high office in bitterly contested elections or who have successfully climbed the ladder of corporate power and prestige. Of course, the fact that editors still consider these stories newsworthy underscores their exceptionality, but even so such cases vividly contradict the stereotype that high political office and business success are beyond the ability of women. And, daily, viewers see on their television screens 'real-life' dramas in which women perform difficult, daring, dangerous jobs: sometimes as police officers armed with clubs and pistols pursuing criminals down crowded streets and wrestling them to the ground; sometimes as lawyers or physicians tackling with aplomb and steely efficiency difficult cases where the fate of a patient or client hangs by a thread, even though, being only human, they are themselves immersed in marital and emotional problems of exquisite complexity. But, you may say, this is merely the stuff of soap opera. True enough, but what should not be forgotten is that viewers of all ages, the impressionable young and the blasé old, are seeing dramatised evidence of what women can accomplish if only society would permit them to freely exercise their talents. And clearly the message of the media is that society must grant women more freedom, that it must allow them greater participation in the labour force and in other sectors of society.

Perhaps at this point the reader has grown a bit restive: this picture of an environment becoming increasingly free of stereotypes seems too rosy. Why all the optimism? Are not sex role stereotypes still present in the schools and the mass media? Indeed they are but not necessarily because the school and the media deliberatly set out to promote them. After reviewing a large number of studies conducted in the last decade and a half, Huston concluded that most teachers do not consistently reinforce sex-typed behaviour. On the contrary, teachers approve of task-oriented achievement behaviour and disapprove of aggression irrespective of the student's gender. Nor do teachers as a rule encourage dependent behaviour in one sex more than in the other.[3]

School curricula and textbooks, however, are another matter. Traditional schools still offer sex-typed courses because they are thought to be peculiarly appropriate to the student's gender, as for example, home economics for girls and mechanics for boys; and some schools scrupuloulsly guide bright boys into advanced mathematics and science courses but tend to be less assiduous in this respect with equally bright girls, frequently to the girl's disadvantage when she seeks admission into college or opts for a programme in engineering or science. Also, as many studies have shown, some publishers insensitively perpetuate sex role stereotypes by letting sex biases creep into the stories and illustrations used in their textbooks at all grade levels.[4] In such stories males are portrayed in a much greater variety of occupations than females, and both males and females tend to be depicted in occupations traditionally regarded as masculine or feminine. But recently, publishers, newly sensitive to these findings and fearful of losing sales, have begun to provide a more balanced picture of men and women in society and the labour force. Furthermore, not only are textbooks changing, so are the curricula. More schools than ever before are stressing non-sexist education, some going as far as to create special programmes designed to exorcise sex stereotyping from the classroom, using special books, discussion materials, and classroom exercises to get their point across. And yet, notwithstanding such remedial efforts, sex stereotyping has not been eradicated from all schools; even in these enlightened times some students receive heavy doses of sex stereotyped material with their formal schooling.

But the power of the school and the media to teach and reinforce sex stereotypes amd sex typed behaviour seems almost trivial when compared with the awesome influence of the peer group. Peers exert an influence upon adolescents that is both the despair of parents and the puzzlement of researchers who have long marvelled at the group's formidable power, particularly in the United States.[5] This power is closely tied to gender and appears very early on the scene. Thus children as young as age 2 have been found to show more attention to peers of the same sex than to those of the opposite sex, and the positive or negative reactions of same-sex peers have more impact upon their behaviour than the reaction of other-sex peers. By age 3, children reinforce one another's sex-typed play and punish each other for deviations from the stereotypes of sex. Boys and girls who play by the rules, who obediently stay within the limits defined by their sex role, and who eschew activities considered wrong for their sex, tend to receive favourable responses from their peers of either sex.[6] These children have friends, whereas those who behave in ways considered inappropriate to their sex come under severe, even savage, criticism and often end up socially isolated. The demand that the sex role rules be strictly observed is, however, more strictly enforced for males than females. Thus boys who play with dolls or display 'feminine' mannerisms and interests, for example, an unusual interest in cooking or sewing, may come under severe criticism, often followed by outright rejection. Girls, on the other hand, are given some leeway to explore the 'masculine' culture for things that might interest them including perhaps a male mode of dress or type of game or sport. The actions of a young 'tom-boy' frequently bring smiles of amusement to the lips of tolerant adults. But this smile usually turns to a frown when the 'tom-boy' grows older, for girls who persist in masculine behaviour do so at their peril and, like boys, will eventually find themselves the objects of reproof, though it seldom takes as harsh a form as that directed at boys.

This pressure to stay strictly within the limits of one's sex role, to think and behave in ways conventionally considered appropriate to one's gender, increases sharply during middle childhood and adolescence. In middle childhood the segregation of boys and girls into separate same-sex peer groups reaches extreme proportions and the tolerance for any deviation from sex-typed thought and action sharply declines. As we have already noted, intolerance deepens whenever isolation makes people increasingly ignorant of each other's true feelings. Early adolescence, with its anxieties and timidities, its rigidities and dogmatisms, does nothing to improve communication between the sexes and, as ignorance increases, the demand for sex role conformity grows louder. Probably not until late adolescence do most boys and girls acquire sufficient familiarity with one another to think of replacing stereotypes with reality and to begin experimenting with non-sex-typical relationships, starting in this way a process of mutual discovery that brings useful knowledge even though it seldom ends in complete understanding.

SEX STEREOTYPING AMONG ADOLESCENTS IN THREE COUNTRIES

Adolescents are buffeted by conflicting winds, some pushing them towards traditional, sex-segregated attitudes and values, others towards modern, egalitarian and stereotype-free perceptions of themselves and the opposite sex. Thus, while it is true that the prevailing winds in an industrial society are modern, strong gusts of traditional opinion can still be felt in almost every area of the adolescent's life, for the media and schools have their traditional sides; on the other hand, the peer group, though usually intolerant of sexual equality, is not immune to industrial influence, and may under some conditions take a modern stance toward the opposite sex. Consequently, the researcher cannot assume that every adolescent living in an industrial society necessarily holds a particular set of attitudes. Only research will settle the question as to whether a particular adolescent accepts or rejects traditional sex role stereotypes, and how prepared he or she is to treat age-mates of the opposite sex as equals.

Among the many traditional stereotypes adhering to sex, we selected for study four that bear a logical relationship to the participation of women in the labour force, to their choice of an occupation, and to their achievement in school and at work. The first stereotype holds that women are less competent than men and less interested in achievement; the second, that women are more dependent than men, that they lack the desire and ability to think and act for themselves and will usually turn to others, preferably men, for help when in difficulty; the third, that women are more concerned than men with personal appearance and will avoid any activity that spoils their looks; and the fourth, that women are more sensitive and empathetic than men.

It seems theoretically sound to argue that anyone who disdains achievement, who lacks self-reliance, and who shuns certain activities for fear of being soiled, will have a difficult time achieving success in a highly competitive industrial world which values achievement and independence and which applauds anyone's willingness to undertake almost any kind of profitable work even though in doing so one's hands and clothes become dirty and one's hair dishevelled. Being sensitive and having the ability to empathise with the problems of others, however need not be a handicap; indeed they are assets to people employed in service occupations, which often require skill in personal relationships and the capacity to see the other party's point of view, and which proliferate quickly in advanced industrial societies possessing a rapidly growing service sector. In short, I am arguing that the first three of these stereotypes work against women in the labour force and serve as justifications for keeping them out of certain lucrative positions that require flexibility, self-reliance, and competitiveness. But the last stereotype works to women's benefit, predisposing employers to see in women personal qualities of critical importance for good performance in service jobs – no small advantage over men in a competitive job market.

In order to determine the degree to which adolescents think stereo-typically we presented them with a six part question, each part a statement that could be applied to a male or female. We asked: 'Are the following more like a boy or a girl: (1) tries to do better than other people, (2) is generally better at doing things, (3) does things without asking for help, (4) does things they don't want to do just to make others like them, (5) doesn't do some things because they don't want to spoil how they look, (6) avoids hurting other people's feelings. Statements one and two concern competence and competitiveness; three and four, self-reliance and the willingness to placate others; five, anxiety about personal appearance; and six, sensitivity to other people's feelings. The adolescent's responses could range along a five-part continuum from 'a lot more like a boy', to 'a little more like a boy', to 'like both equally', to 'a little more like a girl', to 'a lot more like a girl'. To each response we assigned a weight from 1 to 5, with 5 being the most stereotypic response, 4, somewhat stereotypic, 3, neutral ('like both equally'), 2, less stereotypic, and 1, the least stereotypic.

Table 6.1 shows the mean scores of females and males in three countries to each of the six statements; note that the higher the score the most stereotypic the response, and the closer the score to the number three the more the respondent believes a trait is equally typical of both sexes. The data show that the boys and girls in all three industrialised economies, despite the widely disparate histories and cultures of their countries, resemble each other in that they tend to reject sex role stereotypes; nonetheless, some differences between the sexes and countries can be seen in Table 6.1, differences intriguing enough to warrant examining each stereotype separately.

Turning first to the stereotype about competitiveness and competence, the data show that American and Italian males are slightly more inclined than females to think stereotypically; that is to believe boys 'try to do better than other people'. But the British adolescents take a slightly different position: the girls think more stereotypically than the boys. However, the differences between the sexes in all three

Table 6.1   Mean Acceptance of Sex Role Stereotypes, by Sex and Country

	United States		Britain		Italy	
	Female	Male	Female	Male	Female	Male
Tries to do things better?	3.14*	2.40	3.50	3.40	2.82*	2.95
Is better at doing things?	2.99*	3.52	3.03*	3.72	2.87*	3.23
Does not want to spoil looks?	4.20*	1.93	4.16*	1.85	4.00	3.98
Does not ask for help?	3.62*	3.78	3.60*	3.77	3.93	3.94
Does things it dislikes?	3.13*	2.96	2.96*	2.77	3.24	3.19
Tries not to hurt others?	3.80*	2.39	3.94*	2.42	3.66*	3.23

Ns for United States   Ns for Britain   Ns for Italy
Female: > 1499 < 1505   Female: > 495 < 502   Female: > 664 < 669
Male: > 1521 < 1531   Male: > 528 < 536   Male: > 646 < 656
*$p < 0.01$

countries on this question are small; moreover, the mean scores cluster around 3, indicating a strong tendency to select the response 'like both equally'. In fact, 55 percent of the American girls see no difference between the sexes on this issue, a view shared by 45 of the American boys; the Italian adolescents are quite similar to their American peers, and even the British select 'like both equally' more frequently than any other alternative. For the most part, then, on the question of competitiveness, boys and girls tend to think alike.

Responses to the statement on actual competence, however, reveal a difference between the sexes: males in all three countries are more likely than females to think stereotypically, as might be expected from their response to the statement on competitiveness; but this time the differences between the sexes are noticeably large, though never as much as a full point. Thus the mean score for American males is 3.52, females 2.99; British males, 3.72, females, 3.03; Italian males, 3.23, females, 2.87. These differences reflect the strong belief shared by boys in all three countries, that being generally better at doing things is a 'lot more like a boy' than a girl. A further analysis of the data (not shown in Table 6.1), using cross-tabulation by sex and country, tells the story quite sharply: 24 percent of American males, 33 percent of the British, and 18 percent of the Italians believe that being able to do things better is 'a lot more like a boy'; whereas, only 8 percent of the American girls, 9 percent of the English girls and 8 percent of the Italian girls hold this point of view. Nevertheless, despite a tendency for some adolescents to respond stereotypically to this statement, the response, 'like both equally' is the one most frequently chosen by boys as well as girls: about half of the Americans and Italians, and a third of the British, chose this alternative.

The second stereotype concerns self-reliance and the willingness to please or placate others, even at some personal cost. Self-reliance, in the opinion of many adolescents, is a masculine trait: one half of the respondents in the United States and Britain, and two-thirds in Italy, felt that doing things without asking for help is more typical of boys than girls. But although in this area many adolescents appear to hold a traditional (and stereotypic) view of the sexes, it is a view held by about as many girls as boys. For instance, in the United States 50 percent of the girls and 58 percent of the boys said that doing things without asking for help is more typical of boys than girls. Even so, about a third of the American and British adolescents, and almost that many Italians, felt that self-reliance was a trait found as often among girls as boys. Turning now to the adolescents' willingness to do things to make others like them – a trait allied to powerlessness and vulnerability and hence closely tied to dependency – this trait is traditionally thought more characteristic of females than males. But the data in Table 6.1 show little difference between the sexes and countries in their acceptance of this stereotype. It is true that there is a slight tendency for more girls than boys in the United States and Britain to think females prone to placation, but practically no sex differences exist in Italy – despite the stereotype of the macho male and submissive female frequently encountered in descriptions of life in Italy.

Stereotyped thinking seems plainly evident in the responses of American and British females to the question about how concerned the sexes are with personal appearance: the girls' mean scores are much higher than those of the boys; indicating a strong tendency for the girls to accept the traditional judgement that females would give personal appearance priority over performance in the workplace; thus the female mean scores (United States, 4.20; Britain, 4.16) are much higher than the scores of males (United States, 1.93; Britain, 1.85). A cross-tabulational analysis of the data revealed that about 80 percent of the American girls and 78 percent of the British girls believe that not doing some things because one doesn't want to spoil how one looks is more typical of females than males. But it is also true – though this is not evident in the mean scores – that many boys believe vanity is a predominantly male trait: 80 percent of the American and 79 percent of the British boys thought boys more prone than girls to avoid certain activities for fear of spoiling their looks. On the other hand, the Italians, male and female alike, cleave to the traditional stereotype: 74 percent of the girls and 70 percent of the boys believed girls more likely than boys to eschew things that might ruin their appearance.

Finally, the traditional stereotype of females as more sensitive than males to the feelings of others, a consequence presumably of female empathy, finds only limited support among these youngsters. In fact, many American and British males ascribe sensitivity to their own sex rather than primarily to females; thus, while about 60 percent of American and 68 percent of British females believe that the tendency to avoid hurting the feelings of others is more typical of girls than boys, 55 percent of the American and 52 percent of the British boys said that sensitivity to the feelings of others predominantly characterises males. This explains why the mean scores of males and females in Table 6.1 differ so greatly, for very few of the girls considered their male age-mates empathetic and concerned with the feelings of others, an opinion the Italian girls also shared. On the other hand, a large number of the Italian boys (35 percent) as well as girls (55 percent) regard sensitivity to the feelings of others as more a female than a male trait. Even so, it is well to bear in mind that about a third of the respondents of both sexes in all three countries thought a concern with other people's feelings to be a trait found as often among boys as among girls – note the tendency for the mean scores in Table 6.1 to cluster around the neutral number 3.

From this welter of means and percentages a few generalisations can be drawn. First, stereotypes do not dominate the minds of most adolescents, not of either sex nor of any country. In fact, large numbers of boys and girls reject these stereotypes; rather than thinking a trait conventionally ascribed to girls as truly female, they believe the trait equally present in both sexes. Second, when the stereotype is positive, many girls and boys believe the stereotype true of their own sex, as in the case of sensitivity and concern with the feelings of others, notwithstanding the traditional ascription of this trait to one sex or the other. And third, a substantial minority of adolescents – the size varies with the stereotype in question – accepts at least one stereotype even though it reflects badly on their sex and possibly on themselves.

PERCEPTION OF THE OPPOSITE SEX

A deprecating attitude towards one's group and the self-contempt it often induces, reflect the internalisation of hostile out-group judgements and the perception that behaviour at variance with those judgements will evoke anger and bring punishment. Thus the judgement embodied in the traditional stereotype of women, that they are naturally nurturant and non-competitive, that they are non-aggressive and basically uninterested in achievement, carries with it the implied threat that females who behave unnaturally, who compete with men and act self-assertively, will be punished. The threat of punishment may take different forms. The competitive girl may be warned that she will be disliked by boys, most of whom will feel threatened by her behaviour; or she may be told that aggressiveness, the merest hint of self-assertion and independence, will drive eligible young males away, leaving her a lonely spinster, the pathetic object of pity and ridicule. In a traditional society these are not empty threats, and the prudent girl carefully avoids unconventional behaviour – at least until she is safely married.

An industrial society makes such threats less frightening. In modern cities today, unmarried young women, many of them single by choice, have become commonplace: they can be found on the factory floor, in shops and offices; they are not socially isolated or stigmatised. What is happening is that a growing number of women are choosing work and career over marriage and children, for they know that time invested in a career, when successful, often pays handsome dividends in money, prestige and independence. Moreover, the industrial society welcomes competitive, self-assertive, independent women and at the same time disarms the men, who in a traditional society would have been quick to resent an achieving independent female. As we have already noted, an industrial society celebrates an ethic of equality and individual achievement that makes no reference to class, race or gender. That being the case, how can men object to self-assertive women, particularly when the culture supports the right of women to be treated as the equals of men? And what use would such objections be anyway when the economy needs these independent women to work in jobs that require an assertive, self-reliant, independent frame of mind? On what grounds can males object to competition from females when the culture applauds individual achievement, and when the economy positively thrives on the contributions of achievers, female and male alike? And, finally, what reason have women, particularly the young ones who have been exposed since childhood to an industrial ideology that considers many traditional structures and restrictions morally invalid, economically unsound and psychologically damaging, to accept traditional sex role stereotypes or to expect hostility from men when those stereotypes are violated? On the face of it, none whatsover.

But traditional culture dies hard. Values that took generations to develop, perceptions that became deeply rooted in the popular mind, behaviour patterns that served generations well – these sturdy bastions of traditional society are not easily overthrown or abandoned, certainly not by everyone, not even in advanced industrial societies. We should not be surprised, therefore, to find some young people thinking and acting traditionally. But how many is a question that theory alone will not answer; it is an empirical question that only research can answer. We turn now to this empirical question and to research.

How well have adolescents learned the premier homily of the industrial society that achievement depends on personal competence and self-reliance, and that success depends on the individual's willingness to compete in public arenas – the school, the playing field, the state or corporate bureaucracy, or the market place? How many adolescents have made the industrial perspective part of the way they see themselves and other adolescents of the same or opposite sex? We sought to answer these questions by putting the following five-part question to our samples: 'If you did the following things, would a person your age of the opposite sex like you more or like you less?' Two of the 'things' concerned competition and achievement: (1) If you won in a game or sport you were playing with them. (2) If you did better on a test than they did. And three concerned self-orientation and self-reliance: (3) If you did what was best for you, even though it hurt someone else's feelings. (4) If you did something you disliked doing just because a friend wanted you to do it. (5) If you refused to give up when it looked like you were going to lose. To this five-part question the adolescent could make one of four responses: (1) like me a a lot more, (2) like me a little more, (3) like me a little less, (4) like me a lot less. With the exception of part 4, the responses 3 and 4 are the traditional responses. The response 'like me a lot less' was given a weight of 4, and 'a little less' a weight of 3; the modern response 'like me a little more', received a weight of 2, and 'a lot more' a weight of 1. (Part 4's weights were reversed.) When summed these weighted responses provide a measure of traditionalism: the higher the score, the more traditional the perspective, the more the respondent believed that competitiveness and self-assertion would elicit dislike from a peer of the opposite sex.

On the face of it this perception seems unwarranted. After all, are not competition and achievement commendable? And why should anyone be faulted for pursuing his or her own best interest or behaving self-reliantly? Put that way, the perception that the opposite sex would react negatively to one's achievement and independence seems strange. But many teenagers have learned that competition, despite the popular rhetoric that applauds achievement, is seldom entirely welcome, particularly when it comes from a source traditionally regarded as inherently nurturant and supportive – in short, when it comes from a female. Furthermore, competition, whatever the source, inevitably carries with it a suggestion of self-assertiveness, pushyness, and belligerence – qualities, tradition says, especially offensive to males when the competitor is a female.

Table 6.2 presents the mean responses of girls and boys in the three countries to questions about how the opposite sex would react to their behaving competitively and assertively. Recall that the higher the mean score, the more traditional the adolescent's perception of the world. Turning first to the questions on competitiveness and achievement, the data show that most of the scores cluster between 2 and 3, indicating a slight tendency for both sexes to believe that competitiveness and achievement (winning in a game or doing better in a test) would evoke hostility from peers of the opposite sex. This tendency is strongest in

Table 6.2 *Mean Perception of Opposite Sex, by Sex and Country*

	United States Female	Male	Britain Female	Male	Italy Female	Male
Won in a game or sport?	2.35*	2.07	2.66*	2.48	2.04	1.98
Did what was best for you?	2.98	3.06	3.06	3.09	3.47	3.44
Did better in a test?	2.71*	2.55	2.77*	2.59	2.46	2.39
Did something you disliked?	2.31*	2.41	2.53	2.51	2.62*	2.37
Refused to give up?	2.00	1.94	2.20	2.14	2.40	2.43

Ns for United States	*Ns for Britain*	*Ns for Italy*
Female: > 1446 < 1491	Female: > 449 < 475	Female: > 640 < 657
Male: > 1437 < 1513	Male: > 465 < 500	Male: > 633 < 652

*$p < 0.01$

Britain, and weakest in Italy, but in no country is it particularly marked. Winning in a game or sport is perceived as somewhat less threatening to the opposite sex than doing better in an exam. Many girls in all three countries thought this would be troublesome to boys; thus 64 percent of the American girls thought they would be liked less if they did better in a test; 71 percent of the British and 48 percent of the Italian girls concurred. It is important to remember, however, that many of the boys felt the same way; 55 percent of the American, 59 percent of the British, and 44 percent of the Italian boys believed they would be liked less if they did better than girls in a test. But on the whole, the mean scores in Table 6.2 reveal that the sexes differ little in how they perceive members of the opposite sex reacting to competitiveness and achievement.

Nor do attitudes towards self-assertiveness and self-absorption distinguish between the sexes. Very few adolescents, male or female, American or British or Italian, think the single-minded pursuit of self-interest ('doing what is best for you, even if it hurt someone else's feelings') will meet with approval. On the other hand about half think that doing something one dislikes in order to accommodate a friend would be liked, and many teenagers believe a stubborn refusal to give up when it looked like one were going to lose (arguably a sign of self-assertion and self-reliance) would be approved by peers of the opposite sex. The Americans and British are slightly more convinced of this than the Italians. In summary, notwithstanding the popular notion that men are more likely than women to dislike competitiveness and self-assertiveness in the opposite sex, the data show remarkably few differences between the sexes in how such behaviour is perceived when evidenced by members of the other gender.

SEX ROLE BEHAVIOUR

Up to this point we have focused on the adolescent's cognitions and perceptions: what girls and boys believe, how they see each other, and what they imagine the reactions of peers would be to their behaviour. Now we turn to the behaviour itself. As regards self-reliance, self-confidence, and self-assertion, how differently do girls and boys behave? Are girls, as tradition maintains, more timid and submissive than boys? Are girls more concerned about the opinion of others, more unsure of themselves, more easily discouraged and hence more willing to turn to others for help? If so, this is bad news for women, for these diminish one's chance of success in a competitive world. Timid people do not fare well in the hurly-burly of the market place, and success often eludes those who put appearance above performance, who lack the confidence to take on difficult assignments, and who depend upon the help of others when the going becomes rough.

But the views and prejudices of tradition aside, what evidence is there that young women today behave with less assurance, determination, self-assertion, and spunk than men of their own age? Regrettably, little that is not polemical and anecdotal, which, while occasionally insightful, is hardly enough upon which to base a serious generalisation. For that reason we put the following seven-part question to our samples: 'How often do you do the following things: (1) Are too shy to raise your hand when you know the answer; (2) Ask someone for help with a personal problem; (3) Give up without really trying very hard; (4) Act dumber than you really are; (5) Avoid doing something because it would spoil how you look; (6) Worry that other people your own age would think you are stuck up; (7) Do what other people your own age would want you to do even if you don't want to?' To each of these questions the teenager could make one of four responses: never, seldom, sometimes, often. Each response was weighted from 1 to 4: 'never', 1; 'seldom', 2; 'sometimes', 3; and 'often', 4. Thus the higher the adolescent's weighted score, the more often they behaved timidly and diffidently, the more often they submitted to peer pressure, the more often they tried not to appear dowdy, vain, independent, and bright.

The mean scores of students in the three countries are shown in Table 6.3, each question considered separately. As expected, the data show more similarities between the sexes than differences: adolescents of both sexes behave with equal degrees of self-assertion and independence. Thus according to their own reports, girls are not markedly more likely than boys to behave submissively ('do what other people want you to do, even when you don't want to'), or to hide their light under a bushel ('Act dumber than you really are'). In fact most adolescents tend to avoid such behaviour, as the mean scores, which cluster around 1 or 2 (the answers 'never' or 'seldom') clearly indicate.

Nevertheless, there are some differences between the sexes in Table 6.3 that run counter to our hypothesis about the homogenising effects of industrialisation on the sexes: the mean scores of the girls tend to be higher than the scores of the boys when the questions touch upon self-reliance, interpersonal relations, and impression management. Girls appear more concerned than boys about the effect they are having on others, about looking mussed-up and appearing vain. On closer

Table 6.3 Mean Sex Role Behaviour, by Sex and Country

	United States Female	Male	Britain Female	Male	Italy Female	Male
Avoid doing something that might spoil how you look?	2.42*	2.21	2.23*	1.85	2.56*	2.37
Act dumber than you really are?	2.10*	2.95	2.19	2.15	1.66*	1.78
Ask help with personal probs?	2.72*	2.18	2.53*	2.07	2.87*	2.49
Are too shy to raise your hand?	2.16*	1.85	2.43*	1.89	2.17*	1.84
Worry people will think you are stuck up?	2.21*	1.85	1.93*	1.54	2.28*	2.13
Give up without trying very hard?	2.17*	1.97	2.29*	2.03	1.91	1.98
Do what others want even when you don't?	2.19	2.13	2.22	2.12	1.71	1.81

Ns for United States	Ns for Britain	Ns for Italy
Female: > 1495 < 1506	Female: > 495 < 499	Female: > 660 < 667
Male: > 1529 < 1540	Male: > 545 < 551	Male: > 648 < 657

*$p < 0.01$

inspection, using cross-tabulations rather than means, we found that 46 percent of the American girls, 40 percent of the British, and 55 percent of the Italian, say they 'sometimes' or 'often' avoid doing something because it would spoil how they look as compared with 38 percent of the American boys, 23 percent of the British, and 42 percent of the Italian. Girls are almost twice as likely as boys to worry that people will think them vain and conceited. For instance, 40 percent of the American girls sometimes or often worry that people will think they are 'stuck up', as compared with 24 percent of the American boys; the British give much the same responses, and the Italians are also inclined in the same direction, though the sex differences are smaller.

The girls are somewhat more likely than the boys to be shy and easily daunted. About 41 percent of the American girls said they are 'sometimes' or 'often' too shy to raise their hands when they know the answer; only 28 percent of the boys gave this response. British girls are even shyer: 55 percent said they were too shy to raise their hands, as compared with 30 percent of the boys. The percentages for the Italians divide in much the same way: shyness keeps 40 percent of the girls and 27 percent of the boys from raising their hands in class. Girls are also more likely than boys to say they lack stick-to-it-tiveness ('give up without really trying very hard'). Thus 31 percent of the American girls and 42 percent of the British said they 'sometimes' or 'often' gave up, as compared with 26 percent of the American and 31 percent of the British boys. On this item the difference between Italian girls and boys is negligible. Finally, girls are more likely than boys to ask for help. Thus 64 percent of the American, 56 percent of the English, and 70 percent of the Italian girls said they 'sometimes' or 'often' asked someone to help them with a personal problem, whereas only 38 percent of the American, 33 percent of the British, and 51 percent of the Italian boys gave this response.

It may be that these sex differences are smaller than they appear. Perhaps girls are simply more willing than boys to admit to being timid, shy, dependent, preoccupied with appearance, and in need of succour. Such admissions for girls, it could be argued, are still socially acceptable in some circles, whereas similar confessions by boys run counter to the conventional image of the self-controlled and self-reliant male, stubbornly persevering and often negligent about personal appearance. A boy who candidly admits to timidity and weakness leaves himself open to the charge of being effeminate, something most boys will do anything to avoid. If this argument is correct, it makes even more remarkable the willingness of some boys to admit to non-traditional behaviour, to being fearful and dependent, and it helps explain why some girls persist in behaving traditionally, despite the efforts of industrial society to reduce the differences between the sex roles of males and females.

The following section looks at a system of traditional beliefs and behaviour called the Chameleon Syndrome. We will examine its sources and functions, show its effects on the expectations girls bring to their relationships with boys, and explore its impact on the choices women make after marriage.

THE CHAMELEON SYNDROME: SOURCES AND FUNCTIONS

The Chameleon Syndrome is a sub-type of a personality complex called chameleonism: mercurial behaviour that fluctuates to suit the expectations and anticipations of others.[7] Like the reptile chameleon who changes colour to blend into the physical environment, the human chameleon assumes, often unconsciously, a protective façade that permits it to fit safely into a potentially unfriendly social environment. Chameleonism is not tied exclusively to sex nor does it serve any special sexual purpose, but the Chameleon Syndrome is specifically linked to the sex role.

People with a Chameleon Syndrome are strongly attached to the traditional sex role and feel deeply apprehensive about the reactions of others to any behaviour that violates conventional sex role prescriptions. But, since these prescriptions vary with gender, the content of the Chameleon Syndrome will differ between the sexes. For instance, in a traditional female the existence of the Chameleon Syndrome shows itself in her willingness to modify her behaviour to suit the expectations of males who are perceived as being hostile to competitive and self-assertive women. Believing she will be punished if she behaves competitively and self-assertively, the female with a Chameleon Syndrome disguises who she really is, suppresses her self-expansive tendencies, and seeks securtiy and acceptance by pretending to be something she is not – compliant and self-abasive.

In contrast to the form it takes among females, the Chameleon Syndrome in a traditional male shows itself as competitive and aggressive behaviour that is intended to project an image of self-confidence and competence, for males need not conceal their skill or suppress ambition, nor are they ordinarily encouraged to be passive and dependent. Quite the contrary, aggressiveness and competitiveness are widely valued as essential masculine characteristics and hence encouraged, whereas compliance and dependency is considered effeminate and discouraged. Possibly some males fear that being assertive will cost them the approval of females, perhaps some males conceal their competence for fear of offending females; certainly many males behave dependently, but compliant, passive, self-abasive behaviour, particularly where relationships with females are concerned, is not rooted in the traditional male sex role. Therefore, though he may possess these traits, though he may be timid and secretly yearn for succour, the male yielding to the dictates of the Chameleon Syndrome must hide his fear behind a façade of self-assertive and sometimes blustery self-confidence.

This section focuses upon the Chameleon Syndrome in females. We will argue that the Chameleon Syndrome is a by-product of intensive and continuous sex role socialisation by parents, teachers, peers and others, that seeks to prepare females for marriage. For marriage remains an important goal for most people in contemporary industrial societies, despite the current controversy over its viability and the proliferation of alternative life-styles, whose salience reflects the pressures society places on women and men to fulfil sex role expectations.

Most adults in Western industrial societies marry. For example, as of 1986, only 22 percent of American males and 14 percent of females age 30 to 35 years had never married. The American marriage rate remains high in both an historical and a cross-cultural context. Once mated, Americans appear addicted to the marital condition, for although the divorce rate has been rising for decades, four out of five divorced persons eventually remarry. Not everyone, of course, chooses to marry. The recent rise in age at first marriage may indicate a trend toward remaining single, possibly because more young people view it as an attractive alternative to marriage; nevertheless, the percentage wanting to remain single continues to be small.[8] In this study, only 10 percent of the Americans, 9 percent of the British, and 7 percent of the Italians said they did not intend to marry, numbers which may decline as the teenagers grow older, as the pressure on them to marry increases and as marriage becomes more attractive.

The attraction marriage holds for most people is a product of intense social and psychological pressures, some of which give the marital condition appealing properties – emotional and sexual gratification, security, and parentage – while others make the unmarried state a condition of emotional deprivation and a target of social reproof. But although neither sex escapes the pressure to marry, it falls more heavily on females than on males. Bachelorhood is socially acceptable but spinsterhood alarms almost everyone. Indeed, popular and professional opinion often join in warning women against the perils of spinsterhood. For instance, Judith Bardwick, a psychologist and expert on women, believes that a concern with familial relationships is functional for women and a prerequisite for success in other spheres, a condition not required of men, for whom occupational achievement is an important measure of successful manhood.[9] As a result, unlike the traditional male who finds his identity in work, the traditional female makes womanhood synonymous with marriage and good performance of the domestic role. These women feel incomplete unless they are successful at the roles of wife and mother.

But before marriage can take place a mate must be found. To help insure that this occurs, parents, peers, the mass media and other agents of socialisation instruct girls on how to attract and hold a man.

Traditional girls are advised to appear responsive to male needs, to nurture the fragile male ego whenever possible, to be sensitive to cues indicating approval or disapproval and to modify their behaviour accordingly. Aggressive or competitive behaviour threatening to conventional males must be avoided or disguised; attitudes of compliance and passivity must be encouraged because the female is expected to play a passive role in courtship – or appear to be doing so. Underlying this advice is the tacit assumption that females operate in a buyer's market in which males are the buyers. The probably unintended and frequently unrecognised effect of traditional female sex role socialisation is the development in many traditional girls of the Chameleon Syndrome.

THE CHAMELEON SYNDROME INDEX

The Chameleon Syndrome is composed of three interrrelated cognitive, perceptual, and behavioural parts which interact to form an integrated whole. These parts and their content for females are as follows:

A. Sex Role Stereotypes. This cognitive component concerns the extent to which an individual attributes to females certain traits stereotypically defined as feminine. Although the list of such traits is long, we shall focus on only three: (1) *sensitivity,* an awareness of and concern with the feelings of others; (2) *compliance,* a willingness to sacrifice one's own needs in order to satisfy the needs of others; and (3) *appearance orientation,* a concern with physical attractiveness and the avoidance of activities which might detract from one's appearance. These three traits have an important characteristic in common: a concern with the reactions of others and with the maintenance of good interpersonal relationships. That these traits are commonly considered feminine is confirmed by the research of Broverman, *et al.* who found them to be attributed more often to females than to males.[10]

B. Perception of the Sex Role Reward Structure. This perceptual component focuses on how the individual perceives the reactions of members of the opposite sex to behaviour which conforms to or violates the prescriptions of the traditional sex role. The Chameleon Syndrome in females denotes the expectation that non-assertive, self-sacrificing behaviour will be approved.

C. Sex Role Behaviour.   This behavioural component taps the degree to which the individual is compliant, dependent, and self-abasive. The Chameleon Syndrome (female version) involves constraints on behaviour unacceptable to males, such as being too smart, appearing unattractive, and thinking too highly of oneself. Conversely, the Syndrome encourages compliance with the wishes of others, expressions of dependency, and a tendency toward self-disparagement, all designed to attract conventional males who like submissive, dependent females in need of support from a dominant partner.

Each component of the Chameleon Syndrome may be viewed as a step in the developmental process in which the syndrome is formed. The process begins with the attribution of stereotypic characteristics to one's own sex. It gains impetus when the individual perceives that behaviour not in keeping with the stereotype will be punished, whereas behaviour that conforms to the stereotype will be rewarded. It culminates in defensive, non-assertive behaviour designed to ward off disapproval and gain social acceptance. This behaviour brings the developmental sequence full circle, for it reinforces the stereotype and reflects the syndrome-generated perception of the opposite sex.

If, as we maintain, there is a version of the Chameleon Syndrome that is more characteristic of females than males, then an empirical measure of the syndrome derived from the components described above should differentiate between girls and boys. To test this hypothesis a Chameleon Syndrome Index was constructed from a larger pool of items examined in the previous pages. As can be seen in Chart 6.1, the index is composed of three components and fifteen items in all, with each component given an equal weight. One component was designed to assess sex role stereotyping, another the adolescent's perception of the sex role reward structure, and the last chameleon-related behaviour. The procedure employed in constructing the index was as follows. First, the response weights for the Sex Role Stereotyping items (questions 1, 2 and 3) were reversed for the male respondents; the weights for females remained as shown in Chart 6.1. Thus a high score indicates that the respondent, regardless of sex, attributes chameleon-like behaviour to his or her own sex. Also item 4 weights were reversed so that the responses to this question would move in the same direction as the other four within the component.

Three separate sub-indices were then constructed by summing each respondent's weighted answers to the items subsumed under a component. Scores were computed only for respondents who answered all

Chart 6.1   The Chameleon Syndrome Index

A. Sex Role Stereotypes

Are the following more like a boy or a girl?
1. Does things they don't want to do just to make others like them.
2. Avoids hurting other people's feelings.
3. Doesn't do some things because they don't want to spoil how they look.

> *Responses:* 1 = A lot more like a boy
> 2 = A little more like a boy
> 3 = Like both equally
> 4 = A little more like a girl
> 5 = A lot more like a girl

B. Perception of Sex Role Reward Structure

If you did the following things, would a person your age of the opposite sex like you more or like you less?
4. If you did something you dislike doing, just because another friend wanted you to do it.
5. If you won in a game or sport you were playing with them.
6. If you did better on a test than they did.
7. If you refuesed to give up when it looked like you were going to lose.
8. If you did what was best for you, even though it hurt someones else's feelings.

> *Responses:* 1 = Like me a lot more
> 2 = Like me a little more
> 3 = Like me a little less
> 4 = Like me a lot less

C. Sex Role Behaviour

How often do you do the following:
9. Act dumber than you really are.
10. Do what other people your own age want you to do, even when you don't want to.
11. Worry that people your own age will think you are stuck up.
12. Give up without really trying very hard.
13. Are you too shy to raise your hand when you know the answer.
14. Ask someone to help you with a personal problem.
15. Avoid doing something because it would spoil how you look.

> *Responses:* 1 = Never
> 2 = Seldom
> 3 = Sometimes
> 4 = Often

---

questions in the sub-scale. The higher the summed positive score, the more the respondent attributes stereotypic behaviour to his or her sex, the more the respondent perceives herself or himself liked less for assertive, competitive, self-oriented behaviour, and the more the respondent seeks to disguise competence, worries about the reactions of others, and displays a need for social support. In order to insure that each component contributed equally to the total index score, despite differences in the number of questions and response weights, sub-index scores were then standardised by means of the z transformation, using the mean and standard deviation obtained from the group of respondents who had answered all the questions in that sub-index.

Correlation analysis showed the three sub-indices to be positively correlated. Thus for the Americans the Pearsonian correlation coefficient of Sex Role Behaviour with Perception of the Sex Role Reward Structure is 0.10 ($p < 0.001$), and with the Sex Role Stereotype, 0.21 ($p < 0.001$); the correlation of the Perception of the Sex Role Reward Structure with Sex Role Stereotyping is 0.07 ($p < 0.001$). These modest correlations indicate that each component of the Chameleon Syndrome Index is tapping a relatively distinct phenomenon. However, the fact that the correlations are positive permits us to group the components under a single conceptually meaningful label – the Chameleon Syndrome. A composite Chameleon Syndrome Index score was computed for each respondent by summing that person's standardised sub-index scores, and separate Chameleon Syndrome index scores were computed for the American, British, and Italian samples. The reliability coefficient (alpha) for the fifteen-item index is 0.52 for the American and British samples: an adequate level of reliability. Unfortunately, the alpha for the Italians is 0.32, too low to justify constructing an index for this group. Consequently, the data analysis that follows is restricted to the Americans and the British.

The data confirm our expectation that there is a form of the Chameleon Syndrome, as conceived and operationalised in this study, which is more pronounced among females than males. On each component of the syndrome, females, on the average, score significantly higher than males. To begin with, females attribute sensitivity, compliance and a concern with personal appearance more often to females than to males, while males see these as characteristics of the opposite sex. Females are also more likely than males to report that they would be liked less by members of the opposite sex if they behave assertively, compete successfully, and pursue their own interests without regard to the reactions of others. Finally, girls are more likely than boys to report that they conceal their competence, behave in dependent and compliant ways, and worry about the reactions of others to their appearance and behaviour. The differences between the sexes in the Chameleon Syndrome come even more sharply into focus when we compare male and female scores on the Chameleon Syndrome Index. The data in Table 6.4 show a mean score of 1.22 for American and 1.30 for British females, as compared with − 1.19 for American and − 1.29 for British males (scores range from − 6 to + 7). With each component of the Chameleon Syndrome significantly distinguishing between the sexes and all moving in the same direction, the cumulative effect of the composite index is a striking difference between male and female mean scores. A '*t*' test of the difference between the mean scores for girls and boys shows the difference to be significant at the 0.0005 level.

Table 6.4 *Mean Chameleon Syndrome Score, by Sex in the United States and Britain*

| | Chameleon Syndrome Score | | | |
| | United States | | Britain | |
	Mean	(N)	Mean	(N)
Females	1.22	(1397	1.30	(421)
Males	− 1.19	(1343)	− 1.29	(417)
	$t = 40.59$		$t = 24.74$	
	$p < 0.0005$		$p < 0.0005$	

The relationship between sex and the Chameleon Syndrome becomes even stronger when one considers the lack of a relationship between syndrome scores and other social variables. A one-way analysis of variance of the American data revealed that among both males and females the Chameleon Syndrome Index is not related to socioeconomic status as assessed by parental occupation, nor to parental level of education, nor to maternal employment. No relationship was found between the Chameleon Syndrome score and certain other demographic characteristics often associated with adolescent behaviour and personality. Thus the Chameleon Syndrome is unaffected by family size, birth order, or whether the respondent lives in an intact nuclear family or in some alternative arrangement. The largest F ratios are for mother's education ($F = 2.25$) and ordinal position ($F = 1.02$); the smallest are family size ($F = 0.33$) and maternal employment ($F = 0.02$). In no case is an F value statistically significant at the 0.05 level.

An analysis of the British data reveals very similar findings. It appears, then, that as regards the female version of the Chameleon Syndrome, sex overrides other status characteristics: being female is more important than the social class to which one belongs or one's demographic position in the family.

Since the Chameleon Syndrome Index was designed specifically to assess a special kind of chameleonism in females, and given our intention to examine the relationship of the Syndrome to the pressure put on women to marry and to be domestically oriented, the analysis from this point will deal exclusively with females. We will focus on why and how some girls acquire the Chameleon Syndrome, and on its effects on their orientation towards marriage, work after marriage, and children. We believe that the Chameleon Syndrome develops during the process in which girls learn the traditional sex role. Two aspects of this process will be explored: socialisation by parents and by peers of the opposite sex.

PARENTAL SOCIALISATION OF THE CHAMELEON SYNDROME

The Chameleon Syndrome in females originates in the family as a product of the process in which traditional parents instruct daughters on the behaviour and attitudes appropriate to their sex. Two aspects of this socialisation process are central to the syndrome's development: a strong emphasis on interpersonal relationships, and a high level of parental control.

An emphasis on close interpersonal relationships lies at the very core of the traditional female sex role. Entrance into the wife–mother role is contingent upon establishing and maintaining such relationships, as is continued role occupancy, while the disruption of a primary relationship with a suitor or husband threatens a conventional woman's estimation of herself as a woman: her major social roles are endangered, her social identity is jeopardised, and her sense of self is put in question. Consequently, for many females the cultivation of relationships with males becomes a concern of paramount importance, absorbing tremendous time and energy and requiring the development of strategies to enhance relationships. It is not surprising, therefore, that many girls are urged to develop the skills thought essential for good relations with others. Such girls are warned to avoid any action prejudicial to these relationships: aggressiveness must be controlled, feelings of anger must be concealed, and opinions offensive to others must be left unexpressed. The effect of these instructions is that some girls come to believe that good interpersonal relationships are enormously important, indeed essential, if they are to function effectively, not merely as a person but also as females.

Data supporting the contention that many parents place great stress on interpersonal relationships in the socialisation of females can be found in the work of Block.[11] She reports that females are urged to develop close ties with others, encouraged to talk about their troubles, and advised to seek comfort and reassurance from others. Hoffman concludes in a review of research findings on child development that affective relationships are more important for females than males.[12] Even achievement behaviour among girls often appears to be more motivated by a desire to please and to be socially accepted than by mastery strivings.

Strong differences in the amount of control traditional parents impose on their children emerge as they reach adolescence. Girls may then be subjected to what Newson and Newson call 'chaperonage'.[13] Girls are more restricted than boys and more likely to be asked where they are going, with whom, and for what purpose. Understandably parents feel that females are more vulnerable to harm than boys. After all, the fear of sexual attack which infests the thoughts of concerned parents is not without some basis in fact. As a consequence, parents are more protective of girls than boys, and less likely to be concerned with the effects of over-protectiveness. One effect of protectiveness is dependency – a characterological trait more apt to be accepted in girls than boys.

Closely controlled under the guise of being protected, their dependency strivings accepted or even encouraged, and warned that expressions of anger and self-assertion will cost them valued relationships, some girls come to feel weak and vulnerable, grow fearful of being abandoned and alone, and develop strategies for maintaining relationships. One such stragegy is the Chameleon Syndrome. Traditional girls learn that chameleon behaviour keeps friends, since arguments are avoided and differences smoothed over by disguising one's true feelings and actions. Moreover, the Chameleon Syndrome brings rewards from parents who hold conventional beliefs about the female sex role and who respond positively to behaviour which conforms to those beliefs. Thus, as an extra bonus, females who engage in conventional sex role behaviour, of which the Chameleon Syndrome is a part, enjoy a sense of acceptance and security that conformity to sociocultural expectations usually brings.

In this study, several parental socialisation practices related to the development of the Chameleon Syndrome were assessed through the responses of adolescents to five questions about how their parents think and behave. The respondents were presented with the following five statements and asked, 'Are the following more like your father, more like your mother, like both equally, or like neither?'

1. Seems unhappy when you don't have lots of friends.
2. Tells you that people won't like you if you show them you're mad at them.
3. Thinks it's better to keep your opinions to yourself rather than argue with someone.
4. Won't let you solve your problems for yourself.
5. Treats you as though you're younger than you really are.

The first item assesses parental emphasis on interpersonal relationships, in this case on the importance of having friends; items 2 and 3 concern the suppression of behaviour that might jeopardise a relationship; and items 4 and 5 reflect the adolescent's perception that parents are controlling her behaviour.

The relationship of parental socialisation to the Chameleon Syndrome was first examined by constructing a separate index for each parent. This was done by summing the number of times a mother or father was chosen in response to the five items that make up the index. Both indices are positively related to the girl's Chameleon Syndrome score, but the relationships are not statistically significant. A composite Parental Socialisation Index was then constructed by giving a score of 1 to any response in which a parent, either singly or collectively, was chosen; the response 'like neither', indicating an absence of such parental behaviour, was given a weight of 0; each adolescent's responses were then summed across five items, producing an index with scores ranging from 0 to 5, the higher the score, the more intense the socialisation. Parental Socialisation Index scores were then trichotomised, as shown in Table 6.5, into low, medium, and high intensity groups.

The relationship of this composite Parental Socialisation score to the Chameleon Syndrome is shown in Table 6.5. The data show a positive relationship between intensity of perceived parental pressure and the girl's Chameleon Syndrome Index score. The more parents are perceived as concerned with interpersonal relationships, the more worried they appear about behaviour that might endanger these relationships, and the more restrictively they behave, the higher the girl's Syndrome score. The mean scores for the low socialisation groups are 0.97 for the

Table 6.5 Mean Chameleon Syndrome Score, by Intensity of Parental Pressures towards Chameleonism in the United States and Britain

Intensity of parental pressure toward Chameleonism	Chameleon Syndrome Score			
	United States		Britain	
	Mean	(N)	Mean	(N)
low (0–1)	0.97	(469)	1.10	(122)
medium (2–3)	1.32	(645)	1.39	(200)
high (4–5)	1.49	(217)	1.34	(73)
	$F = 9.68$		$F = 1.55$	
	$p = < 0.005$		p: not significant	

Americans and 1.10 for the British, as compared with 1.49 for the American high group and 1.34 for the British. An analysis of variance revealed that this relationship between perceived parental pressures and the Chameleon Syndrome is highly significant ($p < 0.005$) for the Americans. Differences between parental groups are significant for the British when the comparison is between high and low groups, but not when all three groups are considered, primarily because the medium and high groups are very similar. The relationship between perceived parental pressures and the Chameleon Syndrome is unchanged when socioeconomic status was introduced as a controlling variable.

Given the data's cross-sectional nature, it is not possible to state unequivocally that a casual nexus exists between perceived parental socialisation and the Chameleon Syndrome. Nor can we be sure, even assuming a nexus exists, in what direction causation flows. Possibly the syndrome affects how parents are perceived as well as itself being influenced by parental pressures. Most probably the syndrome and parental socialisation interact in an ongoing process, reinforcing one another, but since both theory and research indicate that parents play a significant role in a child's general development, it seems reasonable to conclude that parental influences are also important in the development of the Chameleon Syndrome.

PEER SOCIALISATION AND THE CHAMELEON SYNDROME

Sex role socialisation may begin in the home, but interaction with peers of the opposite sex gives sex role learning special meaning and saliency. Parents may tell their daughter what to expect when interacting with males but it is actual experience that transforms these expectations into reality. Of course, the fact that mutual learning occurs when boys and girls interact is not in question. The crucial question is: what is learned and in what kinds of relationships?

A partial answer – one of great importance for an understanding of the development of the Chameleon Syndrome – is that adolescents acquire stereotypic images of sex roles (or have earlier ones confirmed) from one another, and that this learning occurs primarily in the dating relationship. Thus Lambert, in an empirical study of adolescents, reports a clear tendency for teenagers who interact in situations where sex and sex roles are salient (such as dating relationships) to think and behave in sexually stereotyped ways.[14] In another study, McDaniel argues that females discover the inappropriateness of assertive behaviour during the dating process and learn that a receptive role incorporating deference and dependence and vicariousness is approved by males.[15] In effect, McDaniel is saying that females acquire the Chameleon Syndrome during the dating process, which may be true enough but is it that simple? The dating process is a complex one. The character of the dating partner, the number of dating relationships, the social milieu in which dating occurs, and the seriousness with which it is taken, are only a few of the factors that affect the dating process. Identifying and disentangling the effects of all of these factors on the dating process is beyond our ability. But, at the very least we can separate the effects of frequency of heterosexual interaction from the effects of the quality of that interaction, or, to be more specific, the commitment adolescents develop toward one another.

In this study we asked adolescents how often they interacted with peers, under what circumstances, and with what degree of seriousness. We began by asking them these three questions: (1) In the last week, how many times have you talked on the telephone with someone of the opposite sex? (2) In the last month, how many times have you gone to a boy–girl party? (a) In the last month, how many times have you gone out alone on a date with a person of the opposite sex? A simple additive scale indicating frequency of heterosexual interaction was constructed by summing the respondent's answers across these three items. To our surprise, we found that sheer frequency of interaction is negatively related to the Chameleon Syndrome, contrary to what McDaniel's analysis would suggest. However, this relationship appears to be an artifact of age: the frequency of interaction with peers of the opposite sex is positively related with age, while the Chameleon Syndrome is negatively related to age. When age is controlled, the relationship between frequency of interaction with peers of the opposite sex and the Chameleon Syndrome score disappears.

If frequency of interaction is not significantly related to the Chameleon Syndrome, what aspects of the male–female dating relationships do affect it? The finding that age is negatively related to the Chameleon Syndrome provided a clue as to where to look for an answer. It did so by causing us to ask ourselves this question: In so far as the dating aspect of the heterosexual relationship is concerned, how do older adolescents differ from the younger ones? One answer is that older adolescents have fewer dating partners and are more likely to describe the relationship as serious. Thus in response to the question, 'In the past twelve months, how many people of the opposite sex have you gone with?' American adolescents in the 11th and 12th grades reported slightly fewer relationships than those in the lower age groups: 1.1 for the 11–12th graders, 1.2 for 9–10th graders, and 1.4 for the 7–8th graders. More significantly, the commitment to a dating partner is greater among the older adolescents. The respondents were asked, 'How serious are you about the person you are presently going with?' Responses ranged on a five-point scale from 'not at all serious' to 'very serious'. The higher the score, the more serious the relationship was thought to be. The relationship between age and commitment proved to be linear and positive: the mean score for the American 7–8th graders is 2.0, 2.1 for the 9–10th graders, and 2.7 for the 11–12th graders. In all the above relationships the British are very similar to the Americans.

This combination of seriousness and restrictiveness in the number of people they consider themselves 'going with' helps explain the lower Chameleon Syndrome scores of the older adolescents. Consider the data in Table 6.6 in which type of dating relationships is cross-tabulated with mean Chameleon Syndrome score. Older adolescents (those in the 11th and 12th grades) who report only one steady relationship in the past year and who describe that relationship as 'serious' have lower mean Chameleon Syndrome Scores (American, 0.58; British 0.50) than adolescents who have had several relationships, none of which involve serious commitment (American, 1.86; British 1.50). A similar pattern is found among the younger age cohorts: Syndrome scores are lowest among adolescents who report a single relationship and highest among respondents who are 'not going with anyone' or who have had dating relationships with several different males.

Collectively, the data on heterosexual peer involvement suggest a

Table 6.6   Mean Chameleon Syndrome Score, by the Type of Dating Relationship for 11th and 12th Grade Females in the United States and Britain

| Type of dating relationship | Chameleon Syndrome Score | | | |
| | United States | | Britain | |
	Mean	(N)	Mean	(N)
Not involved in a steady relationship	1.09	(241)	1.50	(92)
One steady relationship in past year				
Not seriously involved	1.30	(15)	0.25	(4)
Seriously involved	0.58	(121)	0.50	(20)
Several relationships in past year				
Not seriously involved	1.86	(16)	1.50	(26)
Seriously involved	1.01	(70)	1.35	(31)
	$F = 3.82$		$F = 2.50$	
	$p < 0.005$		$p < 0.05$	

developmental process during which changes in the nature of the dating relationship ultimately weaken the Chameleon Syndrome by making it less necessary. In its early stages, the dating relationship tends to be role-bound and superficial. Young adolescents, who typically lack the experience of having had intimate relationships with peers of the opposite sex, tend to think and behave stereotypically and, being relatively unfamiliar with the dating process, they tend to exert pressure on one another to engage in sex-typed behaviour. The younger female, constrained to behave as expected rather than spontaneously and involved in multiple superficial relationships, can hardly help feeling insecure. That she responds to this situation with Chameleon-like behaviour is not surprising. But a serious, long-term relationship offers adolescents the chance to get to know one another as persons, not merely as role incumbents, and gives them the opportunity to check stereotypic images of the opposite sex against personal experience. Moreover, a stable, serious relationship makes it less necessary for older adolescents to disguise their true feelings; they can afford to behave more naturally towards one another. Essentially, then, longer and more serious relationships tend to mitigate the effects of traditional sex role socialisation on adolescents and reduce the need for females to think, perceive, and behave in a Chameleon Syndrome fashion.

This is not to say that long-term, serious dating in adolescence precludes the possiblility of the Chameleon Syndrome re-emerging in a different situation at a later time. After all, dating ordinarily precedes marriage, but no one would argue that marital relationships are entirely free of chameleonism. But, should not the Chameleon Syndrome, diminished by serious dating in adolescence, continue to decline in the intimacy of marriage? Not necessarily. The learning that occurs in adolescence may not be generalised to adult heterosexual relationships. It may be that some of the attitudes and behaviour acquired during long-term serious dating are age-specific or linked to particular individuals, with little or no carry-over to adult relationships. Furthermore, the Chameleon Syndrome, like all role-linked attitudes and behaviour, reflects the expectations of others, which in turn vary with the situation. Obviously, marital roles and expectations are markedly different from those involved in adolescent dating and, as we shall presently see, dating patterns and marriage orientation are independent of one another, though both are related to the Chameleon Syndrome – albeit in different ways. It is entirely possible, therefore, that stereotypic, guileful defensive attitudes and behaviour, learned as a by-product of conventional sex role socialisation in childhood but partially abandoned during serious and long-term dating, may emerge again after marriage in response to the expectations of new persons performing new roles in a new situation.

DOMESTIC ORIENTATION AND THE CHAMELEON SYNDROME

The traditional female sex role encompasses behaviour and personality traits that are deliberately inculcated in girls during the socialisation process because of their presumed value to women who perform the roles of wife and mother. Girls who plan to give these roles a central place in their lives can be said to be strongly oriented toward domesticity, which includes, among other things, attitudes towards early marriage, towards children, and towards work outside the home after marriage. In this study we argue that an adolescent strongly oriented towards domesticity would want to marry early, would want to have several children, and would want to avoid work outside of the home when the children are young. If our hypothesis that the Chameleon Syndrome in females develops as a by-product of traditional sex role socialisation, in which the preparation for marriage plays an important part, is correct, then the data should show a positive relationship between the Chameleon Syndrome and domestic orientation.

A Domestic Orientation Index was constructed from answers to the following four questions:

1. About how old will you probably be when you get married?
2. If you could have exactly the number of children you want, what number would that be?
3. How likely do you think it is that you'll have a paid job while your children are young?
4. How would you feel if you had a paid job while your children were young?

The adolescents' responses to these questions were standardised, intercorrelated, and found to be positively related; they were then summed to form a Domestic Orientation Index. This index has a 0.69 reliability coefficient (alpha).

The hypothesised relationship between the Chameleon Syndrome and domestic orientation is supported by the data, as can be seen in Table 6.7 in which the domestic orientation scores are divided into thirds on the basis of the response distribution. Adolescents with a high domestic orientation (the upper third) have the highest mean Chameleon Syndrome score (Americans, 1.36; British, 1.47); those with the lowest domestic orientation (the bottom third) have the lowest Chameleon Syndrome scores (Americans, 0.98; British 1.09). An analysis of

Table 6.7   Mean Chameleon Syndrome Score, by Level of Domestic Orientation in the United States and Britain

| Domestic orientation | Chameleon Syndrome Score | | | |
| | United States | | Britain | |
	Mean	(N)	Mean	(N)
Low	0.98	(439)	1.09	(152)
Medium	1.30	(385)	1.36	(143)
High	1.36	(560)	1.47	(126)
	$F = 7.20$		$F = 2.62$	
	$p < 0.001$		p: not significant	

variance of the data showed the relationship to be significant for the Americans at the 0.001 level; the British barely miss the 0.05 level of significance, though for both countries the trend is the same. These results are not altered when the adolescent's social class is controlled.

The relationship between domestic orientation and the Chameleon Syndrome comes into even sharper focus when we compare females who plan to devote their adult years exclusively to the roles of wife and mother (that is, those who intend not to work even when their children are older) with females who do not intend to marry. Thus the mean Chameleon Syndrome score of American females who do not intend to marry is 0.52; whereas females who do not intend to work after marriage have a mean score of 1.28; the difference between the means is significant at the 0.025 level.

But what if the difference between these two sub-groups – the one high on domestic orientation, the other low – is due to some physical or psychological abnormality that makes females with no domestic orientation unsuitable as marriage partners? Perhaps they have been rejected by males and, feeling unlovely and unwanted, they react by rejecting the domestic role. This possibility was explored by examining whether the two groups have had different dating experiences. If the group with no domestic orientation has in fact been rejected by males, the data should show a marked difference in the frequency and quality of their relationships with males as contrasted with the experiences of the girls with a strong domestic orientation. No differences were found between the two groups in their frequency of dating nor in the number of dating relationships in the past year. Clearly, females who say they are opting out of the traditional female role have not been rejected by males.

But is not the relationship between the Chameleon Syndrome and long-term serious dating inherently contradictory? We have shown that females with a history of serious dating score low on the Chameleon Syndrome, yet girls who score high on domestic orientation tend to have high Syndrome scores. Are not these two groups composed of the same people? Are not the girls who are involved in long-term dating also those with high domestic orientation scores? The answer is no. A cross-tabulation of domestic orientation and type of dating relationship showed these two variables not significantly related to each other. The modal dating category for each level of domestic orientation is 'no steady relationship', the second largest category for all three levels is 'one steady relationship in the past year'. A strong domestic orientation is not an outgrowth of serious dating; rather it is a set of attitudes that females learn when they are socialised into the traditional sex role. This socialisation process transmits both a cultural mandate to marry and have children, as well as a set of beliefs, perceptions and behaviour that we have called the Chameleon Syndrome.

In summary, the Chameleon Syndrome is an accommodative response, found most frequently among traditionally socialised females, to a social environment perceived as hostile to behaviour that violates traditional sex role expectations. The Syndrome is composed of three parts, each representing a distinct cognitive or perceptual or behavioural facet of the whole. All parts of the Syndrome develop out of a developmental process that eventually produces the integrated whole we call the Chameleon Syndrome. The index of the Chameleon Syndrome presented in this chapter assesses the adolescents' conceptions of their sex, their perceptions of how peers of the opposite sex will respond to behaviour that deviates from conventional sex role expectations, and the degree to which they engage in guileful, compliant, self-abasive behaviour. The data show that females attribute stereotypic traits of sensitivity, compliance and a concern with personal appearance more often to their own sex than to males, while males see these as characteristics of the opposite sex. Females are also more likely than males to report that they would be disliked if they were assertive and competitive, or pursued their own interests without regard to the reactions of others; girls are also more likely than boys to report that they conceal their competence, behave in dependent and compliant ways, and worry about the reactions of others to their appearance. When the three component scores were summed together into a single index in which each component has an equal weight, a comparison of the scores showed a Chameleon Syndrome, *in its female version*, to be significantly more prevalent among girls than boys.

Like all role-prescribed behaviour, the Chameleon Syndrome is learned; it develops as part of the process in which some girls are taught the attitudes and behaviour believed necessary for performing the traditional female sex role. Parents play an important role in this socialisation process: the data show that Chameleon Syndrome scores are highest among girls whose parents are restrictive and controlling, who emphasise the importance of close interpersonal relationships and who discourage self-assertive behaviour as a threat to such relationships. The Chameleon Syndrome is also learned from peers of the opposite sex, particularly in superficial dating relationships. Such relationships generate an atmosphere of insecurity, encourage females to act in stereotypic ways, and hence are highly conducive to learning the Chameleon Syndrome. Obversely, Chameleon Syndrome scores are lowest among females whose relationships with males are long term and more serious, since relationships of this type permit girls to put more emphasis on being themselves, and less on living out the female sex role. Finally, since a major goal of traditional sex role socialisation is the preparation of girls to perform the roles of wife and mother, it is not surprising that the data show a positive relationship between Chameleon Syndrome scores and a desire to marry early, to stay home rather than work after marriage, and to have children.

Although the Chameleon Syndrome powerfully affects the domestic expectations of traditional females, its influence on modern females is minimal. For the modern woman rejects the world view and behaviour patterns embodied in the Syndrome and forms her domestic expectations in a social context that emphasises equality between the sexes and that encourages the complete and unfettered participation of women in the labour force. In the next chapter, we shall examine the relationship between domestic expectations, the sex role, and the orientation of adolescent females to the world of paid employment.

7 Sex Differences in the Status Attainment Process

Expectations drive and direct achievement: they influence the willingness of people to marshal their energies, to engage their talents, and to compete against standards of excellence – their own and those of society. Low expectations put a modicum of achievement within the reach of most people and serve to protect the cautious and the timid, the lazy and the dull-witted against frustration and disappointment. But excessively low expectations can cramp the spirit and depress achievement. Not expecting much, the timid and cautious may settle for too little, for less perhaps than they would have been capable of achieving had they raised their sights, taken more risks, and put forth the greater effort that higher expectations would have required. In contrast, high expectations encourage achievement. To be sure, high expectations invite disappointment, for the more difficult and distant the goal the more improbable success becomes; but just as the overly cautious are held back by a fear of failure, so the ambitious and adventuresome are lured on by a vision of success. Expecting much, they give themselves room to grow; risking much, they stand much to gain.

An extensive body of research has established that educational and occupational aspirations and expectations powerfully affect educational and occupational attainment.[1] Thus, as a general rule, the higher the educational aspirations of adolescents the more likely they are to work hard at getting good grades in secondary school and the more likely they are to enter college and earn a degree, the almost essential ticket for admission into the world of lucrative employment in a credentialised society. The occupational aspirations and expectations of adolescents have been found to affect, indirectly and directly, the level of occupational success attained in adulthood, particularly among males. Of course, aspirations do not determine achievement; common experience tells us otherwise. Hopes, wishes, dreams and aspirations oft-times come to nothing when chance and fortune are unfriendly, when intelligence and talent are insufficient, when energy and perseverance are meagre. Nevertheless, as a general rule, the higher the occupational aspirations and expectations of adolescents the higher the income and prestige of the occupations they will hold some years after completing school.

But this rule must be treated cautiously, for the data to support it vary greatly from study to study. As Marini and Brinton point out, most research on the congruence between aspirations and occupational attainment define congruence in terms of similiarity between aspirations and the attainment of an occupation in the same occupational category. But studies vary in the inclusivity of the categories they use: the more inclusive the category, the higher the degree of congruence found. To confuse the issue even further, sample variability and age of subjects also affect the findings. Still, these caveats aside, substantial degrees of congruence between high school age aspirations and adult attainment have been found, ranging from 80 percent six months after graduation to 50 percent five years after high school. Other studies, however, report the degree of congruence drops sharply 10 years after graduation from high school. Perhaps the best and most recent of the studies, reported in 1980, involved an 18-year follow up of Wisconsin high school seniors. Correlations of 0.46 for females and 0.54 for males were found between the status level of occupation aspired to in high school and the status of the occupation attained 18 years later.[2]

Assuming that research has correctly assessed the effect of aspirations on actual occupational attainment, it is important for an understanding of sex differences in occupational attainment to know that occupational aspirations tend to be sex-typed. Young women tend to choose typically 'female' occupations, whereas young men tend to choose 'male' ones. Data collected in 1979 from a nationally representative sample of American youth, aged 14 to 22, found many young men and women inclined towards occupations traditionally assigned to their own sex. Moreover, not only are the occupational choices of youth differentiated by sex, but the range of choices is also affected: 47 percent of the young women aspired to the ten occupations most often aspired to by females; 39 percent of the young men aspired to the ten occupations most often aspired to by males.[3] This tendency for some young people to see the occupational world in sex-typical terms must surely affect, at least to some degree, the sex-typicality of the actual choices made and their eventual level of occupational attainment.

Some researchers see in the sex-typed aspirations and expectations of women an explanation of their inferior position in the labour force. That women are still under-represented in the higher echelons of Western occupational structures cannot be denied. Nor can it be denied that the relatively lower occupational attainment of women, given their large numbers in the labour force, reflects in part the discrimination they encounter seeking work and on the job. Among other things, discriminatory employment practices limit women's occupational choices and channel them into positions with restricted chances for promotion. But job discrimination does not tell the whole story, for it would be a mistake to assume that restrictions on female occupational attainment begin when women enter the job market. Quite the contrary: barriers to female achievement occur early in the occupational attainment process, long before women enter the labour force as adults.

Sex difference in occupational attainment are, in part, a consequence of the soclialisation of some females and males into traditional sex roles, a process which begins early in a child's life, and which severely limits the occupational choices of young people of both sexes. Traditional sex role socialisation transmits behaviour patterns and belief systems which differentially affect the educational and occupational expectations of girls and boys, by, among other things, restricting career choices and channelling activities into areas considered proper for a particular sex. Traditionally socialised males and females learn to aspire to positions conventionally allocated to them in the occupational structure. For traditional females this means wanting to become clerical, operative, or service workers: secretaries, assemblers, teachers, nurses, beauticians. Conversely, it has meant not wanting to be a mechanic, not planning to become a business executive or aspiring to enter the liberal professions.

Sex role socialisation does more than incline individuals to choose occupations traditionally assigned to their sex: it also fosters needs, values and skills that cause some women not to enter the labour force at all, and others to do so late or intermittently. For traditional sex role socialisation places more emphasis on achievement and occupational success in the rearing of boys than girls; consequently, occupational achievement appears less crucial to female self-worth and less necessary for obtaining social approval. Female self-esteem among traditionally socialised women is built around success in marriage and the skilled performance of domestic duties. These women were taught early to value interpersonal skills, attractiveness and popularity, for these are important factors in attracting a mate. They were also taught that competitiveness and achievement will jeopardise relationships with males, many of whom, women were told, feel threatened by assertive, competent females. And since a career and success in marriage, particularly when children are involved, are traditionally considered incompatible goals for females – but not for males – traditional women, including some with exceptional talent, do not develop high occupational aspirations, or else abandon them during courtship or upon marriage.[4]

But it is well to remember that traditionally socialised women are a dwindling breed. The industrial economy does not need them, and their skills, more domestic than economic, bring little reward in the market-place. The family says it misses them but does little to keep them at home; on the contrary, they are being pushed into the labour force to earn the money the family requires to meet its pressing needs. The polity grows nostalgic reflecting on its heroic past, wives in the kitchen, mothers in the nursery, and yet it does little to make it easier for women to play their traditional roles as wives and mothers when they serve also as breadwinners. Where are the publicly-supported day-care centres? Where are the corporate policies and programmes that help rather than punish women for becoming mothers? The paucity of such pro-grammes tells us far more about the true value placed on the traditional sex role than any number of pious pronouncements from the pulpit or the political podium.

Traditional women have not, of course, entirely disappeared from view. They can be seen in certain television programmes resurrected from the 1950s; they can be found, though with far less frequency than in the past, among certain American ethnic groups of Hispanic or East European or Mediterranean origin, among peasants in the villages of Southern Italy, and even occasionally in families located in the villages and small towns of rural Britain. We have even encountered them in the pages of this book. These are the girls who accept traditional stereo-types of the sexes, who worry that ambitious, self-assertive behaviour by girls will offend boys, who adopt the Chameleon Syndrome as a means of winning over, or at least not driving away, their peers of the opposite sex. But as the numbers in our tables show, they are a small minority.

The majority of young women in today's industrial society are not timid and cautious, not compliant and self-effacing, not riddled with self-doubt to the point where they become incapable of competing with men, as traditional socialisation would have made them, not willing to choose only those occupations traditionally regarded as appropriate to their sex. In fact, many young women today seem less bound than men by traditional limits on occupational choices. One American study found that females are more likely than males to make cross-sex occupational choices. Thus a 1978 study, based on a national sample, reported that only 4.1 percent of the males aspired to female occupations; in contrast, 34.5 percent of the females aspired to male occupations.[5] Several American national and regional studies point to a steady drop of sex-segregated occupational aspirations of young women. Leuptow found that the percentage of Wisconsin high school girls planning to enter predominantly female occupations dropped from 79.7 percent in 1964 to 49.8 percent in 1975.[6] Garrison examined changes in the occupational expectations of Virginia high school seniors between 1970 and 1976 and found that an index of sex segregation in occupational distributions had dropped from 43.6 in 1970 to 38.2 in 1976.[7] Herzog examined changes in the sex segregation of occupational plans between 1976 and 1980 for national samples of high school seniors and found that the index of segregation between male and female choices declined from 49.8 percent in 1976 to 36.3 in 1980.[8] In sum, all three of these relatively recent studies indicate declining sex segregation in the occupational goals of American high school seniors.

We will argue in this chapter that the variables that affect male educational and occupational expectations similarly affect those of females, and that the same casual model can be used to explain educational–occupational expectations of both sexes. This argument seems to run counter to the position of other researchers, who found the variables in their explanatory models of educational–occupational expectations differently related to sex.[9] We grant that our explanatory model works somewhat differently for the sexes, but these are primarily differences of degree, differences in strengths of effects between the paths of variables in the casual model. The variables and the direction of cause between them are much the same for both males and females.

Our casual model relates sex differences in educational and occupational expectations to several exogenous variables (socioeconomic status, mother's and father's education, and family size) whose effects, direct and indirect, will be shown to vary in strength but not direction with the sex of the adolescent. Certain social psychological and achievement-related intervening variables (mental ability, academic achievement, parental expectations, and self-assessment) mediate the effects of family background on status expectations. As we shall see, the direct and indirect effects of these intervening variables on status expectations vary by sex in ways which can be interpreted as logical consequences of sex role socialisation, but the casual linkages between variables are the same for both sexes.

References to educational–occupational expectations and to socioeconomic status appeared early in our analysis of the data. Hence, to help the reader, we shall describe again how these variables were measured; the measurement of other variables will be discussed as the relevant data are presented. Data on educational expectations were obtained from answers to the question: 'How far do you actually expect to go in school?' We phrased the question this way hoping to elicit responses that not only tap educational aspirations, but also include an appraisal of how realistic such hopes are. Students reported their occupational expectations in response to the question: 'What job do you think you'll probably end up having when you are your parent's age?'. Worded this way, the question encourages realistic expectations linked to a middle point in their life-cycle, as distinct from fantasies associated with youthful careers. Responses were coded into six categories that fit the way occupations cluster in standard indices of occupational prestige. Each category was given a weight, ranging from one to six. In this sytem, which corresponds to the index of socioeconomic status described in an earlier chapter, a high score indicates a high-status aspiration. Females who chose the occupation 'housewife' fall outside the index and will be discussed later. The respondent's socioeconomic status was determined by the occupation of the family's principal wage-earner, usually the father, although when the mother was the main provider, her occupation was used.

The validity of applying to both sexes an occupational status scale derived principally from descriptions of the male labour force has been questioned.[10] Some maintain that the status hierarchy varies by sex, thus necessitating a separate index for females. Others argue that the prestige hierarchy is essentially invariant with respect to sex, and that the socioeconomic hierarchy is nearly invariant – a position which we accept.[11] Also we assume that the occupational prestige hierarchy is relatively stable over time.

Current adult educational and occupational attainment form the context within which adolescents develop their own status expectations. Hence it has been argued that the expectations of adolescents tend to resemble the existing sex-differentiated status attainment structure. Not that adolescents consciously seek to replicate the status structure, but they cannot help observing its character nor entirely escape being influenced by it. In addition, since traditionally socialised adolescents have been taught to believe that the sex-typing of occupations is both proper and functional, in accepting the existing status structure they evince both a desire to conform to sex role expectations and an appraisal of what is realistically possible.

SEX AND EDUCATIONAL EXPECTATION

Previous research has shown educational expectations to be antecedent to educational attainment and the latter to be related to occupational attainment.[12] These studies show educational attainment to be closely associated with sex; males are more prominent at both ends of the educational continuum: they are more likely than females either to drop out of high school or to complete four years of college. Females are less likely to drop out of secondary school, more likely to obtain some intermediate, technical–vocational training, but less likely to complete college. If the current adult sex structure of educational attainment affects the formation of adolescent educational expectations, the educational expectations of the adolescents in this study should closely parallel the attainments of their sex.

But adolescents are responding to more than their perception of how educational attainment is currently distributed between the sexes. They are also reacting to a society that is increasingly insistent upon women's participation in the labour force, to a labour market that is increasingly open to women's entry into jobs at every status level, and to a complex techno-service economy that increasingly has made advanced formal education a prerequisite for admission into the more prestigious and lucrative tiers of the work force. This being the case, girls today would be foolish to replicate in their own plans the existing educational distribution between the sexes, just as some of their mothers and grandmothers had been unwilling to settle for the *status quo* of their times. In fact, as industrialisation advanced, certainly well before the turn of this century, some women in the past quickly took advantage of every new opportunity to increase their level of education and to gain new skills. Today's women want a level of education at least as high as that of men, or even higher; and some women feel the need to collect every possible credential available to them, as assets in what they still perceive to be an unequal contest with men. They are right to do so, if they expect to succeed in the industrial world. We believe most adolescent girls recognise this, and consequently their educational expectations do not on average differ from those of boys.

Testing this hypothesis with our data presents a methodological problem that, while not insuperable, requires some explanation. The problem flows from the differences in the secondary and post-high-school systems of the United States, Britain and Italy. We sought to minimise these differences by selecting secondary schools in the three countries that resembled each other, and in fact the public high schools of the United States and the comprehensive schools of Britain have much in common. But the secondary schools of Italy are more specialised than those in the other two countries; also, since 14 is the legal age at which Italian adolescents may leave school, the secondary school in Italy is more selective in terms of the average student's ability and social status than in the United States.

To complicate matters even further, many British and Italian secondary schools contain a sixth form or 13th year, required only of those students who wish to go on to the university, which means that on average the British and Italian students in these samples tend to be more advanced academically than the Americans. In addition, the requirements and significance of secondary and post-secondary diplomas, certificates, and degrees vary considerably by country. No doubt these differences are important, but examining them closely would take us needlessly far afield. We need only emphasise again that our interest is not in making comparative judgements about the educational systems of the United States, Britain and Italy, judgements implying that educational expectations are higher or lower in one country than in another. Rather we wish to compare the expectations of boys and girls within each country, controlling for age or grade whenever necessary or possible. In this way, we hoped to discover how effective industrialisation has been in eliminating sex differences in educational expectations.

The adolescents were asked, 'How far do you actually expect to go in school?' They were given five possible responses to choose from: (1) not to complete secondary school, (2) to graduate from secondary school, (3) a post-secondary technical or business school, (4) a college or university, (5) a post-college professional or graduate school. The numbers given to these alternative responses are weights assigned to each alternative; obviously, the greater the weight the higher the educational expectations. British students in the sixth form, and Italian 13th graders, were excluded in order to make the age and grade groups roughly comparable across the three countries. In this section and in the following ones, only subjects who provided full and codeable responses to all the questions employed to index the variables are included in the analysis; hence table *N*s are smaller than the total sample size and change with the variables under consideration.

The data in Table 7.1, which give the educational expectations of adolescents sorted by sex and country, show no significant sex differences in the level of educational expectation of Americans and Italians, and only very small differences between British females and

Table 7.1 Percentage of Type of Educational Expectation, by Sex and Country

Type of education expectation	United States Female (%)	(N)	United States Male (%)	(N)	Britain Female (%)	(N)	Britain Male (%)	(N)	Italy Female (%)	(N)	Italy Male (%)	(N)
Not complete high school	0.5	(7)	0.9	(12)	9.0	(24)	4.4	(12)	3.0	(15)	3.9	(20)
Graduate high school	22.0	(286)	22.2	(290)	65.9	(174)	57.9	(157)	26.2	(131)	23.2	(117)
Tecinical/business school	17.7	(230)	16.3	(212)	17.6	(20)	17.7	(48)	12.4	(62)	17.3	(87)
Four year college	40.3	(522)	40.4	(526)	14.1	(37)	16.6	(45)	44.2	(221)	43.5	(219)
Professional or graduate school	19.5	(253)	20.2	(264)	3.4	(9)	3.4	(9)	14.2	(71)	12.1	(61)
	100.0		100.0		100.0		100.0		100.0		100.0	

chi-sq. = 2.31
p: not significant

chi-sq. = 17.09
p < 0.002

chi-sq. = 6.45
p: not significant

males; even these differences vanish in the upper reaches of educational expectation. For example, the American data show that both males and females, on the average, expect to attain an educational level somewhere between post-high school graduation and graduation from a four-year college. And a further analysis revealed no significant sex difference in expectation levels by age; expectations decline slightly in the oldest age groups, but, by the 11th and 12th grades, American males and females have identical mean educational scores. We also found that educational expectations rise as socioeconomic status increases, a familiar finding; but this is true for both sexes.

The modal response category in the United States and Italy, encompassing about 40 percent of both males and females, is graduation from a four-year college. Furthermore, 20 percent of the American adolescents, male and female, and 12 to 14 percent of the Italians, expect to attend graduate or professional school. The expectations of the British adolescents are lower: the modal response category for this group is graduation from high school. Only with the British sample are the sex differences statistically significant. Even so the actual differences are quite small, as they are in the other two countries.

Why do the educational expectations of adolescents not resemble the actual pattern of previous adult attainment? Perhaps because our samples do not represent their countries as a whole, but we think it more likely that the norms surrounding educational attainment have changed. More young people today, of both sexes, continue their education beyond high school than was the case in their parents' generation. This increase in the general level of education among young adults has affected the expectations of adolescents still in school. Also, education is becoming more utilitarian for females, most of whom expect to enter the labour force. In short, post-high-school education has become as necessary in antecedent to high occupational attainment for females as it has long been for males.

SEX AND OCCUPATIONAL EXPECTATIONS

In the past both boys and girls tended to have stereotypical occupational expectations: boys concentrated in the conventional masculine categories of executive–professional and skilled manual jobs, girls in the equally conventional feminine categories of lesser-professional and clerical–secretarial work. And since work in the feminine categories often carried with it less money and prestige, it follows that girls did not aim as high, occupationally speaking, as boys. Added to this is the tendency of traditional women to prefer marriage and family to paid employment and career, a choice which contributes to their decision not to enter the labour force at all or to stay there only as long as work outside the home was compatible with family responsibilities.

But, as we have already noted, sex role stereotypes are breaking down as everyday reality gives the lie to many once-sacrosanct beliefs about feminine and masculine aptitudes, dispositions, and behaviour. It is not longer shocking to find women performing skilled blue-collar work. Who now stands aghast at the sight of women on the assembly line welding metal, working amidst noxious fumes and sparks and other conditions once thought beyond their capacity to endure? Who now turns around and stares at women in the cabs of large buses or trucks manoeuvring their vehicles through heavy traffic conditions once thought too intimidating for the female temperament to bear. Nor is it any longer surprising to find women in executive offices and professional settings. Who now wonders at the sight of women attorneys defending their clients in the courtroom or women physicians attending their patients in the hospital?

Some people, of course, are astounded and others offended at what sex roles have come to, at the kind of work men and women are doing in some sectors of the economy. But these traditional souls tend to come from remnants of older generations, principally in the working class, from people with only a high school education or less, and from people whose ties to their Hispanic, Mediterranean or East European origins remain strong. And yet even they must yield eventually to the exigencies of their circumstances: to the instability of the family that drives women into the labour force, to the pressures of rising taxes and inflation that overwhelm the family budget, to the simple, painful, unrelenting, imperious need so many people feel for more money. It often boils down to this: the husband's income, adequate in his parents' generation, no longer suffices to meet the family's needs, particularly when those needs have escalated to include expensive electronic appliances, exotic vacations, a state-of-the-art automobile or recreation vehicle. And if women must work, why should they not seek jobs in the better paying fields that heretofore have been reserved for men?

To young people of both the sexes the answer seems obvious or, rather, the question hardly ever arises. Women should and must enter the labour force; they have every right — indeed the obligation — to do as well there as they can, and if this means competing with men, so be it. To use a current expression, women are urged to 'go for it'. Most girls see this as a natural right, one that no civilised, enlightened society would deny them; and the boys, almost totally disarmed by the liberal industrial ethic, appear untroubled at the prospect of finding women in jobs their mothers or grandmothers would never have dreamed of holding. We must remember, however, that traditionalism has not entirely vanished among contemporary adolescents, even in advanced industrial societies; hence, some young people still make traditional choices as regards family and work but their number is small, and hence we believe that the differences in occupational expectations between the sexes has become equally small.

This conclusion seems straightforward and easily testable through survey research, as in fact has been done on the national level. But testing this hypothesis on the trans-national level presents the researcher with serious problems. For the same occupation may not possess identical amounts of power and prestige or deliver identical amounts of income across all three countries, despite the fact that they are all highly industrialised. For example, most physicians in Britain and Italy work for the state, whereas they tend to be private entrepreneurs in the United States, and private work almost everywhere pays more than government employment, at least in capitalist societies. And, to cite a few more examples of national differences, skilled manual workers, especially if self-employed, enjoy more prestige in the United States than in Britain and Italy; teachers are more highly valued (though not better paid) in Europe than in America; businessmen, including small merchants and shopkeepers, tend to hold higher positions in their communities in the United States than in Britain or Italy. On the other hand, the rank ordering of occupations is roughly the same across all three countries: physicians enjoy more prestige than plumbers, teachers more than secretaries, shopkeepers more than sales-clerks, foremen more than machine operators, and so forth. Consequently, it is possible to group occupations into categories that form a single hierarchy of prestige, valid for all three countries, and then to compare the occupational choices of adolescents in terms of where their choices fall on the hierarchy. Drawing upon previous research on the prestige of occupations, we constructed a hierarchy of occupations composed of six categories, as follows in ascending order: (1) unskilled and semi-skilled work, (2) skilled manual, (3) clerical, technical, (4) small business, lower administrative, (5) managerial, lesser professional, (6) executive, professional, large entrepreneurial.

We asked the students in all three countries what job they thought they would have when they reached the age of their parents, and urged them not only to name a specific job but also to include a general description of the work they would be doing. Putting these jobs into the hierarchy described above was tedious but not difficult, particularly when we could draw upon previous research in social stratification that contained a ranking of occupational prestige based upon the judgements of national samples. Using this information, we were able on our own to rank the occupational choices of American students with relative ease. but we thought it wiser to draw upon foreign experts for help in categorising the occupational choices of the students in Britain and Italy; therefore, a British team worked with the British data and an Italian team with the Italian data. Each team was composed of two researchers who understood the stratification systems of their respective countries and whose judgements were highly reliable.

Table 7.2 shows the relationship between sex, country, and adolescent occupational expectation. In this table, occupational expectations are organised into three status groups: the lowest status group contains occupational expectations that fall into categories 1 and 2, composed essentially of unskilled, semi-skilled and skilled manual jobs; the middle status group contains expectations that fall in categories 3 and 4, jobs in the clerical, technical, lower administrative, and small business domains; and the highest status group, which contains expectations in categories 5 and 6, the managerial, lesser professional, executive professional, and large entrepreneurial spheres of work.

The data in Table 7.2 provide only ambiguous support for the argument that the sexes have different occupational expectations. Thus, although adolescent males in Britain and Italy were slightly more likely than females to expect to hold high status jobs when they become adults, the reverse is true for the American sample: more American girls than boys expect to fill high status positions. And in all three countries males appear more willing than females to settle for the low status jobs, mainly manual work, that hold little appeal for most females, particularly those with conventional attitudes about the kind of work that would be appropriate for their sex role. On the other hand, middle status jobs, the lesser professional, white-collar occupations, attract more female than male interest in all three countries. On the average, apart from sex differences in preferences for particular occupations – i.e. more girls than boys want to be beauticians, more boys than girls expect to be automobile mechanics – the sexes do not differ strikingly in the overall status of their occupational expectations. For example, if we assign each occupational category a particular weight, ranging from 1 (low status) to 6 (high status), and average the responses

Table 7.2 Percentage of Level of Occupational Expectation, by Sex and Country

| Type of occupation expectation | United States | | | | Britain | | | | Italy | | | |
| | Female | | Male | | Female | | Male | | Female | | Male | |
	(%)	(N)	(%)	(N)	(%)	(N)	(%)	(N)	(%)	(N)	(%)	(N)
Low	7.6	(79)	28.3	(287)	29.4	(63)	44.9	(110)	5.6	(22)	18.0	(78)
Medium	40.1	(419)	27.0	(274)	50.0	(107)	28.6	(70)	58.1	(229)	39.7	(172)
High	52.3	(546)	44.7	(453)	20.6	(44)	26.5	(65)	35.3	(143)	42.3	(183)
	100.0		100.0		100.0		100.0		100.0			

chi-sq. = 156.8
p: < 0.001

chi-sq. = 22.55
p < 0.001

chi-sq. = 42.6
p: < 0.001

for each sex, the mean scores for the sexes in the American samples are almost identical: 4.2 for the females, 4.1 for the males.

If, as the data indicate, gender has little or no effect on the educational expectations of adolescents, and only a modest effect on their occupational expectations, why do people continue to believe that its impact is greater than it is? Three sets of converging forces keep this largely erroneous belief alive. First, traditional sex roles stubbornly refuse to disappear, and it was traditional culture that gave gender its significant impact on educational and occupational expectations. Girls who took their directions from traditional culture saw the value of education in a familial context, as an asset that would help them attract a suitable husband, as a means of acquiring a fund of knowledge that would prove useful in keeping a home and rearing children, and as an ornament that would enrich the quality of family life. Education as an instrument of social mobility was considered appropriate for boys but not for girls. The traditional girl contemplated with satisfaction a life devoted to the family: she entered the job market only briefly before marriage, exited after marriage, re-entered it only under duress, and left it as soon as possible. While this tradition and its accompanying sex roles are fast disappearing, vestiges survive to this day; moreover, and perhaps equally important, the news of tradition's demise has not reached the ears of some people who, believing the impact of gender on educational expectations to be far greater than it actually is, continue to respond to echoes of the past.

Second, notwithstanding the rapid movement of young women today into every sector of the economy, some degree of sexual differentiation in the labour force not only still exists, it is often highly visible to the most casual observer. Thus most of the skilled manual trades remain male preserves. How frequently does the plumber who responds to a call for service turn out to be a women? And secretarial and clerical jobs are so frequently filled by women that a male receptionist or typist causes eyebrows to rise in amused disbelief. What is a man doing in a women's job? True, the recent surge of women into the corporate and professional spheres of the economy is changing the popular perception of the labour market; no longer is the structure of the labour force seen as the inevitable reflection of a sex-segregated society.

But enough sex segregation in the workplace still exists to excite comment and alarm when someone is found in a sex-inappropriate job, triggering a search for its explanation. Explanations, of course, vary. Some focus on prejudice and discrimination as the main mechanism that coerce both men and women into filling conventional positions; others conclude that the sex-segregated labour force simply reflects a common perception of the kind of work that is possible, permitted, and pleasing to males and females. Although coercion implicitly tinges this explanation, its essential emphasis is on voluntary choices made by males and females. Boys and girls, it is said, are simply attracted to different kinds of jobs, an attraction explained by the existing occupational structure, which is still visibly sexually segregated in some areas.

The third set of explanations, though it draws upon the previous two, focuses primarily upon the family network in which adolescents are embedded and upon its psychological consequences. Girls, it is said, receive less parental financial support than boys for their educational and occupational aspirations, and girls are also under less parental pressure to excel in school and in the occupational world. In addition, even though they do as well in school as boys, girls tend to derive less psychological benefit from good academic performance. High grades in school and superior performance on intelligence tests do not necessarily point the sexes in the same direction, educationally or occupationally. Boys take academic performance as useful predictive evidence of how well they will fare in college or in the labour market, and raise or lower their expectations accordingly. Girls, in contrast, tend to shrug off academic facts and let cultural pressures and subjective evaluations overly influence their educational and occupational choices. Believing that sex roles set firm limits on what they can do, girls respond less vigorously than boys to parental statements about getting ahead or to information on how well they could do in the world of work. Good grades and high test scores are absorbed, digested, and frequently ignored; as a result they have less effect on the expectations and self-esteem of girls than on boys.

In fact, most girls, it is said, build self-expectations and self-esteem on grounds other than academic performance: on attractiveness and popularity, on the approval of peers, especially boys, on the establishment of enduring and satisfying relationships with other age-mates. As a result, parental expectations about school and work, and teacher evaluations about competence, while not entirely irrelevant, play a decidedly secondary role in the complex process that forms the adolescent female's educational and occupational expectations. This being the case, male and female educational and occupational expectations require separate explanatory models, with different variables arranged in quite different causal sequences.

I do not accept this conclusion. Whatever its validity in the past, the notion that males and females follow distinctly separate paths to status attainment ignores the effects of industrialisation and modernity on the individual and on society. Competence counts in an industrial society, for male and female alike, and academic performance is an early indicator of competence. Self-confidence counts, for male and female alike, and self-esteem is one aspect of self-confidence. Family support counts, for male and female alike, and family background and parental expectations are measures of family support. In an economy increasingly open to women and deeply dependent upon their full participation in the labour force, separate paths to economic success for the sexes cannot endure – they would not be countenanced.

A MODEL OF STATUS EXPECTATIONS

The causal scheme presented here is a variant of a model widely employed in contemporary research on the status expectations of males. I believe it can be used as well to explain the status expectations of females. In our version of the model, the variables and the linkages between them, their direction in the casual flow, and the contributions each variable makes to the end effect, are much the same for both sexes. The model, shown in Figure 7.1, treats two sets of variables as causal antecedents to status expectations. The first set includes exogenous family background variables: mother's and father's education (MOEDUC, FAEDUC), socioeconomic status (SES), and family size (FAMSIZE). The second set is composed of intervening social-psychological and achievement-related variables: perception of parental expectations (MOEDEX, FAEDEX), self-assessment (SAS), mental ability (IQ), and academic achievement (GRADES). Exogenous variables operate primarily through the intervening variables, which have both direct and indirect effects on expectations. Path coefficients between the variables in the model are given in Tables 7.3 and 7.4.

Educational and occupational expectations appear in this model as separate, though correlated, dependent variables. We posit no unidirectional path from one type of expectation to the other; thus some individuals may first aspire to an occupation and then plan to obtain the necessary education, while others may do the reverse. The predicted paths in the model are the same for both variables and are not treated as causally related to each other, though in all probability the two types of expectations interact in a way that produces mutual causation. Since

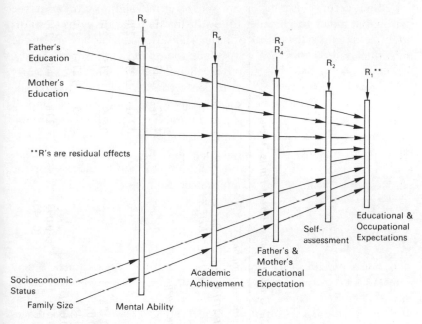

Figure 7.1 A Causal Model of Status Expectations

more respondents provided codeable responses to the question on educational than on occupational expectations, the calculations of path coefficients, prior to the inclusion of occupational expectations, are based on the larger sub-sample. Only the calculations of the direct paths to occupational expectation are based on the smaller sample size. This has the effect of increasing the reliability of the path coefficients in the earlier part of the model.

Our path analysis is based on a sub-sample having the following characteristics. First, we included only 11–12th grade students, reasoning that their expectations would be more concretely formed and realistic than those of the younger students. Second, only those students from whom we could obtain complete information on all of the variables in the model were included. Also, since parental education and parental educational expectations were assessed separately, only respondents who provided data on both parents were included in this stage of the analysis. Unfortunately, this reduces the sample and limits the extent to which the results can be generalised to larger populations.

It was not possible to construct strictly comparable models for the

Table 7.3 Coefficients of a Model of Status Expectations for 11-12th Grade Females, Trivial Paths Deleted

Dependent variables	Predetermined variables									Constant	R^2	N
	FA-EDUC	MO-EDUC	SES	FAM-SIZE	IQ	GRADES	FA-EDEX	MO-EDEX	SAS			
	Metric Coefficients†											
IQ	—	3.251 (0.818)	1.390 (0.507)	−1.619 (0.418)						94.043	0.176	270
GRADES	—	0.155 (0.071)			0.047 (0.005)					0.181	0.274	270
FAEDEX	0.249 (0.065)	0.142 (0.084)	−0.101 (0.041)		0.010 (0.006)	0.125 (0.063)				0.599	0.215	270
MOEDEX	—	0.243 (0.060)	0.047 (0.036)	−0.094 (0.031)	0.010 (0.005)	0.157 (0.047)				0.535	0.278	270
SAS	—				—	0.415 (0.031)	—	0.098 (0.040)		0.291	0.480	270

Educational expectation	—	—	0.054 (0.020)	—	—	—	—	0.105 (0.031)	0.613 (0.042)	0.240 (0.040)	0.077	0.719	270
Occupational expectation	—	—	—	—	—	—	0.097 (0.056)	0.504 (0.078)	0.245 (0.077)	2.391	0.377	206

Standardised Coefficients

IQ	—	—	—	—	—	0.105	0.613	0.240	
GRADES	0.247*	0.171*	−0.216*	0.474*		0.097	0.504	0.245	
FAEDEX	0.119*	—	−0.140*	0.100	0.128*				
MOEDEX	0.112	0.075	−0.166*	0.137*	0.206*				
SASCHOOL	0.245*	—	—	—	0.604*	—	0.116*		
Educational expectation	—	0.090*	—	—	—	0.137*	0.629*	0.208*	
Occupational expectation	—	—	—	—	—	0.117	0.455*	0.185*	

† Standard errors in parentheses.
* Significant to the 0.05 level.

Table 7.4 Coefficients of a Model of Status Expectations for 11-12th Grade Males, Trivial Paths Deleted

Dependent variables	Predetermined variables									Constant	R^2	N
	FA-EDUC	MO-EDUC	SES	FAMSIZE	IQ	GRADES	FA-EDEX	MO-EDEX	SAS			
	Metric Coefficients†											
IQ	—	2.025 (0.846)	2.419 (0.490)	-1.979 (0.480)						98.241	0.182	248
GRADES	0.109 (0.096)	0.229 (0.102)	0.120 (0.074)	—	0.040 (0.007)					-1.130	0.232	248
FAEDEX	0.417 (0.059)	—	—	—	—	0.156 (0.044)				1.113	0.252	248
MOEDEX	0.129 (0.055)	0.278 (0.069)	—	—	0.009 (0.005)	0.150 (0.044)				0.178	0.239	248
SAS	—	—	—	—	0.009 (0.003)	0.343 (0.027)	0.145 (0.033)			-0.426	0.573	248

expectation					0.006 (0.003)	0.060 (0.032)	0.261 (0.040)	0.322 (0.046)	0.170 (0.060)
Occupational expectation					0.015 (0.008)	—	0.429 (0.116)	0.290 (0.119)	0.322 (0.120)

(cont.)		
0.059	0.669	248
-0.038	0.442	175

Standardised Coefficients

Variable							
IQ	—	0.149*	0.306*	-0.241*	0.322*		
GRADES	0.082	0.135*	0.123		—	0.203*	0.335*
FAEDEX	0.408*	—			0.103	0.219*	0.368*
MOEDEX	0.142*	0.241*			0.132*	0.604*	0.162*
SAS	—	—				0.197*	
Educational expectation	—	—			0.076	0.100	
Occupational expectation	—	—			0.120	—	0.321*

(cont.)		
0.335*	0.162*	
		0.212*
0.190*		

† Standard errors in parentheses
* Significant to the 0.05 level.

American, British and Italian samples. British schools do not administer intelligence tests nor do they grade students in the same way, and
without these variables the American and the British models would not
have been comparable. Italian schools also eschew formal intelligence
testing; however, they assign grades much as do American schools. A
modified model was constructed for the Italians with only one variable
missing, mental ability; but the absence of this variable makes valid
comparisons between the American and Italian models impossible;
hence a model of status expectations based on the Italian data is not
included in this section, though the general trends of the two models are
similar.[13]

THE EFFECTS OF FAMILY BACKGROUND

Our interpretation of the effects of family background on expectations
will focus on two phenomena that, in the past, differentially affected
females and males: financial resources and role modelling. In a traditional society, sex influences how parents distribute family resources, to
whose needs they accord priority. Also, sex affects role modelling by
inclining the child to incorporate the actions, beliefs, and expectations
of the parent of the same sex.

Beyond high school the cost of education escalates rapidly, often to
the point where a college education becomes impossible without
substantial financial assistance, the most common source of which in
the United States is the family. But family resources are never limitless,
indeed they are frequently very restricted, and hence many parents
cannot avoid the difficult decision as to how to allocate their scarce
resources among their children. One rule that helped parents in the past
decide whom to educate, when claimants for their help outnumbered
their resources, was that preference should be given to males in order to
ensure their occupational advancement – a consideration seen as more
crucial for males than females. The data provide two pieces of
information from which we can draw inferences about family resources: the occupation of the principal wage earner and family size.
The first tells us something about family income, the second about
family outflow.

In the conventional view, limited family resources depress female
expectations more severely than male, especially educational expectations, a condition of considerable importance for occupational
attainment because the cost of school typically occurs early in the

occupational attainment process, and prohibitive educational costs may stop the process in its tracks. But our data provide little support for the conventional view, as Table 7.5 clearly demonstrates. It is true that father's occupational status (SES) and family size (FAMSIZE) have greater total effects on female than on male educational expectations, but the differences are trivial; on the other hand, SES has a greater effect on male than female occupational expectation, though the reverse is true as regards the effects of family size. But again the differences between the sexes are extremely small. On balance, the model shows that, contrary to the standard view of the status attainment process, family resources as measured by family status and family size do not differentially affect the educational and occupational expectations of girls and boys.

THE EFFECTS OF ROLE MODELLING

A second factor said to differentially affect male and female expectations is role modelling. Typically, children model the parent of the same sex and in this fashion learn the roles appropriate to their sex. Since educational and occupational attainment affect how parents perform their roles, and may in fact be perceived as aspects of the parental role, children who model themselves on a particular parent may use that parent's attainment to define their own self expectations. As regards expectations, mother's status attainment can have a stronger impact on the traditional daughter than the father's on the son, for traditional females have fewer high-status educational and occupational role models available to them.

The data in Table 7.5 show that the educational and occupational attainments of same-sex parents have slightly more impact on the adolescent's status expectations than those of the opposite sex: mother's education has a greater total effect on the girl's educational expectations, while father's education has a greater effect on the boy's. In addition, mother's education has a greater effect on female than on male educational expectations, while the reverse is true for father's education. The difference between the effects of mother's and father's education on the adolescent's educational expectation is greater for females than males.

The same pattern holds when both parents' occupational attainments are related to the respondent's occupational expectation. Father's occupation has greater total effects on male than on female

Table 7.5 Direct, Indirect and Total Effects of Status Expectations, 11-12th Grade Females and Males

Indep. Variable	FAEDUC	MOEDUC	SES	FAMSIZE	IQ	GRADES	FAEDEX	MOEDEX	SAS
				Educational Expectation: Females					
Direct effects	—	—	0.054 (0.090)	—	—	—	0.105 (0.137)	0.613 (0.629)	0.240 (0.208)
Indirect effects	0.026 (0.016)	0.258 (0.269)	0.053 (0.097)	−0.098 (−0.179)	0.017 (0.238)	0.213 (0.285)	—	0.024 (0.024)	—
Total effects	0.026 (0.016)	0.258 (0.269)	0.107 (0.187)	−0.098 (0.179)	0.017 (0.238)	0.213 (0.285)	0.105 (0.137)	0.637 (0.653)	0.240 (0.208)
				Educational Expectation: Males					
Direct effects	—	—	0.071 (0.120)	—	0.006 (0.076)	0.060 (0.100)	0.261 (0.335)	0.322 (0.368)	0.170 (0.162)
Indirect effects	0.184 (0.223)	0.176 (0.181)	0.071 (0.120)	−0.038 (−0.060)	0.013 (0.181)	0.151 (0.252)	0.025 (0.032)	—	—
Total effects	0.184 (0.223)	0.176 (0.181)	0.071 (0.120)	−0.038 (−0.060)	0.019 (0.257)	0.211 (0.352)	0.286 (0.367)	0.322 (0.368)	0.170 (0.162)

Occupational Expectation: Females									
Direct effects	—	—	—	—	—	—	0.097 (0.117)	0.504 (0.455)	0.245 (0.185)
Indirect effects	0.024 (0.029)	0.255 (0.205)	0.047 (0.068)	−0.085 (−0.136)	0.016 (0.187)	0.197 (0.232)	—	0.024 (0.021)	—
Total effects	0.024 (0.029)	0.255 (0.205)	0.047 (0.068)	−0.085 (−0.136)	0.016 (0.187)	0.197 (0.232)	0.097 (0.117)	0.528 (0.476)	0.245 (0.185)
Occupational Expectation: Males									
Direct effects	—	—	—	—	0.015 (0.120)	—	0.429 (0.321)	0.290 (0.212)	0.322 (0.190)
Indirect effects	0.261 (0.186)	0.163 (0.131)	0.064 (0.103)	−0.030 (−0.053)	0.015 (0.122)	0.228 (0.234)	0.047 (0.037)	—	—
Total effects	0.261 (0.186)	0.163 (0.131)	0.064 (0.103)	−0.030 (−0.053)	0.030 (0.242)	0.228 (0.234)	0.476 (0.358)	0.290 (0.212)	0.322 (0.190)

Standard Coefficients in parentheses.

occupational expectation. Mother's occupation was not used in the regression analysis since its inclusion would have sharply reduced the sample size; this variable, however, was correlated with occupational aspirations, using pairwise deletion of missing cases. The correlations between mother's occupation and female occupational expectation is greater ($r = 0.25$, $p < 0.001$) than with male occupational expectations ($r = 0.15$, $p < 0.001$), and greater than the correlation of father's occupation with female occupational expectations ($r = 0.21$, $p < 0.001$).

Further evidence of the mother's effect on a daughter's expectations can be seen in the relationship of mother's work status to the girl's orientation toward working after marriage. Respondents' answers were coded 1 if their mother was working full-time, 2 if working part-time, and 3 if not working outside the home. Daughter's work orientation was coded 0 if she did not expect to work outside of the home as an adult (i.e., expects to be a full-time housewife) and 1 if she expected to work. The data show that working mothers tend to have daughters who also expect to work ($r = -0.19$, $p < 0.001$); daughter's work orientation is also significantly correlated with mother's occupational status: the higher the status of the mother's occupation, the more likely the daughter will expect to work ($r = 0.18$, $p < 0.001$). None of the other family background variables is related to daughter's work orientation, not even SES. Thus a girl whose father is a physician is as likely to expect to be a full-time housewife as is a daughter of a plumber.

But not many American girls (nor British, nor Italian) expect to be full-time housewives; nor will modelling their mothers necessarily cause them to want to become full-time homemakers. For unlike most girls of the past, the large majority of contemporary girls have mothers who are in the labour force, and the model these mothers present to their daughters often includes elements of energetic, assertive, competitive activity in paid employment where success brings rich rewards in money, prestige and power. These mothers, often as well educated as their husbands and working at jobs in many ways comparable in income and prestige to their husbands', will not depress their daughters educational and occupational expectations. On the contrary, they boost such expectations and have helped produce a generation of ambitious girls who proudly assert their intention to 'have it all' – family and career, and all the advantages men have long possessed and which they see their mothers now enjoying.

MENTAL ABILITY AND ACADEMIC ACHIEVEMENT

Research on white males has shown that status expectations are heavily influenced by mental ability and academic achievement: the higher the mental ability and grades, the higher the educational and occupational expectations.[14] It could be argued that it hardly needed more research to make this point. After all, the linkage between ability and academic performance, apart from being obvious, has been endlessly reported in professional journals. And the connection between academic performance and educational-occupational expectations seems entirely logical in a meritocratic industrial society that puts enormous emphasis on formal education as a condition for admission into the attractive sectors of the economy. Grades are both markers of how well one has done and signposts to where one should proceed. Students who are doing poorly in secondary school usually recognise the inadvisability of their proceeding on towards college, set their educational sights accordingly, and so inescapably close off avenues to many kinds of work. In so far as males are concerned, the relationship of ability and school grades on educational and occupational expectations seems reasonably clear.

But the impact of mental ability and academic achievement on the expectations of females requires more research. Not that mental ability and academic achievement are unrelated to status expectations among females, but the relationship may be less clear and less powerful for females because their effects are weakened by the constraints that traditional sex role socialisation and the female sex role place on girls. No doubt most parents approve of achievement by females, and no doubt parents say so; but the message traditional parents send to girls is a contradictory one: achievement is fine, the message says, but it must not interfere with marriage and raising a family. Furthermore, as she grows older the traditionally socialised girl finds her parents putting ever greater stress on the importance of developing qualities that will enable her to attract a mate. She is urged to acquire interpersonal skills, to improve her personal appearance, and to strive for popularity with boys. Concern with future occupational achievement may have to yield to these new demands. Moreover, a traditionally socialised girl is warned by parents (and peers) that exceptional occupational achievement will jeopardise her relationships with males, many of whom are said to resent competitive, achieving females – a perception of the male sex which may explain why women who abandon aspirations for a professional career also believe that men disapprove of bright, competitive women.[15]

A measure of mental ability (IQ) was obtained from intelligence tests administered by school authorities to most of the students in the study. Student self-reports provided data on academic performance (grades). They were asked, 'On the average, what grades have you received since last September?' Responses ranged from mostly 'A's to mostly failing grades. These self-reports were then checked against the school records of 27 percent of the sample; a correlation of 0.77 was found between self-reported grades and information obtained from school records. By puting these measures into our model we were able to determine whether mental ability and academic performance have different effects on the expectations of boys than on girls.

Mental ability (as measured by IQ score) and academic achievement have no more effect on the educational expectations of boys than of girls. As the data in Tables 7.3, 7.4 and 7.5 show the total effect of IQ on the educational expectations of females is 0.017; on males it is 0.019. Also girls and boys are responding to information about academic performance, the grades they receive in classes and their ability to cope with academic demands, in precisely the same way: the higher the grades the higher the educational expectations (girls 0.213, boys 0.211). This relationship and the lack of differences between the sexes holds true in a model that controls the effects of other theoretically important contributors to educational expectations.

Nor are the effects of mental ability and academic ability on occupational expectations markedly different for girls than for boys. True, the total effects of these variables on occupational expectations are higher for boys than girls, but the differences between the sexes are trivial. Thus, as Table 7.5 shows, the total effect of mental ability on occupational expectations for girls is 0.016, for boys, 0.030; and the total effects of grades on expectations for girls is 0.197, for boys 0.228. We need, however, to consider these findings in relation to another: females tend to have higher grades, at least in some subjects, than males, but they do not significantly differ from males in their status expectations. This could be interpreted to mean that females need to achieve higher levels of academic excellence in order to have the same level of occupational expectations held by boys.

PARENTAL EXPECTATIONS

Initially, parental expectations are formed on the basis of their own attainments: parents expect their children to do at least as well as they have done, preferably better. But in time parents adjust their expectations according to the child's ability and interest, as demonstrated in part by academic achievement, all the while keeping in mind their ability to finance the child's education should that be necessary. Measures of each parent's expectation were obtained from respondents by asking this question: 'How far does your mother actually expect you to go in school?' The same question was asked with respect to father's expectations. The responses were coded using the same categories and values employed in obtaining the respondent's own educational expectation.

Both parents' educational expectations have direct effects on male and female status expectations, but the effects of the like-sex parent are greatest on females. For daughters, the mother's expectation has a greater effect than that of the father as regards both educational and occupational expectations. For sons, the father's expectation outweighs that of the mother only for occupational expectations. The effects of a parent's educational expectation on either the respondent's occupational or educational expectation are greater for the adolescent of the same sex than for the adolescent of the opposite sex.

Sex does not greatly influence how the antecedent variables affect parental expectations. Thus family size has a direct negative effect on parental educational expectations on both daughters and sons – a finding that runs counter to the argument that the strain family size puts on financial resources much more strongly affects females than males because parents are less willing to allocate scarce resources for the education of girls than boys. The adolescent's sex does not modify the effects of academic achievement on parental expectations. Academic achievement has a substantial effect on parental educational aspirations for both boys and girls, and the mean level of parental educational expectations is not significantly different for males and females even though females tend to have higher grades than males.

The relationship between mother's and father's educational attainment and each parent's educational expectation for the respondent is complicated by the interaction between the sex of the parent and that of the adolescent. When the parent and adolescent are of the same sex, that parent's educational expectation is based on his or her own individual attainment, and not that of the other parent. As can be seen in Table 7.5, each parent's educational attainment directly affects his or her educational expectations of the child. But when the parent and the adolescent are of different sexes, the parent appears to consider the educational attainment of the other parent as well.

SELF-ASSESSMENT

How far individuals expect to go in school, and how high they aim to climb on the occupational-status ladder, reflect to some degree their assessment of their ability to attain these goals. As already noted, one kind of ability closely related to status attainment is the ability to do well in school. Obviously, self-assessment of academic ability limits educational expectation: persons with low academic self-assessments of themselves are less likely to expect to enter or complete college than those with high self-assessments, other things being equal. As part of a larger set of items dealing with self-assessment students were asked: 'In general how good are you at school work?' Response categories ranged along a five-point continuum from 'not good at all' to 'excellent'.

Several variables in our model have direct effects on self-assessment of academic ability, and hence indirect effects on status expectations. As can be seen in Table 7.5, past academic performance by both sexes has the strongest direct effect on self-assesssment – indicating that self-assessment is rooted, to some extent, in reality. Also, only the educational expectations of the same-sex parent have a direct effect on self-assessment.

Where the sexes differ is in the effect of mental ability on self-assessment. Mental ability has a significant direct effect on self-assessment among males, but this is not the case for females. Among girls, the effects of mental ability on self-assessment are mediated by academic performance. Why should this be so? Perhaps boys tend to have a greater sense of their ability, independent of the external validation that academic grades provide and, hence, the direct effect of a boy's mental ability on his self-assessment. Girls, on the other hand, may need strong inputs from others, parents, peers and teachers, in the form of reactions to their academic performance before mental ability can affect self-assessment.

The effects of self-assessment on expectations varies within each sex group. Among girls, self-assessment has a greater effect on educational than on occupational expectations, while among boys the effect of self-assessment is greater on occupational than on educational expectations. Comparing the effects of self-assessment on expectations across the sexes, on the other hand, provides another perspective. In this case, the data show that the effects of self-assessment on educational expectation are greater for females than males; the effects of self-assessment on occupational expectations, however, are greater for males. This suggests that males, to a greater extent than females, see academic ability as pertinent to occupational attainment; females seem to consider it more relevant to educational attainment.

In summary, the distribution of women in the American occupational structure cannot be explained in terms of job discrimination alone; the effects of sex role socialisation on educational and occupational expectations must also be taken into account. Conventionally socialised females are directed towards domestic goals and away from occupations which put them in competition with males. Thus, in this study, fewer adolescent girls than boys expect to fill jobs at the top of the status hierarchy: a much smaller proportion of females than males expect to become professionals, executives, entrepreneurs, or managers. Both sexes have, on the average, similar educational expectations, but the correlation between educational and occupational expectations is lower for females than males, indicating a slippage between the two types of expectations that can have negative consequences for female occupational attainment.

While female and male expectations can be predicted by the same model variables, the process is by no means identical for both sexes. First, the model accounts for more of the variance in male than females occupational expectations, a finding which may reflect the model's emphasis on achievement as the major causal element linking the variables to one another. Expectations in this model are functions of objective mental ability and academic performance, and of the evaluations of the adolescent and others of that ability and achievement. But achievement is a matter rife with conflict for traditionally socialised females, who fear that high occupational expectations, particularly in areas dominated by males, will evoke disapproval from males. It is this fear which weakens the relationship between ability, achievement and occupational expectations among females. Hence it is not surprising that the model – originally formulated to account for status attainment among males – is somewhat less effective in predicting female than male occupational expectations.

Second, the model accounts for more of the variance in educational than occupational expectations, and predicts slightly better for females then males, although the difference is not substantial. Since there are no sex differences in either the mean level or distribution of educational expectations, this finding suggests that sex role norms are less salient in the formation of educational expectations than of occupational expectations.

Finally, the exogenous family background variables, such as SES, family size, and mother's education, have greater total effects on females than males. Intervening social-psychological and achievement-related variables, for example, academic achievement, mental ability, and self-assessment, are also associated with occupational expectations, but to a lesser extent for females and males. The differential effect of these variables on female and male expectations reflects, in part, the impact of traditional sex role socialisation on some adolescents, which channels their interest and energy into areas considered appropriate to their sex, consequently reducing the expectations of these females that they will some day fill high-status jobs.

8 Domestic Roles and Occupational Choice

Married women entering the labour force today face a challenge their ancestors seldom encountered: how to reconcile the conflicting demands of family and career. Either set of demands can be enormously time-consuming, energy-depleting, and emotion-draining; and when women take on both assignments they soon discover that there simply are not enough hours in the day, not enough resiliency in the body, not enough flexibility of the mind to do both jobs properly. Superwomen, perhaps, can juggle successfully the demands of family and careeer, of employers who require complete commitment to the job, of husbands who insist on the services of a wife, of children who want total attention to their needs, without wrenching physical and emotional costs. No doubt such women exist, but ordinary women, torn by conflicting demands and desires, often end up exhausted, nerve-wracked, and guilt-ridden.

The problem is that the modern industrial system has not made performing either the family or the work role easier. Modern technology, which promised to take the drudgery out of housekeeping, has not made homemaking easy. It is true that less brute strength and less backbreaking labour is required to do the job than in the past, but on the other hand, the standards of good housekeeping have risen, sometimes to ridiculous heights. The washing machine has indeed made laundering easier, but it is no longer enough merely to clean a shirt; it must also be free of the dreaded ring around the collar. Vaccum cleaners and floor polishers have eliminated much stoop labour, the modern housewife is seldom found on her hands and knees scrubbing floors, but she is expected to keep the kitchen floor forever bright and shiny, and no dust must ever spoil the pristine surface of her furniture or rugs.

And, contrary to the expectations of some people, the small nuclear family, congenial though it is to the needs of the industrial system, has not made the wife–mother role any less demanding. In fact, the role may have become more difficult. Today there are few kinsfolk around to provide support in troubled times, and fewer people to help lighten

181

the burden in ordinary ways, providing babysitting, helping with the heavy cleaning, giving friendly advice, being trusted confidente when the soul cries out for a sympathetic ear. Regrettably, husbands tend to be less helpful than might be expected in an enlightened modern society. Many modern husbands, men fully at ease with a rapidly changing workplace, men ever ready to jettison old ideas and practices, often turn out to be traditional spouses who want their meals served on time, their homes kept neat and tidy, their children trained in conventional manners and decorum – all this without their becoming more than intermittently involved in the whole tiring business. And the children, though not as numerous in today's small family as in the past, still demand inordinate amounts of attention. Consequently, though she may have fewer children to contend with than did her mother or grandmother, the modern mother finds herself expected to devote as much time to her smaller family as her predecessors had given to a much larger brood. In short, though time and attention are less fractionated today than in the past, the sum total of time and energy consumed is probably unchanged. Indeed, the emotional investment that mothers make in their children may have increased because they must focus all their hopes and fears on a few heads rather than dividing them more thinly among a larger group of progeny. But this can be a terrible gamble, for by covering fewer bets the parent risks suffering devastating losses when children turn out disappointingly.

Nor has the environment on the job become easier for women. Less brutally exhausting, perhaps; cleaner and safer, probably; more remunerative and prestigeful, very possibly. But easier? No. If anything, the pressures on women at work have increased. Women in the work force today are expected to bring to their jobs all the energy, talent and motivation that employers have long expected of men – a willingness to work full-time at tasks that often involve long hours and overtime, a commitment to the job that often requires putting the needs of the employer above those of the family, an acceptance of intense competitive pressures in a framework of excellence that makes failure as fully possible as success. These pressures coexist with equally imperious demands at home from husband and children who clamour for attention to their needs. As a result, the ambitious and conscientious employee–wife–mother may find herself caught in a bind, a classical case of role conflict in which she is pulled in opposite directions, made to feel vulnerable and guilty by the people she loves, needs, or fears, people who can reward her with advancement and love, or punish her with demotion and rejection.

All too frequently she cannot depend on understanding and help from either her employer or her family. Her employer is usually oblivious or indifferent to her predicament, and if forced to pay attention may grow resentful. The mother who is called away from her job to attend to a child with a sudden high fever or broken bone from an accidental fall will get her employer's grudging permission to leave – the law or the union may give him no alternative – but frequent absences from work to care for the sick at home may put her job in peril or mark her down as someone unsuitable for promotion to a high responsible position. Her family may want to be helpful but they too have desires and responsibilities, and all too humanly they tend to put their own needs above those of the mother. It is still uncommon for husbands to leave their own work to care for a sick child rather than expect their wives to do so. And sick children, or even healthy ones, can hardly be expected to subordinate their wants, which are ordinarily imperious and tied to a deeply egocentric view of the world, to the work needs of the mother. Women in modern societies would be wise not to expect a rose garden when they enter the world of paid employment. Wealth and prestige and excitement can be found there, but it is a place that also abounds in tensions and problems.

DOMESTIC ORIENTATION IN TRADITIONAL SOCIETIES

Women in traditional, pre-industrial, sex-segregated societies do not face these problems. Traditional societies tend to put woman firmly in her place: the home. And in this setting her daily activities make for a full day. According to one observer of life in a traditional Brazilian village, a woman's routine involves the following chores: 'fetching water and firewood, washing and ironing clothes, cleaning house, bearing children, caring for children, training the children in acceptable conduct, helping care for domestic animals, working in the field when needed, sewing and embroidering.'[1] With a workload this heavy, women have little time and less inclination to enter the paid labour force. Of course, in some societies men help with the housework and the care of children – though no society gives over to men the primary responsibility of socialising the young – but in many places men seldom lift a finger to help their wives and regard with pity and scorn any man who has been seduced or coerced into doing what they consider to be woman's work. Even when the men assist their wives at home, they do so along lines congruent with the prevailing stereotypes of masculinity.

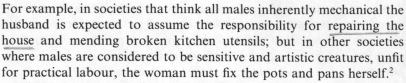

For example, in societies that think all males inherently mechanical the husband is expected to assume the responsibility for repairing the house and mending broken kitchen utensils; but in other societies where males are considered to be sensitive and artistic creatures, unfit for practical labour, the woman must fix the pots and pans herself.[2]

Within the home traditional folk follow a strict code that explicitly distinguishes between male and female responsibilities. According to this code, housework is woman's work. The male who routinely cooks or cleans or cares for children leaves himself open to ridicule, with the sharpest jibes often coming from female neighbours. Hence, except in emergencies, few men have the courage or the desire to expose themselves to mockery by deviating from their traditional sex role. In rural Brazil, for example, most men and women are very clear in their minds about who should do the housework: the woman. You can see the sexual division of labour starkly reflected in the males conception of what constitutes a good woman. For example, here are some remarks made by several unmarried young men who apparently know what kind of woman they want:

> A good woman works hard and is obedient. She takes care of her family as she should. She washes clothes, straightens up the house and looks after her husband.
>
> A woman's work is to cook and wash clothes.
>
> I want a woman who is a hard worker and will do everything around the house.
>
> Without a woman it would be much harder to get the cooking done and the clothes washed and take care of the livestock.[3]

And so it goes: all the ethnographies of village life in Brazil report that labour in the home is stictly divided according to gender.

The traditional community has nothing to lose by keeping the wife housebound for, unlike the industrial city, it has little use for sustained female labour outside the home. It is true that women in the rural community and traditional small town sometimes help their husbands in the field, the store, and the workshop, but such non-domestic work is sporadic and usually compatible with child-care since children often accompany their parents into the store or field, either working beside them or slung on the mother's back. Consequently, with no strong need for women to be in the labour force and with a tradition of male dominance in the home, the traditional community is far more likely than the industrial society to believe that a woman's proper place is in the home caring for her husband and children. A governmental inquiry into the condition of women in Nissoria, a rural community in Southern Italy, explicitly affirmed this point of view. According to its report, 'a moral woman ought not to work for wages in the country-side. This work is meant only for the most miserable; for those abandoned by their husbands or for widows or for girls who are disgraced ... Women should work at home.'[4] Although this report was published in 1910, its point of view is still alive today in rural Italy.

Even when men and women work together in the field, they typically perform tasks assigned to them according to a gender-linked division of labour. Thus in Caporotondo, a southern Italian village, custom dictates that the 'threshing is done by men. One trots the mule, another shovels the pulses under its feet, but if there is only one man the shoveling is done by the women. Winnowing is done by both men and women. A wife and her mother and daughter usually do the hand sorting ... Olives are harvested by spreading a cloth under a tree and shaking the branches one by one. Men shake; women pick out the olives from the twigs and leaves, and put them in sacks.'[5] But close cooperation at work between the sexes is relatively uncommon. Most often men and women work in separate places and at tasks that are not shared even though interdependent.

Sexual segregation occurs in other areas besides work. At play and at worship, in community affairs and in public entertainment, traditional men and women tend to separate into same-sex groups, even when assembled in the same room. For example, in Pisticci, a town near the heel of the Italian peninsula, men and women carry their traditional sense of separateness into the house of prayer itself. For even though the church has abandoned its practice of holding separate masses for different categories of family members, hoping thereby to mould the family into a ritual group, the sexes stubbornly maintain their distinct sense of apartness. During services, as Davis tells us, 'the men usually sat apart from the women and children, and would arrive and leave separately and at different times.'[6] A continent away, Donald Pearson noted similar patterns of sexual segregation in Cruz das Almas, a rural Brazilian community: 'At Mass and other religious ceremonies, the men tend to occupy one side of the church and the women the other . . . . At festivals, either religious or secular, women are to be seen only talking together among themselves. Rarely does a woman converse with a man, except be he a relative of the family. At dances, the women sit together and the men remain apart. There is no conversation between partners during a dance'.[7] When men and women are systematically separated into separate groups, when they work at different though interdependent tasks, when critical areas of their lives seldom intersect, then the sexes acquire different interests and skills, different attitudes and values – in short, they develop sex-related sub-cultures, in which the domestic role is an important element.

Traditional parents accept the sexual division of labour and its related sex role cultures as part of the natural order of things and teach their daughters that the destiny of women is to be wives and mothers, that domestic roles should take precedence over all other roles, including occupational ones. Not that work is unimportant, but traditional girls build their lives around the family and give to work and careeer a subordinate role. Even in today's industrial society, traditional girls remain strongly familistic; they want to marry relatively early, to have larger than average-size families, to eschew paid work while their children are still young.

ROLE CONFLICT AND OCCUPATION

Traditional girls today still feel drawn to the kinds of occupations an earlier era considered singularly appropriate for women – jobs mostly in the service sector. That these jobs usually pay poorly, that they give their holders little prestige and less power, is secondary; what matters most are certain characteristics of the job that traditional girls find exceedingly attractive.

To begin with, traditional female jobs tend to be in safe environments populated mainly by women, and hence minimally competitive with men. Competition between women, while never entirely absent, is muted, for the emphasis is on service, on helping others with health, physical, intellectual or emotional problems – an emphasis eminently congruent with the traditional image of the woman as someone who is naturally nurturant. Such work tends not to be overly demanding or excessively time-consuming, and there is no obligation to take the headaches of the job home at the end of the day: the secretary can leave her office troubles at the office, the teacher enjoys a short work day and long vacations, the dental technician need not concern herself with other people's plaque when she puts her tools down at day's end. These women and others like them with similar 'female' jobs tend to have sufficient time and energy left over to care for their families after the office or shop has closed. Equally important, such jobs usually permit relatively easy exit when family considerations require the woman's presence at home, even for long periods at a time, and allow quick re-entry, often into the same job or one similar to it when she is no longer needed at home. She can usually pick up her typewriter or textbook or thermometer where she left off, with little injury to her prospects.

The accommodations women make to the conflicting demands of their family and work roles are more than practical solutions to role conflict; they also reflect the acceptance or rejection of beliefs about the female sex role, beliefs that affirm and reward stereotypic feminine behaviour. The traditional female sex role, as we have already noted, requires that women be nurturant and empathetic, helpful and responsive, cooperative and non-competitive. Believing these are socially desirable ways of behaving, traditional women find performing service-type, people-oriented jobs psychologically and socially rewarding. And, warned against appearing aggressive, tough, independent, and excessively smart, they avoid top level postions that may put them in conflict with other people, especially men. These women often choose to be administrative assistants rather than executives, nurses rather than doctors, teachers of mathematics rather than professional mathematicians. In this way they maintain a psychological consistency across domestic and occupational roles, and enjoy the sense of security and acceptance that the conformity to society's expectations usually brings.

Not all females, of course, expect to enter traditionally female occupations. Influenced by industrialisation, by the feminist movement, by new patterns of socialisation, and by the obvious fact that many women now occupy dual domestic and family roles, many adolescent females have acquired a conception of their role as women which does not conform to traditional definitions. These females tend to think about both sexes in non-stereotyped ways, to value non-domestic roles for women, and to be less restrained in exhibiting independence, assertiveness, and competence. They have not lost interest in the wife-mother role; it is just that for them other social roles have increased in importance. To these females, the desire for marriage and a family no longer means that they must assign to the work role a subordinate position in their lives.

Industrial societies, of course, do not limit women to domestic work in the house. On the contrary, they lure women out of their homes with promises of good pay and exciting work because industrial societies, capitalist and socialist alike, especially in their early stages, hunger for cheap labour and women help assuage this appetite. At first the jobs are sex-typed and poorly rewarded, but eventually women are recruited into better positions, not necessarily for altruistic reasons but partly because society is bombarded with complaints about sexual inequality, and partly because it worries about human talents that remain undeveloped, skills that can find no employment, and achievements that are lost to society – even achievements by women.

But even in advanced industrial societies the traditional division of labour in many homes remains almost intact – a division, as we know, that assigns most of the responsibility for doing housework to women. Whether rich or poor, school drop-out or college-trained professional, the majority of married women find themselves burdened with more than their share of the cooking, the washing and cleaning, and the care of young children. Granted, the egalitarian ethic, when applied to the division of labour in the home, argues strenuously against an unfair and sexually-determined distribution of domestic responsibility and work; nevertheless, traditional attitudes in this area persist despite the heavy burden it lays on working women.[8]

The traditional division of household labour and the strains it creates for working women are known to most young people. Their minds are equipped with sensitive radar tuned to receive signals from diverse quarters, from parents and kinfolk, from friends and peers, from the mass media of communications. At home, youngsters with working mothers sense the travail of women saddled with heavy domestic as well as careeer responsibilities. In school, teenagers hear the chatter of friends speculating about the future, about marriage and work, about the desirability of having children and what problems they cause. In the mass media, they encounter stories of harassed working women struggling to keep their bosses happy, their husbands satisfied, and their children content. Women who fail to meet these expectations are excoriated, held up to censure, and blamed for divorce, child neglect, and juvenile delinquency. To many a teenager, the working mother's world must seem filled with people who have grievances against her. There is the husband, coming home to a cold supper, who wonders: where is my wife? The child, coming home to an empty house, who calls out: where is my mother? She is at her office, perhaps, preparing a report for her boss, but paradoxically that report may suffer because her mind is on her problems at home. Small wonder that many an adolescent girl who contemplates a married life coupled with full-time employment believes it will be beset with problems.

Faced with hard choices, unwilling to choose between work and family, and wanting it all, some girls fall back on fantasy. They think the state will build modern child-care centres equipped with competent, dedicated personnel who will take the care of children off their shoulders. They believe a two-salaried family can easily afford a full-time servant, a live-in one possibly and certainly one that is competent and responsible. They expect to find exceptional husbands, sensitive men willing to do their share of the housework and able to take pleasure in the everyday task of raising the children. Perhaps all this will indeed come to pass. But the odds, at least in the short term, are against it. A state-supported network of reliable day-care centres would be prodigiously costly, and most governments today, caught in straitened financial circumstances, will resist it as long as they can. Even more problematical is the availability of reliable servants in an industrial society. As industrialisation develops, servants become scarcer and much more expensive, the costs rising to the point where only the rich can afford them. For why should women – in the past, most servants were young females – do housework and care for other people's children when better, less confining and more lucrative jobs are available in factories, shops, and offices? As for the liberated, enlightened, caring, compassionate male, the ideal mate, he may well be around or in the making, but most studies show his number to be as yet very small. In brief, whatever its psychic rewards may be, fantasy affords a poor basis upon which to make crucial choices about work and family.

Other girls, unwilling to base their choices on fantasy, begin to plan their lives while still in secondary school. They plan to delay marriage until after their training is completed, which may mean spending years at college and post-graduate school or in professional work; they plan to have small families with no more than two or three children, or perhaps only one or none at all; more subtly and often unconsciously, they resist old ideas and take on instead the modern values and perceptions that will make it easier for them to compete with men in the world of work. Thus modern girls reject traditional sex role stereotypes, hostile pictures of women that portray them as dependent, vain, vulnerable creatures, eager to please others and fearful of competition, inferior to men in the hurly-burly struggle of the industrial world; they believe, rather, that women, even though they may be wives and mothers, can excel in the workplace if they wish. Modern girls see no reason why the traditional division of labour, sexually segregated, with women doing most of the housework, should be forced upon them, and they will resist it. They expect to change the world, and they face the prospect of entering the labour force without inordinate trepidation because they see no sector of the job market, despite some residual discrimination, as forever closed to them; nor do they consider the odds irremediably stacked against them in their competition with men for the brass ring of success on the economic merry-go-round.

When young women with modern plans, beliefs, values and perceptions enter the job market, they do not feel compelled to choose occupations in the 'pink ghetto', the financially deprived sector of the economy inhabited by secretaries, librarians, sales clerks, nurses, teachers, and similar denizens in a world of work traditionally set aside for women. The ambitious and talented among them set their sights rather higher: they seek entry into the prestigious, prosperous, exciting world of commerce, industry, science and the professions. Rather than becoming legal secretaries, they elect to become lawyers; rather than settling for work as nurses, they want to be physicians; rather than choosing to be clerks and book-keepers, storing and sorting information for others to use, they want to become data analysts, accountants, account executives, corporate managers; rather than working as laboratory technicians, repetitively processing other people's material and seldom having the chance to be innovative, they prefer to be biologists and chemists, scientists intellectually equipped and institutionally postioned to generate new information and to take novel paths to discovery.

Some modern women, perhaps less talented or ambitious, rich or lucky than others, opt for certain trades or service occupations once dominated by men, such as bus driving, real estate agenting, claims adjusting, and bartending. This is not to say that all modern girls reject every job in the traditional woman-saturated work world: nursing, teaching, clerical and social work, still attract girls who are modern in every respect but their choice of career, rather, our point is that modern attitudes and values predispose more girls than ever before to choose occupations in fields once reserved almost exclusively for men.

In one important respect, men have a much easier time of it than women: the domestic and occupational roles of males are in the main complementary. In most Western societies, at least until very recently, men were expected to assume the major burden of financially supporting their families, a responsibility that freed them from most of the domestic chores. Even today, the husband-father role is primarily that of breadwinner, though no doubt many men enjoy the emotional side of family life and make important contributions to the affective content of familial relationships. But the domestic chores, housework and spending time with children, must not interfere with the major responsibility of the adult male, the economic support of the family, which is made possible through his work in the labour force. Perforce the domestic responsibilities devolve upon the female, a condition that many men regard as a major disadvantage of the female role.[9] Believing they will be able to escape most of the domestic chores in the marriage, males feel free to make occupational plans without giving much concern to the domestic side of their sex role.

Modern girls resent the double standard implicit in the traditional attitude toward working women. Women are asked to choose between family and job, men are not; nor are men condemned for devoting themselves to their job, for spending long hours working overtime and on weekends in the office or on the factory floor. On the contrary, such men are called hard-working and conscientious, good providers who enjoy social approbation and generous salaries. Take, for example, James R. Randall, the President of Archer Daniels Midland Company, an international commodities firm. Mr Randall arrives at his desk by 6.30 every morning and works on weekends. For this he is handsomely rewarded (his annual salary is more than $500 000) and held up as an exemplar of corporate dedication and efficiency. Nothing is said about the possible adverse effects of this schedule on his family.[10] But a woman who kept this work schedule would most likely come under attack. Where is she when the children get out of school? What excuse can she give when the family picnic must be called off because a problem at the office demands her presence? The male excuse that work must come first is not acceptable to society when offered by a female. In effect, the double standard converts what is a virtue for men into a vice for women.

RESEARCH PROCEDURES AND FINDINGS

In the following pages, we will present data that show how the domestic role differentially affects the occupational choices of adolescent girls and boys. First, we will show that the domestic role tends to be viewed differently by the sexes, that girls and boys have different expectations as to when they will marry, as to the number of children they would like, and as to their degree of participation in the labour force after marriage. Second, we will show how the domestic role, expanded to include sex role values and stereotypes and perceptions of the opportunity structure, affects the occupational expectations of adolescents. And third, we will show that adolescent girls who are drawn to typical service-oriented 'female' jobs tend to have the values, perceptions and expectations traditionally associated with the domestic role.

The domestic role, as the term is used here, encompasses a body of values and norms that specify the responsibilities and activities of men and women performing their roles as spouses and parents. Among other things, the domestic role defines the division of labour and authority in the family; it directs and controls the expression of affection, anger and aggression between husbands and wives and between parents and children. As we have already noted, the traditional domestic role assigns to women the primary responsibility for keeping house and caring for children, never easy tasks to perform in the past, and not made any easier in modern industrial societies by the pressure on women to enter the labour force. Men who fulfil the major responsibility of the domestic role by being good providers and protectors of their spouse and children are not expected to involve themselves in the routine care of the house and of the children.

The domestic role, rooted as it was originally in an agrarian economy, could not long resist the force and pull of industrialisation. The reasons for this are threefold. First, the industrial society openly applauded individual achievement and supported equality of opportunity in the labour force and before the law, powerful values that underminded the social and psychological foundations of the traditional domestic role. It was not that the industry society wilfully set about to weaken the roles of wife and mother: only the shrillest misogynist or most radical feminist denigrated these roles. It is rather that the rewards for good performance in the domestic role becames trivial and perfunctory. The good wife and devoted mother receives (when she does) only the most routine of rewards – a kiss, praise, and a card on Mother's Day. Virtue in this area, as in so many others, has become its own reward. The real rewards – money, power, and prestige – go to the occupational achiever, someone who has shown exceptional ability in the world of paid employment, someone whose accomplishments in the workplace set him or her apart from the herd.

Second, the modern stress on equality, initially linked only to economic and political matters, inevitably spilled over into the domestic sphere, affecting the relationships between husbands and wives and between parents and children. If the sexes are equal, as the egalitarian ethic vigorously maintained, why should the burden of housework and child care fall only on the shoulders of women, or the responsibility for bringing home the bacon be assumed only by men? Justice and a fair reading of the egalitarian script called for the abandonment of traditionalism in the division of labour and the establishment of a system in which domestic responsibilities and economic opportunities are shared by men and women equally. And thirdly, the industrial economy, particularly its service sector, ineluctably drew women into the labour force, diverting their time and energy from domestic activities to other pursuits, enlarging their view of the world and of their sex, and enhancing their sense of personal efficacy, their belief that they could compete successfully with men for wordly success. Before these powerful forces the domestic role had no choice but to change.

SEX ROLE COMPONENTS OF THE DOMESTIC ROLE

We chose to measure changes in the domestic role indirectly. Rather than ask teenagers how they would divide domestic labour, affection and authority with their future spouses, decisions perhaps too complex, emotional and remote to evoke realistic responses at their tender age, we asked them at what age they expected to marry, how many children they would like to have, and whether they intended to work outside the home while their children were still young. Granted, these decisions are also some years away, but the questions benefit from concreteness: the answers to them take the form of an age, a number, a yes or no, statements about future actions in specified circumstances. These questions were put to all the students, but only the responses of the upper division students, minus the British sixth-formers and Italian 13th-graders, are examined here. Although this drastically reduced the size of the sample, it had the positive effect of making the national groups more comparable and of limiting the analysis to data obtained from an older age group whose responses were presumably more concretely formed and realistic than would be those of the younger students.

We used the following questions to tap domestic expectations: (1) 'About how old will you probably be when you get married?; the responses were coded from 1 (for '16 or younger') to 6 (for '30 or older'); (2) 'If you could have exactly the number of children you want, what would that number be?'; the response categories ranged from 0 ('none') to 7 ('seven or more'); (3) 'How likely do you think it is that you will have a paid job while your children are young?'; response categories ranged from 1 ('very likely') to 4 ('not at all likely'). Age at marriage, family size and labour force participation all affect the performance of domestic roles, influencing the maturity, time and energy that role players bring to their tasks and to their relationships with spouses and children. The traditional pattern has been for people to marry early and have large families, for women to restrict their entrance into the labour force until their children are grown, and for the domestic role to be more salient for females than for males.

The data in Table 8.1 show that females expect to marry earlier than males and expect to have more children; females are also much less likely than males to expect to work while their children are small. Overall, females are more likely than males to see the domestic role as consuming a good deal of their energy, beginning early in their adult lives, and expect their domestic role to take them out of the labour force while they are young adults, whereas the males do not. A series of one-way analyses of variance revealed that the differences between the sexes are statistically significant at the 0.001 level or better. At first inspection, it would seem that industrialisation has not eliminated the traditional differences between the sexes in their orientation toward domestic roles.

But the data in Table 8.1 do not tell the whole story; the decline of the traditional domestic role that accompanied industrialisation and the movement of females into the labour force is greater than the mean scores indicate. This decline can be better seen in the distribution of the adolescents' responses to particular questions, as expressed in percentages. Consider, for example, the responses of the American females to the question about working after marriage. Asked to anticipate what they would do when they became adults (their parents' age), the overwhelming majority, 82 percent, said they expected to work and to have a family simultaneously. Only 10 percent expected to be full-time

Table 8.1 *Means of Domestic Expectation Variables, by Sex and Country*

	United States		Britain		Italy	
	Female	Male	Female	Male	Female	Male
Expected age at Marriage	3.84*	4.19*	3.50*	3.82	4.62*	4.86
Desired family size	2.68*	2.32*	2.69*	2.30	2.38	2.38
Labour force participation	2.47*	1.19*	2.67*	1.34	2.55*	2.02

Ns for United States
Female: > 472 < 507
Male: > 478 < 532
*p < 0.001

Ns for Britain
Female: > 179 < 183
Male: > 190 < 197

Ns for Italy
Female: > 169 < 191
Male: > 186 < 220

housewives; an even smaller number, 8 percent, did not expect to marry, thus in effect making paid work the focus of their lives. When it comes to working while their children are still young, the data show that most teenagers have fallen away from the traditional standard: only 9 percent of the girls said they were 'not at all likely' to work while their children are young, as compared with 14 percent who thought it 'very likely'. Perhaps equally significant, the movement away from the traditional point of view is not yet completed; about 77 percent of the teenagers took a middle position on this issue, saying that working while their children are still young is 'not very likely', or only 'somewhat likely'. For the most part, the responses of the British and Italian females resembled those of the Americans. It appears then, that while few girls expect to play the traditional domestic role of housewife and mother, many are still somewhat uncertain as to what other options to pursue.

STEREOTYPES AND LABOUR FORCE PARTICIPATION

Decisions about working or remaining at home are rooted in the adolescent's beliefs about the nature of men and women. Girls who hold sterotypic beliefs about the sexes, who believe that women are dependent, vulnerable, non-competitive creatures, prone to empathy and vanity; who think women's proper place is in the home caring for husband and children; and who believe that men's place is in the labour force earning money for their families at jobs suitable to their more aggressive, competitive natures – these girls find the traditional domestic role more attractive than do girls who think achievement, competition, and equality as natural a condition for women as for men.

Support for this conclusion can be seen in Table 8.2 in which measures of sex role stereotyping and sex role values of teenage girls are related to their domestic role preferences – expectations about marriage, work, and family. An internally consistent, reliable measure of sex role stereotyping was described in an earlier chapter, and it is this measure which appears in the table. The sex role values index, however, is a new measure; it assesses beliefs and values girls have about occupational and domestic roles. This index, a Likert-type scale, is composed of the summed responses to three statements, as follows; (1) 'It is still best for a man to earn the money for a family, and for a woman to stay home and take care of her family and house', (2) 'Women's work and men's work should be different in nature', (3)

Table 8.2　Mean Sex Role Values and Sex Role Sterotypes, by Life-style Expectation for Females in Three Countries

	Sex Role Values			Sex Role Stereotypes		
	USA	Britain	Italy	USA	Britain	Italy
Family only, will not work	7.41	7.47	5.67	4.04	4.74	5.33
Family with employment while children are young						
Not at all likely	7.11	7.10	6.88	5.03	4.35	3.13
Not very likely	6.42	6.68	5.88	3.68	4.15	3.05
Somewhat likely	5.63	6.10	5.25	3.74	4.58	3.51
Very likely	5.33	6.40	4.57	3.55	3.27	3.17
Employment only, does not expect to have children	4.84	4.68	5.43	2.96	3.91	3.13
$F =$	10.84	5.92	5.82	4.42	1.96	0.89
p	< 0.001	< 0.001	< 0.001	< 0.005	not significant	not significant

'Mothers should work only if their family needs the money'. Response categories ranged from 'strongly disagree', which was given a weight of 1, 'disagree', a weight of 2, 'agree', a weight of 3, to 'strongly agree', a weight of 4; thus the higher the score the more traditional the sex role value. The inter-item reliability coefficient (alpha) for this measure is highly satisfactory in all three countries.

As can be seen in Table 8.2, adolescent females who do not expect to have children, or who think it 'very likely' that they will work even while their children are young, are more likely to reject traditional sex-role values than are those with more traditional attitudes about working after marriage. For example, the mean sex role values score of American adolescents who do not expect to have children is 4.84; the score for those who think it 'very likely' that they will work when their children are young is 5.33; both scores indicate relatively modern sex role values. In contrast, girls who do not expect to work afer marriage tend to hold traditional values: their mean score is 7.41. Girls who expect to work after marriage but who think it 'not at all likely' that they will work while their children are young have a mean score of 7.11. These girls find the traditional division of labour both natural and proper; they accept a way of life that keeps them at home and sends the husband out into the labour force. On the whole, the British and Italian teenagers resemble their American peers: among all the groups, the girls who express a willingness to work while their children are still young tend to reject traditional sex role values.

A similar pattern exists with regard to sex role stereotyping: the more the girl indicates a desire to work after marriage, even when her children are young, the more likely she is to reject stereotypical thinking. Again, consider the mean scores of American females. Table 8.2 shows that girls who do not expect to have children, or who believe it 'very likely' that they will work even while their children are young, have significantly lower mean scores, 2.96 and 3.55 (low scores indicate a rejection of sex role stereotypes) than do girls with more traditional domestic expectations. Thus adolescents who do not expect to work after marriage ('family only') have a score of 4.04; and those who believe it 'not at all likely' that they will work while their children are young have an even higher score, 5.03, a score that indicates that these girls tend to regard their own sex as basically non-competitive, dependent, compliant, and vain – ideas that modern girls vehemently reject. Again, the responses of the British and Italian girls resemble those of the Americans, although the association between stereotyping and life-style expectation is somewhat weaker; nevertheless, the basic trends are the same among teenagers in all three countries.

Unfortunately, nothing in these data enables us to fix the causal nexus between work expectations and sex role values or sex role stereotypes. As a rule, cross-sectional survey data make casual inferences risky and ambiguous, and such is the situation here. Do work plans cause the adolescent to hold certain values, or is it just the other way around? The data do not say. In all probability, work expectations and sex role values and stereotypes are interrelated, each an integral part of the domestic system, each subject to the industrial forces impinging on the family and the individual. Changes in one part of the role system produce changes in other parts as well, thus setting in motion an interactional sequence that helps explain the awesome power of industrialisation to alter people and the domestic role. Influenced by industrialisation, captivated by the ethos of domestic achievement and equality, and aware that millions of women today pursue dual family and career goals, modern girls have come to believe that having a family and a career simultaneously is both proper and satisfying. And since they no longer believe that either the family role or the work role must be sacrificed if both are to be performed adequately, they anticipate entering marriage and the labour force without crippling anxiety and emotional conflict, expecting that the demands of both roles can be fitted into their lives, that somehow time and energy will be found to be wives and mothers as well as gainfully employed workers.

The modern girl not only gives paid work an important place in her plans, she also raises her occupational sights. Since she expects to work while she has small children, or perhaps expects not to have children at all, this kind of girl can consider a wide range of occupations, including those in fields that require continuous labour force participation. And unburdened by stereotypes that portray her sex as weak and dependent, less restrained about appearing aggressive and competitive, the modern girl need not seek refuge in the 'pink ghetto'. She need not rule out an occupation merely because tradition has defined it as masculine; and she can aspire, without ambivalence, to jobs which require assertiveness; her possession of this trait increases the probability of her being successful, making these occupations even more attractive, particularly when they pay well and possess high status. Confident of her right to compete for any job she finds attractive, the ambitious girl with modern domestic expectations seeks a family structure compatible with high status work, with social mobility, and with success in a labour market bustling with activity and competition.

The connection between the domestic role and the work role became clear when we correlated the domestic expectations of adolescents holding dual role expectations with their level of occupational expectation. The reader will remember that occupational expectation is measured on a six-part scale, with unskilled jobs given a weight of 1 at one end of the scale and executive-professional work a weight of 6 at the other. These correlations necessarily omit the most traditional females, the small group that does not intend to work outside the home, as well as the least traditional girls who do not expect to marry or have a family, omissions that attenuate the correlations somewhat but do not change the basic relationship between domestic expectations and occupational expectations.

The correlations revealed that the higher the girl's occupational expectation, the later she expects to marry, the fewer children she intends to have, and the more willing she would be to enter the labour force while her children are still young. Consider, for example, the American girls; the correlation of occupational expectation with expected age of marriage is 0.39, with desired family size −0.13, and with labour force participation −0.21; the correlation is negative in the latter case because the response 'not at all likely to work' was coded 4, whereas the response 'very likely' was coded 1. The correlations for the

British and the Italians differ somewhat from those of the Americans, but the basic trends in all three countries are the same: the more the female sets limits on her domestic role, the more free she feels to seek work in the upper reaches of the occupational status hierarchy. This relationship is not changed when socioeconomic status (and IQ for the Americans) are controlled.

The domestic expectations of males, on the other hand, are not significantly related to occupational expectations. The American correlations, for example, range from 0.01 to 0.05; all statistically insignificant, as are the correlations for the British and Italian males. We included all the males in this analysis since the conventional role for males subsumes the option to work and have a family simultaneously. And in fact no male student in these samples expected to have a family and not work outside the home, a condition similar to the 'housewife' category for women. Moreover, we found that the inclusion of the less traditional males, those who said they did not expect to marry or to have a family, did not significantly alter the correlation between desired family size and occupational expectation. Apparently, adolescent males see the domestic and occupational roles as separate spheres of their future lives; for them domesticity is unrelated to the occupation they expect to hold one day.

Not so with the adolescent females: in many of their minds the two roles are inextricably connected. As we have seen, whether an adolescent female believes that as a young mother she will stay at home or work at paid employment is associated with the prestige of the occupation she expects to have on reaching her parents' age. But since occupational prestige and type of occupation are analytically different, though empirically related, we thought it useful to examine how domestic expectations influence teenage girls to choose particular types of occupations. By looking at the relationship of type of occupational expectation to the domestic role, we hoped to obtain a better understanding of the factors underlying the dramatic changes that have occurred in the occupational distribution of women in the labour force in the last few decades.

In Table 8.3 we present the type of occupation females expect to have, cross-tabulated with their expected labour force participation. Students (about a third) who did not provide codeable information on occupational expectation are not included in this table, a sizeable reduction that reflects an uncertainty about the future natural to adolescence, not a systematic bias in the data, judging from an

Table 8.3 Percentage Distribution of Occupational and Labour Force Participation Expectations, by Sex and Country

	United States Likelihood of Working			Britain Likelihood of Working			Italy Likelihood of Working		
	not very	some-what	very	not very	some-what	very	not very	some-what	very
Semi-skilled, skilled manual	3.4	6.5	5.0	34.3	4.1	40.0	0.0	0.0	0.0
Clerical, sales secretarial	31.8	28.2	15.0	34.2	41.7	20.0	2.6	3.3	9.4
Technical, lower admin.	20.5	13.7	20.0	15.1	29.2	13.3	50.0	50.0	37.5
Lesser professional	40.4	43.5	38.3	13.7	20.8	13.4	26.3	20.0	28.1
Executive, entrepreneur, professional	3.9	8.1	21.7	2.7	4.2	13.3	21.1	26.7	25.0
N =	143	124	60	73	22	15	38	30	32
	chi-square = 22.2 $p < 0.01$			chi-square = 12.4 not significant			chi-square = 7.43 not significant		

examination of the 'don't knows' and 'no answers'. The missing responses to the question on occupational expectation are not significantly related to sex, socioeconomic status, IQ or grades.

As expected, the data revealed a marked relationship between anticipated labour force participation and type of occupational choice; thus girls who say they are 'very likely' to work while their children are young are more likely to choose executive–professional work, careers that demand long-term commitment and continuous participation, than are girls who answered 'not at all likely' or 'not very likely'. Girls who plan to stay at home while their children are young tend to have traditional occupational expectations: their choices incline toward clerical–secretarial work or toward lower administrative and lesser professional jobs, teachers, nurses, office managers, technicians, and the like, jobs which permit some flexibility of scheduling and work pace, and which enable mothers to attend to family needs without excessive damage to their prospects in the workplace. Consider, for instance, the American girls. As Table 8.3 shows, of those American girls who said it was only 'somewhat' or 'not at all likely' that they would work while their children are young, only 3.9 percent expected to hold an executive–professional job, whereas 3.8 percent thought they would end up in a clerical or secretarial position. In contrast, of those girls who thought it 'very likely' they would work while their children are young, 21.7 percent expected to fill an executive–professional position, while only 15 percent expected to do clerical–secretarial work. Expected labour force participation has little effect on the occupational expectations of the British students, and almost none on the Italians. The critical decision for these young people is not whether to work while the children are young but whether to have children at all. About half of the girls who say they do not expect to have children expect to fill professional positions.

The distribution of male occupational expectations provides a useful source of comparison with the females. As might be expected, the male and female distributions are different. Separate analyses show the distribution of occupational expectations of females for each occupational sub-group to be somewhat different from that of the males. But the degree of dissimilarity decreases as the likelihood of continuous labour force participation increases. That is, when the pattern of female and male labour force participation are roughly similar, the distributions of male and female occupational expectations resemble each other more than when the females deviate from the male norm by expecting to interrupt paid employment in order to stay at home with their children. This is not to suggest that the distribution of male occupational choices is more normal or superior to that of females; nor should it be taken to mean the occupational choices of males are without traditional characteristics. On the contrary, many boys expect to hold conventional masculine jobs; for instance, 27 percent of the American boys expect to have a skilled manual job, a type of work long attractive to males.

A MULTIVARIATE ANALYSIS OF OCCUPATIONAL EXPECTATIONS

The domestic role far from exhausts the list of factors that influence a girl's occupational expectation.[11] Also important, as we have seen, are social status, academic potential and performance, educational expectation, sex role values, sex role stereotypes, and the perception of sexism in the labour force. The latter factor critically influences a female's occupational expectation, because whether the occupational world is seen as fair and open to women or biased and closed must surely affect her choice of work: the perception of sexism in the labour market can chill her interest in entering certain fields. For when a girl thinks the cards are stacked against her, when she believes boys receive preferential treatment in the job market, when she supposes positions of authority are given to men but denied to women, then she will tend to gravitate to a traditional female job, one that does not require her to compete with males, one that does not load the odds against her.

A Perception of Sexism index was constructed from the adolescent's responses to four statements. The student was asked whether the following statements were always true, usually true, usually false, or always false: (1) 'Boys have a greater choice of future jobs than girls do', (2) 'It's much harder for a girl to become a doctor or a lawyer than it is for a boy', (3) 'A woman is just as likely as a man to become a boss', (4) 'Boys are more likely than girls to get training for high paying jobs'. Responses to these statements were scored from 1 ('always false') to 4 ('always true'), with the scoring reversed for item 3. The responses were then summed to form a single Likert-type index: the higher the score the more sexism the respondent perceives in the labour market. The reliability of this index (Cronback's Alpha) is 0.61, an adequate degree of inter-item consistency.

With ten factors in our explanatory model, all acting on occupational expectation simultaneously, we needed a statistical technique that would permit an examination of their separate effects on the dependent variable. Discriminant analysis is such a technique, and, as it is well suited to our data, we put it to use. But first a few words about this statistical procedure. Discriminant analysis resembles regression analysis in that it is based on least squares and, like regression analysis, it generates a standardised coefficient for each independent variable; these coefficients, similar to beta weights in regression, tell us the relative contribution of each independent variable to the dependent variable. The larger the coefficient, the greater the variable's contribution to the dependent effect under examination. In addition, discriminant analysis has an important advantage over regression; it permits the examination of the effects of interval level independent variables on categorical dependent variables – in this case, type of occupational expectation.

The categorical dependent variable being examined here is the sex-typicality of the occupational expectations of females. Occupational categories were labelled as 'female' or 'male' when at least 70 percent of all the respondents choosing an occupation in that category were of one sex, and sex neutral when neither sex comprised more than 55 percent of the total. Using these criteria, we were able to put the respondents into one of three categories: sex-typical, sex-neutral, and sex-atypical. For females a sex-typical choice would be a clerical–secretarial position or a lesser professional one; a sex-atypical choice would be an occupation in the skilled manual trades or one in the executive–professional realm; the residual categories are sex-neutral. The analysis was based on data obtained only from those females with dual-role (work and family) expectations, and who provided information on all the ten variables in the model. These variables include the background and educational factors conventionally used as predictors of occupational expectations, as well as the sex role and domestic expectation variables that form the core of our theoretical approach.

Restricting the sample in this way severely reduced the number of respondents who could be fitted into the discriminant model: only 287 American females satisfied our criteria for inclusion in this part of the analysis. The British and Italian sub-groups, having been drawn from samples about one-third the size of the American sample, were too small to be reliably analysed with the discriminant analysis technique. In addition, the British and Italian samples provided no information on IQ, and the British schools provided data on academic performance (grades) that was at best fragmentary. For these reasons the discriminant analysis presented below is based entirely on data obtained from American girls.

Table 8.4 presents a discriminant analysis of the occupational expectations of American females, categorised into three expectation sub-groups – sex-typical, sex-neutral, and sex-atypical – and their relationships to ten independent variables. The analysis revealed a significant separation between the three groups; all the statistically reliable between-groups dispersion could be accounted for by the first discriminant function; no significant between-group co-variation remained after the first dimension had been partialled. In column one, the table presents the standardised discriminant coefficients of each independent variable; the absolute size of these coefficients represents the relative independent contribution of the associated variables to the total separation between the groups. Since a standardised discriminant coefficient is analogous to the standardised regression coefficient, the interpretation should be treated with the same caution accorded to a regression coefficient.

To help the reader understand the relationships of the variables to the discriminant variable, the correlations between the original measures of the variables and the discriminant variable are presented in column two. These correlations or 'loadings' may be interpreted as orthogonal factor loadings if it is remembered that the underlying 'latent discriminant' variable has been generated in order to maximally differentiate between the criterion groups and not because of some inner factor linking the data together. The 'loadings' are bivariate Pearsonian correlations between the discriminant scores and each variable. Also presented are multivariate centroids, imaginary points that describe how closely together the groups fall spatially, and whose coordinates are the group's mean on each of the variables.

The general patterns emerging from the data in Table 8.4 show that girls who expect to have traditionally 'male' occupations (the sex-atypical group) make this choice aware that they will encounter an opportunity structure somewhat closed to females; consequently, they plan to fit the 'male' model by working continuously, by obtaining a higher education, and by limiting their domestic obligations through having a smaller than average family. In contrast, the girls who have traditional 'female' occupational expectations (the sex-typical group) seem to view the sex segregation of occupations as appropriate and valid. They endorse the traditional sexual division of labour, which separates the occupational and domestic spheres, assigning one sphere

Table 8.4   Discriminant Analysis for Sex-typicality of Occupational Expectation Groups, Females with Dual Role Expectations

Standardised discriminant variables	Coefficients	Loadings	'Sex-Typical' Group	'Sex-Neutral' Group	'Sex-Atypical' Group
			Univariate means		
Socioeconomic status	−0.311	−0.330	4.02	4.44	4.97
IQ	0.198	−0.136	107.60	106.40	111.29
Grades	0.083	−0.158	5.81	5.87	6.17
Sex role values	0.203	0.430	6.24	6.18	4.72
Sex role stereotypes	0.009	0.184	2.95	2.84	2.28
Perception of sexism	−0.326	−0.245	10.38	10.73	11.19
Expected age at marriage	0.039	−0.326	3.93	4.07	4.47
Desired family size	0.269	0.410	3.09	2.53	2.08
Labour-force participation	0.568	0.662	2.78	2.18	1.47
Educational expectation	−0.315	−0.486	3.44	3.50	4.25
Multivariate centroids			0.26	−0.30	−1.10

to men, the other to women; they expect to remain at home and to have a larger than average number of children. On all the variables the 'sex-neutral' group falls between the modern and traditional groups.

This exploratory discriminant analysis, however, may capitalise unduly on chance because of the strong optimisation techniques employed. Given this possibility, we subjected the data to a series of predetermined setwise discriminant analyses designed to determine the relative importance of four sets of indicators (domains) as predictors of the separation of the three groups. The sets were entered in the following order: Background variables (socioeconomic status, IQ, grades), Sex Role variables (sex role values, sex role stereotyping, and perception of sexism), Domestic Orientation variables (expected age at marriage, desired family size, and labour force participation) and Educational Expectation. By first entering the Background variables, which are conventionally considered critical to the formation of occupational expectations, we were able to determine the residual discrimination achieved with the other sets of variables. Theoretically, the residual discrimination of the second set of variables, the Sex Role indices, should be significant because the groups are defined in terms of the sex-typicality of occupations, a dimension of sex roles in our society. After the conventional background and sex role variables are considered, a rigorous test of the residual discrimination achieved by the Domestic Orientation variables is then possible.

The contribution of each domain was assessed using the techniques suggested by Rao and by Jennrich.[12] There was significant residual discrimination remaining after the Background variables were entered ($\chi^2 = 60.41$, $p < 0.0001$). After the Background and Sex Role variables had been entered, there was still non-chance residual discrimination in the remaining variables ($\chi^2 = 39.213$, $p < 0.0001$), so the Domestic Orientation variables were entered. With these three domains being used to predict the choice of sex-typed or non-sex-typed occupational roles, Educational Expectation did not add any significant independent discrimination.

This theoretically-based test of the differences between women who intend to pursue 'female' occupations and those aspiring to 'male' or 'sex-neutral' occupations shows that the group differences must be explained by using variables in several domains: the sex role, the domestic role, as well as the Background variables. The significant contribution of the Domestic Orientation variables after the inclusion of the other sets indicates the substantial impact domestic expectations (labour force participation, in particular) have on the occupational expectations of adolescent females.

In summary, the data in this chapter show that some girls still draw a sharp line between the roles of women and men: they continue to believe that marriage and motherhood should be the primary life goals of women; they see the sexes in stereotyped ways; they believe women and men should perform different domestic and occupational roles; and they conform to traditional sociocultural expectations by planning to marry young and have more than the average number of children. Nevertheless, reflecting no doubt current trends, many of them expect to work at some point in their lives.

But in an industrial society, many of the women who decide to work and have a family encounter conflicting demands upon their time and energy: as mothers they are expected to take care of their young children, as employees they are expected to work full-time and continuously. This is less of a problem for women with a traditional view of their sex role: they expect to remain at home while their children are young. Thus early in the selection process they eliminate from further consideration occupations into which late entry or re-entry is difficult or impossible; in effect, most 'male' occupations are ruled out of bounds. Moreover, traditional females, perceiving stereotypic differences between the sexes and believing that mens' and womens' work should be different, are drawn to occupations typed as appropriate to their sex.

Modern young women take a less orthodox approach to domestic and occupational roles. Responding to current occupational and domestic norms, they plan to work while their children are young; they appear unwilling to devote themselves exclusively to the wife–mother role, even during the years when their children are young, because they do not view having a family and working as mutually exclusive. In this respect they are similar to most males, for whom a pattern of domestic and occupational role integration is taken for granted. In brief, modern, innovative females tend not to think stereotypically about the sexes; they reject the traditional approach to occupational and domestic roles. Their liberal sex role attitudes and values, along with an expectation for a continuous labour force participation, allows them to consider a broader range of occupations, including those sex-typed as 'male'.

9 Conclusion

The world has definitely changed. Once most women shunned the paid work force, preferring whenever possible to stay at home and care for spouse and children, willingly making the homemaker's role the focus of their lives; now women take paid employment for granted, even after marriage and into motherhood, and have entered the labour force in such huge numbers that the female presence there will soon equal its proportion in the population. Once, most working women took jobs in rigidly sex-segregated workplaces, unremunerative work, the sort traditionally set aside for women; now women work in all sectors of the economy, including those once considered exclusively male domains, competing with men and achieving noteworthy successes in the arts and sciences, and in commerce and industry. It is no exaggeration to call these changes revolutionary.

Revolutionary change demands attention and cries out for explanation. But revolutions are never simple: their roots are deep and often obscure, their courses tortuous and tension-ridden, their effects continuous, complex and tangled. Some people understand this and, recognising that complex change requires a search for facts and causes that lie beneath the obvious surface, accept explanations that sometimes seem at odds with common sense and are frequently as complicated as the phenomenon they try to interpret. Other people, impatient with complexity and too emotional to think objectively, hunger for simple answers to complicated questions and seek in ideology a comforting explanation of a confusing world that is churning in flux and torn by conflict. Fortunately for these impatient souls an ideology and an organisation to promote it is readily at hand – feminism and the women's movement. Together they provide an explanation for the changes in the condition of women, an explanation that has become the orthodox wisdom: the liberation of women and their successes in the labour force stem from the actions of women themselves, from their rejection of sexual inequality, and from their support of policies that forced a reluctant, male-dominated society to admit women into every nook and cranny of the polity and economy.

More than simplicity makes this explanation attractive; it also appeals to the theatrical imagination, for it contains themes with the emotional punch of high drama. In this modern morality play, the sexes are cast in the roles of antagonists, oppressors and victims, men and women engaged in a protracted battle between good and evil. As in any good morality play, the action has a beginning, a middle and an end, each act filled with struggle and hope and disappointment, yet all eventually ending in the triumph of right over wrong. The final act produces catharsis and a satisfying sense of victory: sexual discrimination and inequality are ended or soon will be, and the future for women (men, too, for they also will benefit from the liberation of women) seems bright.

As an explanation of the changing status of women, the orthodox wisdom has some merit; it certainly contains elements of truth: the women's movement has helped open doors to women. But is also leaves much out; and since it views social change as warfare, it cannot imagine that change may be encouraged and welcomed by the very society the change-makers are trying to alter. Moreover, its image of victory seems to envision a time when the struggle for change ceases and the blissful calm of social equality prevails. That social change often involves conflict can hardly be doubted, though its importance can be exaggerated; but that the course of social change in the condition of women will arrive at a terminal and necessarily happy stage is most unlikely. Social change is not theatre but process, a sequence of actions and events without a specific starting point and with no clear and definite ending. The process, which substantially antecedes the birth of organised feminism, first became visible in the last century during the early decades of the industrial revolution when women were recruited to work in the shops and mills and factories of the newly industrialising West. It gained momentum, though admittedly with occasional interruptions and halts, during the nineteenth century as the industrial economies of Europe and North America, energised by war and economic growth and desperate for workers, brought ever-increasing numbers of women into the labour force. And the process acquired even greater momentum in the present century as the techno-service economy developed, intensifying the need for women workers and multiplying the opportunities open to them. As a result, in order to make it possible for women to work where they were needed, the industrial society began to dismantle the barriers that an earlier traditional society had erected against them.

Some women welcomed these changes and eagerly accepted the challenge to compete with men on an equal footing for the rewards of occupational success. But other women, principally those with a traditional cast of mind, rejected the industrial society's appeal to join its labour force. To them, industrial work seemed dirty, monotonous, coarsening and unfeminine, and unless driven by poverty they resisted the lure of paid employment and stayed at home. It was to encourage these traditional women, who until this century constituted the bulk of womanhood, to enter the labour force that the industrial society began in the last century to change the female sex role and the personalities of the women who played it; for it was apparent that unless the needs of the industrial society and the requirements of the sex role could be made congruent, women would not be able to take their places comfortably and effectively beside men in the workplace.

The traditional sex role required women to devote themselves to domesticity and punished those who were seen as neglecting their families out of a foolish and selfish desire for the excitement and money a paid job would bring; consequently, a modern sex role had to be created which would permit, even encourage, women to be mothers and salary earners and entrepreneurs concurrently. That such a sex role eventually emerged is history, that many women preferred it to the traditional role is obvious, and that it contributed to the movement of women into the labour force and into almost every kind of work is one of the themes of this book. The new sex role put few constraints on the occupational expectations of women. Rather than insist that women work only in fields set aside for their gender, the new sex role encouraged them to take on the kind of work men have long performed and to bring to their jobs the talents and skills long expected of men but heretofore considered unfeminine.

In order to play their new sex role properly women had also to change. Traditional feminine passivity, compliance and dependance had to be put aside and the masculine traits of competitiveness and aggressiveness put in their place. Women had to learn to compete openly with men, to act independently, and to assert themselves in the workplace when the situation required, eschewing the submissive demeanour required of the traditional female. Passivity and compliance, dependency and non-competitiveness, empathy and nurturance are all admirable traits, especially in women in a traditional society that usually values group solidarity and social quiescence above all else; but an industrial society has different goals, and thus needs a different kind of worker in order to function effectively. Because it values efficiency and productivity, an industrial society needs workers who can get a job done, and it rewards people who excel at their work; it is of no practical significance to an industrial society whether the hand or mind that does the job is attached to a male or a female anatomy.

Changing a sex role and the personalities of the people who perform it is no easy task, but the industrial society had favourable circumstances in which to work, and immense resources and powerful allies to help produce the changes it desired. To begin with, it was assisted by two social changes it had helped to foster: urbanisation and cultural modernity. Industrialisation uprooted vast rural populations and sent them reeling to the city to seek work. In the city they encountered new values and expectations and people imbued with a viewpoint, modernity, which derided the traditional culture and espoused individualism and hedonism as important goals. In the city, migrants and natives, men and women, found new opportunities and encountered ideologies that shook them free from traditional norms and set them moving toward new horizons. For with the old culture discredited by industrialisation and modernity, the community lost its ability to enforce the traditional norms of sexual segregation, an ability which had been steadily undermined by the insistence of the industrial systems that workers be free of traditional constraints on their availability, mobility and efficiency. Between them, industrialisation and modernity, usually uneasy allies, changed the old order, replaced the traditional sex role with a new one, and enthroned a new value system whose banner read: Achievement, Individualism and Equality.

The values we call industrial have in fact been around for centuries: an emphasis on achievement, equality and individualism can certainly be found in the literature of Periclean Athens and Medicean Florence. But not until the industrial era did they become general and not until modern times did they reach the top of society's hierarchy of values. And the prized industrial traits of ambition and the need to achieve, of competitiveness and assertiveness, have never been absent from the personalities of women – the image of passive, dependent, compliant female is a stereotype and a myth. These qualities needed only the encouragement and sanction of society to become visible parts of the female personality and evident in the behaviour of women in the workplace. To encourage the development and expression of industrially useful values and behaviour, and to make women feel that it was both necessary and desirable for them to compete with men in the labour market, the industrial society set about socialising females into their new sex role, employing the services of its most potent agents: the family, the school, the mass media of communication. Acting independently, at times hardly aware of each other's methods and goals, these institutions of instructions and persuasion worked to erase differences between the sexes in competence and values, in perceptions of themselves and the opposite sex and the world, and in educational–occupational expectations.

Unlike their traditional forbears, modern parents tend to treat their daughters and sons in much the same way, for they understand that women must compete with men, and hence they try to equip females with the same competences, values and personality traits they have long valued in males. And the schools, with objectives similar to those of the parents and imbued with the principle of academic excellence, seek to instil a passion for excellence in girls and boys alike, responding to performance with an admirable indifference to the student's gender, punishing failure and rewarding achievement in boys and girls impartially. In addition, the media pick up the theme of achievement and give female accomplishments dramatic reality in daily accounts in newspapers and on television screens of female successes in the performing arts, sciences, business and the professions.

The data in this book show how successful the efforts of these agents of socialisation have been: the adolescent girls and boys in our three-nation study have, on the average, similar competences and achievements, values and perceptions, educational and occupational expectations. Girls perform as well as boys in school and engage in many of the same activities; girls and boys hold similar values and see themselves and members of the opposite sex (with some significant exceptions) in much the same way, sharing many of the same stereotypes, possessing many of the same anxieties, and displaying much the same degrees of self-confidence. Girls enjoy levels of self-esteem on a par with those of boys, and respond to threats to their interests with equal degrees of hostility. The notion that females inhibit aggression, bottling up anger or expressing it only in covert and indirect ways, while still true in individual cases, is on the whole fallacious; assertive and active responses to personal and situational challenges are as common among girls as boys. Self-confidence and assertiveness are evident in the educational–occupational expectations of the girls in this study: their expectations are, on the average, as high and as bold as those of the boys. In brief, so far as achievement and its related individual traits are concerned, the chasm of difference between the sexes has narrowed to a trivial gap in most cases or vanished entirely in others.

Aided by changes in the social structure brought about by industrialisation and the rise of the techno-service economy, this diminution of sex differences in achievement-related skills, personality traits, and expectations has produced predictable results: women have not only entered the labour force in large numbers with zest and optimism, they are doing very well there. An enumeration of female successes in the work force would, at this point, hold no surprises for the reader; after all, they have been catalogued in this book and in the media. But what is still surprising, perhaps even perplexing, is the reluctance of some of the most articulate, dedicated and passionate fighters for sexual equality to recognise how far women have advanced towards their goal. As they see it, the war for sexual equality is far from over; granted, some skirmishes have been won, but the big battles lie ahead and their outcomes are uncertain. Prisoners of the past, unable or unwilling to recognise the gains women have made, they act as though nothing basic has changed, and continue to fight enemies that more objective observers believe have already been defeated.

But this behaviour may not be as irrational as it seems. Some passionate fighters for sexual equality may feel that their hard fought victories can be reversed, that past gains can be eroded and lost, and that the attainment of full equality will be pushed unacceptably far into the future. To this group add those fighters who enjoy battle, impassioned belligerents whose lives have been given direction and purpose by the struggle for woman's liberation, and for whom life would lose its savour without the challenges and joys of fighting for a noble cause. These people see social change as a conflict between the forces of progress and reaction, as a struggle having a definite terminal point. Immersed in struggle, they do not recognise that their attention has been distracted from certain major problems which the changes they champion have created for women, for men, and for society, problems that were most unanticipated, and that have become deeply troublesome and horrendously complicated.

The major challenge facing women today in the industrial world is not gaining admission into the labour force – that problem has been solved; not winning places in privileged and remunerative sectors of the economy – that problem is being worked on and in time will also be solved; the needs of society, women and the changing sex role will see to that. Rather, the major challenge confronting women, the one to which not enough attention has as yet been paid, is finding a solution to the difficulties women encounter meeting the demands of their work and domestic roles. Women who are wives–mothers and paid employees at the same time often experience intense emotional and physical stress: there are simply too many conflicting demands, too many things to do, too little time to do them. It has become common to treat women caught in this bind as either victims or villains: victims because they have been put in a situation that must invevitably cause emotional conflict and physical exhaustion; villains because they are often held responsible for marital instability and child neglect, and their attendant social pathologies. Critics claim that women who insist on working damage themselves, their husbands and their children, and for this society is paying a terrible price. Some people would call this a classic case of blaming the victim.

But name-calling will not solve the problem, nor will the problem go away on its own. What is clear from this study is that most girls expect to work, that almost every one of them wants to have children, and that they expect to combine motherhood with paid employment. Most of them have not thought seriously about the problems this combination will bring, an understandable and perhaps excusable mistake given their age and inexperience; but adults cannot fall back on the excuse of youth and naïveté: they should understand that attention must be paid to the difficulties these youngsters will encounter when their dreams collide with reality, when they try to juggle the conflicting demands of the roles society has thrust upon them.

Slowly, industrial societies are moving to alleviate the tensions and strains they have created for women and the family. Some governments require employers to grant women generous maternity leaves, which makes the transition from the work role to the domestic role less traumatic, at least financially; in addition, some women are guaranteed re-employment in the same or a comparable job when their leave ends. On their own, some employers have instituted flexible work schedules that permit women to arrange their lives in ways that reduce the possibility of emotional and physical overload. And some employers have installed day care centres near the office or factory where mothers can leave their children as they report for work. These programmes and practices are helpful but none are universal and most are meagrely funded. The problem is that most employers do not believe it is their responsibility to help women who work both in and outside the home. They see this as a private or social problem that the family or the government must deal with, not something the employer must attend to as a normal cost of doing business. Those employers who do institute programmes to help women complain of its cost, and point to the price they pay when they lose out in the market place to competitors who have evaded their responsibilities to female employees.

This argument should not be dismissed as merely the complaint of cost-conscious businessmen who want to maximise their profits. Social services, whether public or private, are expensive, and the costs must be retrieved either through taxes in the case of the government or through higher prices in the case of private industry. Government could make the burden of helping working women more equitable if it made some programmes mandatory; all employers would then be required to do their part, and conscientious employers would not be punished in the market place for their willingness to behave responsibly. Coercion alone, however, will meet with resistance and evasion, and compliance would be grudging and half-hearted. To forestall this reaction and encourage cooperation, the government could use a system of tax incentives and subsidies to ease the financial burden of instituting programmes designed to help the working woman. Money often lowers barriers to social change that force, efforts at persuasion, and appeals to compassion leave unmoved.

But even if these actions were taken and proved successful, there would still remain unresolved the problems created by that most stubborn of all impediments to sexual equality: the traditional male sex role. Industrialisation has made fewer demands for change on men than on women, and the traditional male sex role has come under much less attack than its companion female role. Being a traditional male is no handicap to men working in most sectors of the economy; on the contrary, independence, self-assertiveness, and a willingness to build one's life around one's work, all components of the traditional male sex role, still bring rich rewards to men. Unfortunately for the working woman, the traditional male sex role does not include the idea of sexual equality, certainly not in the division of household labour. And it is the absence of equality in this area that is helping to make the life of working women with young children so difficult. A significant number of the problems afflicting women in the labour force could be avoided or at least reduced if men would take on more of the day-to-day work of household management and child care. But, as we know, the traditional male believes that his primary job is to protect and sustain his wife and children, he does not see domestic drudgery as part of his role: household work is women's work.

Nevertheless, men and the male sex role are changing, albeit slowly. Increasingly, men are taking jobs in the service sector, where the traditional feminine traits of empathy, nurturance, and cooperativeness are valued, and men must either take on these traits or lose out in their competition with women. Also, the ideology of equality and the fact that almost as many women as men work outside the home are undermining the traditional masculine assurance that men have a

natural right to decide how work and responsibility in the home should
be allocated, and that their role as the family provider excuses them
from becoming involved in domestic work. After all, in many house-
holds men are no longer the sole, or even the major, income-earner. But
perhaps most important of all, modern young women have grown
restive living under the rules of the old regime and are pressing men to
change. Women who work all day, often at jobs as demanding and
well-paying as their husbands', see no justice in a division of labour that
unfairly loads them down, that impoverishes their lives as women and
workers, and that makes their victories in the workplace feel hollow
and joyless.

Women's quest for equality, for the chance to develop their talents
and for the opportunity to succeed at work of their own choosing, is
moving from the halls of legislature and the court, from the factory
floor and corporate office, from the union hall and the political caucus,
into the home and the family. It is in the arena of the family that the
struggle for sexual equality will continue. And it is from this struggle
that the next important changes in the roles of women and men will
come. They may well create some anxiety and confusion: what changes
must be adopted, what conditions accepted, what compromises work
out, no one can now entirely foresee. What is certain is that men and
women are now caught up in changes that have no terminal point, no
time when wins and losses can be finally counted and effects assessed:
the process of change is endless.

Appendix: People, Places, Procedures

Ideally, a study of industrialisation's impact on women and achievement should be longitudinal. In this way data could be collected both before and after the advent of industrialisation, thus permitting the researcher to monitor the temporal sequence in the casual chain linking industrialisation to women and achievement. But this ideal, though attractive, has its problems. Obviously, no one now living can recall from personal experience the condition of women before the onset of industrialisation in the West: indeed, few can remember what happened to women and their place in the economy more than a generation or two ago. It is true that women and achievement could be studied longitudinally in contemporary less-developed countries, hell-bent on industrialisation, but unfortunately this would be so costly in time and energy and money that no one, to my knowledge, has ever tried it.

A more pragmatic approach would be to reconstruct the path from historical materials such as census reports, newspaper articles and books, public records, diaries, letters and memoirs. But these sources, though useful for some purposes, are not entirely satisfactory for our's since the data they yield are usually fragmentary and often lack quantifiable psychological information about personal attitudes, values and needs; in short, they lack the data that would be necessary to test a theory of structural and individual change. I chose, therefore, to work in the present, comparing currently industrialised countries and regions with one another and with places still predominantly non-industrial. Using the comparative method I was able to contrast the condition and achievements of women living in industrialised societies with each other and with those of their peers in pre-industrialised settings, and to locate the social structural and psychological factors that help explain the similarities and differences between the groups. The assumption underlying the comparative method, based logically on Mill's method of difference, is that theoretically predictable similarities among industrialised persons and differences between them and non-industrialised people are due, *ceteribus paribus*, to their degree of exposure to industrialisation. Of course, the comparative method is not without its

217

own shortcomings; thus, lacking measures of change over time, it cannot unequivocally separate cause from effect, nor pinpoint the sequence of events that occur in the process of change. Still it can illuminate similarities and differences between groups that can be plausibly attributed to industrialisation.

THE COMPARATIVE DESIGN

This book is built around research conducted in four countries and three continents over a period of twenty years. Roughly speaking, the research occurred in four phases, each of which tackled a part of the same large problem – how industrialisation affects the family and women. The first phase, itself part of another project that continued until 1978, took place in Brazil over a two-year period, 1963–65. In this phase I compared families in five communities, each of which represented a different point on a rural small town – big industrial continuum. At the non-industrial end of the continuum were two two communities, one an agricultural village located on a large plantation, the other a relatively isolated small town with no industry and a simple social structure; at the other end was an industrialised city with a high degree of occupational specialisation, a complicated social structure, and a huge population of industrialised inhabitants. Two medium-size cities, one industrial, the other not, fell between the extremes. This research provided data on the roles, values and perceptions of women in small non-industrial communities, which could be contrasted with those of women living in a large industrial city. Although the research focused on the impact of industrialisation on family stucture, not on women and achievement (though of course these social phenomena are related), the data serendipitously highlighted the effects of industrialisation on female achievement and on the importance of women as agents of social change. At the time of this research, women in Brazil had begun to move into the industrial labour force in large numbers and the effects of this on family relationships had become apparent. But the impact of industrialisation on female occupational achievement was as yet small, for few women had succeeded in capturing good positions in the economy. This industrialisation process in Brazil had reached a take-off stage but its full effects were yet to be felt by most women.

In the second phase of the research, I turned to the United States where women had become prominent in the labour force, both numerically and in terms of their achievements. Thus changes in the condition of women and in the women themselves could be easily observed in the United States, changes that either had not yet occurred in Brazil or were just beginning to take shape. In 1974–75, I conducted research on women and achievement in three industrial American cities, this time focusing on adolescent girls and boys rather than on adults with families. There were two reasons for this decision. First, adolescents are being touched by industrial change at a very formative stage of their development; the effects, therefore, of industrialisation on the adolescent are major, often visible and, especially important for our purposes, relatively easy to research. Working with adolescents, it is possible to study the process of socialisation through which society and its agents influence the personalities, actions and expectations of young people. Second, teenagers are at the leading edge of social change: in their attitudes, values, perceptions and expectations we can see the shape of things to come. Indeed, it is likely that since these studies were conducted many of these youngsters have demonstrated their interest in achievement through exceptional occupational performance in the workplace.

But it could be argued that the United States is not a representative industrial country: its history, culture, and resources make it unique; perhaps industrialisation has different effects in America from those in other countries. To guard against this criticism, I conducted research during 1975–76 in seven British cities located in a belt of communities stretching from London to Bristol. Like their American counterparts, the British cities are industrialised, either because they possess light or heavy manufacturing establishments or through their proximity to large industrial cities. And like the American samples, British subjects were adolescent girls and boys enrolled in public-supported secondary schools. Although the inclusion of the seven British cities in the research substantially broadened the research design, there still remained a nagging concern, the question of uniqueness, the possibility that the United States and Britain, sharing the same language and other elements in common culture, were not typical of industrialised countries in general. This concern motivated me to add Italy to the list of countries studied. In 1983–84, I conducted research in two northern Italian cities, again focusing on the personalities and behaviour of adolescent girls and boys. No one could argue that Italy is the mirror-image of the United States or Britain, many aspects of its culture and social structure differ markedly from those of the other two countries, and yet in one important respect Italy resembles the others – it is highly industrialised, particularly in the northern region in which the two cities in this study are located. By permitting a comparison of the three industrialised countries with one another and with the traditional norm as displayed in the non-industrial Brazilian communities, this research design makes possible some generalisations about the effects of industrialisation on the behaviour, personalities and expectations of adolescents. If it could be shown that the values, perceptions, expectations and actions of youngsters in industrial societies differ from traditional norms but are similar to one another, and if the similarities could plausibly be attributed to the influences of the social structure and culture of industrial nations, it would support our hypothesis about the impact of industrialisation on women and achievement.

CITIES AND SAMPLES

At the traditional end of our research continuum are two Brazilian communities, Boa Vista and Sao Luiz do Paraitinga; both are located in the state of Sao Paulo. Boa Vista is a small village situated on a large coffee and cattle plantation, whose inhabitants, 50 families in all, are farm workers, poor and mostly illiterate, who earn a precarious living doing various kinds of routine agricultural labour. From this group 38 families were selected and the husbands and wives separately interviewed. Sao Luiz is a small commercial town of about 3500 inhabitants, with no industry other than a small milk-processing plant and a stone quarry. Many of its inhabitants work in the quarry or milk plant, while others provide services for the local farmers. A sample of 128 families was selected from this community, and the husbands and wives were interviewed using the same schedule employed in Boa Vista. The interview, which focused on husband–wife and parent–child relationships, provided data on the degree to which the residents of non-industrial communities in this section of Brazil observed the dictates of the traditional sex roles. These data have been reported in an earlier book (*The Industrial Connection: Achievement and the Family in Developing Societies*) and are not re-examined in detail here; but the data are important nonetheless because they provide a picture of traditional life and thus serve as a background against which the changes that have occurred in the modern world can be compared.

At the modern end of the continuum are twelve cities, three in the United States, seven in Britain and two in Italy. The three American cities are contiguously located in an industrial section of up-state New

York; they are Binghamton, population 54 800; Vestal, 27 238; and Johnson City, 17 126. Binghamton and Johnson City, though not large cities, are highly industrialised, while Vestal, essentially a dormitory town, has many residents who work in nearby manufacturing factories or service centres. These cities were selected because (1) their populations are relatively racially homogenous, (2) they have long histories as manufacturing centres, and (3) they have attracted advanced-technology industries and thus have a high percentage of skilled workers. In addition, Binghamton possesses a branch of the state university, which contributes a certain cosmopolitan air to the surrounding area.

Students were sampled from two senior high schools and two junior high schools in Binghamton, one senior and one junior high school in Vestal, and one senior and one junior high school in Johnson City, nine schools in all. These schools were chosen on the advice of the superintendents of the school systems of each city, who assured us that collectively the schools were representative of the tri-city area. The sample contains students from all the socioeconomic strata in the area, ranging from teenagers who lived on welfare payments to those whose parents enjoyed the incomes of physicians and corporation presidents. In selecting students we used stratified sampling procedures which ensured that approximately equal numbers of females and males and enough students from each age and socioeconomic stratum to permit multivariate statistical analysis of the data would be drawn into the sample. Specifically, we took all the students enrolled in one third of the English classes in each school, after having first stratified the classes by grade and ability grouping. This procedure, though not strictly random, resulted in a relatively representative sample of the students in each school. Approximately 3200 students took part in the study. From this group we eliminated students who failed to complete at least 80 percent of the questionnaire or answered facetiously or mutilated their questionnaires. This group added up to less than 5 percent of the original sample; the final sample included 3049 students.

The British sample was drawn from students attending comprehensive schools in seven cities. Three of these cities are relatively large, Bristol, population 426 657, Reading, 132 939, and Oxford, 108 805, and all have substantial amounts of heavy and light industry. The other cities are much smaller; Stanmore, Langley, Ascot and Henley-on-Thames. None of these have more than 20 000 residents, but all are either located near major manufacturing centres or have some light industry of their own. Geographically, the cities extend in a belt across southern England from London to the west coast; economically, they are situated in the most prosperous section of country; culturally, they are highly urbanised and modern.

In each city we selected a comprehensive school as the source from which to draw a sample. We chose to work in the comprehensive school because it is relatively comparable to the American public school for, like its American counterpart, the British comprehensive school is publicly supported and coeducational, draws students from almost all sectors of the society and has a mixed curriculum of academic and vocational subjects. When this research was conducted about 65 percent of all British students were attending comprehensive schools. Missing from the sample are students attending elite private schools and very selective public secondary schools; still, many of the students in the comprehensive school come from the middle classes and many will enter a university: the proportion of successful Oxford candidates from state schools now almost matches that from independent schools.

We were guided in our choice of particular comprehensive schools by officials at the Foundation for Educational Research in England and Wales who identified for us schools they believed to be representative of the community. Within each school we selected compulsory maths classes in Forms 2 to 6 and administered our questionnaire to all the students present in school on the day of our visit. Completed questionnaires were obtained from 1060 students, approximately 95 percent of those to whom the instrument was administered. Inspection of the completed questionnaires revealed that we had been successful in drawing into the sample students from varying social backgrounds and levels of ability.

The Italian cities, Padua and Verona, are situated in the most industrialised and urbanized region of the country, the north. Padua has a population of 227 528, Verona 259 992; both cities are highly industrialised and prosperous, both are important cities in the Veneto, and both have ancient traditions as centres of learning and art. Since almost all students in Italy attend a public school, it is possible to find in these schools adolescents from all stations of life. On the advice of people in each city, eleven junior and senior high schools (*scuole media* and *superiore*) were chosen as representative of the various types of schools servicing a diverse student population. Some of the schools sought to prepare students for the university and focused upon languages and literature, or science; others were mainly vocationally oriented and sought to train students for jobs upon graduation. In each school we selected classes at different grade levels, making sure that we included classes that were required of all students so as to minimise any selection bias. From these classes we obtained a sample of 1325 students, after eliminating a small number of incomplete or otherwise useless questionnaires.

In none of the schools was the system of sampling random, or are the cities representative of their respective countries. It was never my intention to generalise from the data to national populations, or to make comparisons between nations; rather, I sought, through stratified purposive procedures, to select large samples, roughly comparable in sex, age and class distributions, from which to obtain data to test a hypothesis about the impact of industrialisation on women and achievement. No doubt larger and more representative samples, randomly selected, would have been ideal; but the ideal had to give way to the limitations of practical concerns (money, time, energy) placed upon most research. On the other hand, the cities in this study, though different in size and degree of heterogeneity, are all modern and industrialised, either in their possession of manufacturing establishments or propinquity to industrial centres; hence, the students have been exposed throughout their lives to the culture of an urban, industrial civilisation. The sampling procedure did what it was designed to do: namely, it brought into the study approximately equal numbers of females and males from diverse social backgrounds who had been exposed to the effects of industrialisation. With this group in hand, it was possible to consider whether industrialisation had, as hypothesised, reduced or eliminated differences between the sexes in achievement and related personal variables.

THE FIELD WORK

Gaining access to students in the school classroom was not easy, for many schools and communities have become chary of opening their facilities to social researchers. To begin with, the research takes up classroom time and some teachers object to this; also, the topic of the research may be offensive to some parents and to members of the community. In consequence, considerable time had to be spent meeting with school officials and teachers, explaining the purpose of the research, going over the questionnaire with them, answering their questions and objections, and winning their consent. In the United States I first met with the superintendent of schools in each city, and following that I talked with the principal of each school and with groups of teachers. On the whole, they proved receptive to the purpose of the research and were cooperative. In Britain, I enlisted the help of officials of the Foundation for Educational Research in England and Wales, located in a suburb of London called Slough, who put me in touch with the headmasters of schools in each of the seven cities. Although I was told that British communities are generally not keen about foreign researchers entering their schools, discussions with the headmasters proved successful in every case and, once their consent had been obtained, it was relatively easy to enter the schools and administer the questionnaires. Italy presented a similar challenge: the idea of a foreign researcher entering the school needed time to get used to; hence in the beginning I encountered some difficulty obtaining consent to conduct research in the Italian schools, but with the help of professional colleagues at the University of Padua and Verona, consent was eventually granted; again once the researchers entered the schools the work went smoothly.

The cooperation of the teachers was critical to the success of the field work. To encourage their cooperation we carefully explained the nature and importance of the research (the subject of achievement and women appealed to most teachers, many of whom were female) and emphasised that the administration of the research instrument would be the responsibility of the research team, one of whose members would always be present in the classroom to answer questions. The teacher was a stabilising influence during the administration of the questionnaire, helping to maintain order and finding work for the students to do when they finished quickly. As might be expected, questions of confidentiality inevitably arose. We sought to allay these anxieties by assuring the students that the completed questionnaires would be treated with utmost confidentiality and that no teacher or school official would see them. How much faith the students put in this assurance is not known for certain, but so far as could be seen the overwhelming majority answered the questions candidly. Although occasional instances of student frivolity were evident in the way some questions were answered, most of the students concentrated seriously on filling out the questionnaire, sometimes biting their lips in thought and occasionally raising their hand to seek an explanation of a question that puzzled them.

Because the questionnaire is the keystone around which the research was constructed, much time and effort went into its development. The eventual product was the result of a lengthy process of trial and error, during which the instrument underwent several important revisions. The process began with informal discussions with adolescent boys and girls wherever they could be found: in playgrounds, on the streets, in front of their houses. They were asked how they spent their time, what things they enjoyed doing and were good at, whether they had a boyfriend or girlfriend, what they thought of their own sex and the opposite one, and the like. These informal conversations were the inspiration for many parts of the questionnaire and helped us translate the questions from the language of the adult researchers into the everyday language of teenagers.

The next phase was the preparation of a structured interview with a pre-determined set of topics and questions. Using this instrument, the researchers were able to find out how well the questions were understood, what words were difficult or unclear, and what areas touched off giggles of embarrassment or scowls of hostility. At this point in its development the questionnaire was still much too long and some items had to be dropped; changes in question order and format were also made. The questions were then put in structured form with pre-coded answers so that the answers could be transferred directly from the questionnaire to a data card and thence to a tape. The final round of pre-testing took place in the classrooms of two schools in a city not included in the research sample. The purpose of this pre-test was to discover how long the questionnaire took in a classroom setting (it took about fifty minutes), what difficulties its administration presented, and what problems had been missed in the previous rounds of pre-testing and revision. Only minor changes were needed after the classroom pre-test; after these were made the final version was printed and administered to American adolescents.

But, as it turned out, our work on the questionnaire was not yet finished: before it could be used in Britain and Italy more revisions and pre-testing had to be done. Translating the American questionnaire into idiomatic British English was easy; only a few minor changes were necessary. With the help of the staff of the Foundation and through interviews with small groups of British teenagers, we were able to locate some bothersome American terms and replace them with English ones. The revised questionnaire was pre-tested in the schools of Slough and things went smoothly without any evident hitches. So far as I could tell the questionnaire was as intelligible and meaningful to British adolescents as it had been to Americans. The translation of the questionnaire into Italian was more difficult and time consuming. The work of translation began on the American side with the help of a bilingual Italian who was familiar with Italian adolescents and the schools in Italy. This translation was then compared with the one made by colleagues at the University of Padua, who could call upon the assistance of their students and staff in reconciling the differences between the two translations. The final questionnaire, a combination of two earlier versions, was pre-tested with students in Vicenza, a city near Padua, and found to work as well in Italy as it had in the United States and Britain.

In all three countries the questionnaire was administered by local professional staff, principally graduate students in the United States, researchers at the Foundation in Britain, and university professors in Italy. The writer was on the scene in all three countries and, in the early phases of the research, accompanied the staff into the schools and classrooms, partly to supervise the work and partly to talk with teachers and students. In particular, my informal conversations with students in all three countries materially helped this research. The students were usually lively and friendly; they sometimes asked questions and made comments that ran through my head during the long period when the data were being analysed and the book written. More than they will ever know, they were the inspiration for this work.

Notes

CHAPTER 1

1. That industrialisation has affected feminism and the condition of women has not, of course, escaped the attention of scholars. See, for example, Donald Meyer, *Sex and Power: The Rise of Women in America, Russia, Sweden and Italy* (Middletown, Connecticut: Wesleyan University Press, 1987). But previous research did not focus on the impact of industrialisation on sex roles and personality, nor did it seek, as the present work does, to establish the social and psychological linkages between structural and individual change.
2. Bettina Berch, *The Endless Day: The Political Economy of Women and Work* (New York: Harcourt Brace Javanovich, 1982) pp. 32, 42.
3. Berch, p. 5. Useful information about the current condition of women in the labour force can be found in Ann H. Stromberg and Shirley Harkess (eds) *Women Working: Theories and Facts in Perspective*, 2nd edn (Mountain View, California: Mayfield Publishing, 1988).
4. *The Wall Street Journal*, 25 September, 1986.
5. Barbar Welter, 'The Cult of True Womanhood', in Michael Gordon (ed.) *The American Family in Social-Historical Perspective* (New York: St Martin's Press, 1978).
6. Frederick Engels, *The Origins of the Family, Private Property and the State* (New York: International Publishers, 1972).
7. The gloomy view of industrial life is not, of course, without some basis in fact. Louis Wirth, looking about him in Chicago, was impressed by the bleak impersonality and competitiveness of industrial urban life in the first decades of this century. See his, 'Urbanism as a Way of Life', *American Journal of Sociology* Vol. 44 (July 1938) pp. 3–24. Diatribes against the industrial system continue unabated. Anthropologist Lionel Tiger calls the industrial system unnatural, heartless, impersonal and a producer of evil. See, Lionel Tiger, *The Manufacture of Evil* (New York: Harper and Row, 1987).
8. Jane Kramer, 'Reflections', *The New Yorker*. 24 September 1979, p. 64.
9. Norman Podhoretz, *Breaking Ranks: A Political Memoir* (New York: Harper and Row, 1979) p. 116.
10. John W. Osborne, *The Silent Revolution: The Industrial Revolution in England as a Source of Cultural Change* (New York: Scribner's Sons, 1970) p. 17.
11. Charles R. Morris, *A Time of Passion* (New York: Harper and Row, 1984) p. 230.
12. Daniel Bell, *The Cultural Contradictions of Capitalism* (New York: Basic Books, 1976) pp. 223–4.
13. Marvine Howe, *New York Times*, 5 November 1972.
14. Brazil is not alone in recognising the important role women play in modernising a developing society. The former president of Burkina Faso,

a West African republic, put women in one-quarter of the ministerial positions in his government. 'Development without the participation of women is like using only four fingers of your hand', President Thomas Sankara said. *New York Times*, 23 August 1987, p. 10.

15. Erich Fromm and Michael Maccoby, *Social Character in a Mexican Village* (Englewood Cliffs, New Jersey: Prentice-Hall, 1970) p. 18.
16. This is C. Wright Mills' summary of Talcott Parsons' position. See, *The Sociological Imagination* (New York: Oxford University Press, 1959) p. 31. A fuller presentation of the Parsonian position on the isomorphic relationship between social structure and personality can be found in, Talcott Parsons, *The Social System* (Glencoe, Illinois: The Free Press, 1951).

CHAPTER 2

1. George Murdock, 'Comparative Data on the Division of Labor by Sex', *Social Forces*, vol. 15 (May 1937) pp. 551–3.
2. Joan W. Scott and Louise A. Tilly, 'Women's Work and the Family in Nineteenth-Century Europe', in Alice H. Amsden (ed.) *The Economics of Women and Work* (New York: St Martin's Press, 1980) p. 101.
3. William M. Kephart, *The Family, Society, and the Individual* (Boston: Houghton Mifflin, 1977) p. 74.
4. Scott and Tilly, p. 105.
5. Edward Shorter, *The Making of the Modern Family* (New York: Basic Books, 1975).
6. William N. Stephens, *The Family in Cross-Cultural Perspective* (New York: Holt, Rinehart and Winston, 1963).
7. Bernard C. Rosen, *The Industrial Connection: Achievement and the Family in Developing Societies* (New York: Aldine Publishing, 1982).
8. Alice Kessler-Harris, *Out to Work: A History of Wage-Earning Women in the United States* (New York: Oxford University Press, 1982) p. 13.
9. Kessler-Harris, p. 48. See also, Julie A. Matthaei, *An Economic History of Women in America*, (New York: Schocken Books, 1982) pp. 198–203.
10. Scott and Tilly, p. 94.
11. Scott and Tilly, p. 84.
12. Bettina Berch, *The Endless Day: The Political Economy of Women and Work* (New York: Hascourt Brace Javanovich, 1982) p. 42.
13. The sources for these statistics are as follows. Alba M. Edwards, *Comparative Occupational Statistics for the United States, 1870–1940* (Washington, DC: US Bureau of the Census, 1943); Elyce J. Rotella, *From Home to Office* (Ann Arbor: UMI Research Press, 1981); Kessler-Harris, *Out to Work*; Matthaei, *An Economic History of Women; Women at Work: A Chartbook* (Washington DC: US Department of Labor, Bureau of Labor Statistics, Bulletin 2168, April 1983); The Wall Street Journal, *National Science Foundation Report*, 12 June 1984; Bureau of Labor Statistics, 'Employment and Earnings', vol. 34, no. 1, (January 1987).

14. Scott and Tilly, p. 92. See also L. A. Tilly and J. W. Scott, *Women, Work and Family* (New York: Rinehart and Winston, 1978).

15. Lee Holcombe, *Victorian Ladies at Work* (Hamden, Connecticut 1973) cited in Scott and Tilly, p. 93.

16. C. P. Blacker, 'Stages in Population Growth', *Eugenics Review*, vol. 39 (1947) pp. 88–102. See also, *The Determinants and Consequences of Population Trends*, vol. 1 (United Nations 1973). For more recent data, see H. S. Habakkuk, *Population Growth and Economic Development Since 1750* (Leicester: University of Leicester Press 1972); Ben J. Wattenberg, *The Birth Dearth* (New York: Pharos Books, 1987).

17. *National Center for Health Statistics Report*, September 1987. For an analysis of trends in divorce see J. Ross Eshlemann, *The Family* (Boston: Allyn and Bacon, Inc., 1985) pp. 576–97.

18. Walter Karp, *New York Times*, Book Review Section, 17 August 1986, p. 24.

19. In the United States, the position of young married people was especially difficult in the 1970s and the first half of the 1980s. Average weekly earnings, adjusted for inflation, declined 14.3 percent from 1973 to 1986. As a result, among couples aged 25–34, the percentage of women working outside the home soared in 1986 to 62 percent, twice the percentage in 1961. See, Steven Greenhouse, *New York Times*, Section 3, 13 July 1986.

20. *New York Times*, 29 June 1987, p. 7.

21. Victor Fuchs, *The Service Economy* (New York: Columbia University Press, 1968) p. 14.

22. Ronald K. Shelp, 'Giving the Service Economy a Bum Rap', *New York Times*, 17 May 1987; Louis Uchitelle, 'Service Sector Wage Issues', *New York Times*, 19 December 1986.

23. Samuel M. Ehrenhalt, 'Work-Force Shifts in the '80s', *New York Times*, 15 August 1986.

24. Yves Sabolo, *The Service Industries* (Geneva: International Labour Office, 1975); Joachim Singlemann, *From Agriculture to Services: The Transformation of Industrial Employment* (Beverly Hills: Sage Publications, 1978); Russell Lewes, *The New Service Economy* (London: Longman, 1973); *New York Times*, 26 January, 1986.

25. Daniel Bell, *The Coming of Post-Industrial Society: A Venture in Social Forecasting* (New York: Basic Books, 1973).

26. George Gilder, *Wealth and Poverty* (New York: Basic Books, 1981), p. 213.

27. Cited in Louis Uchitelle, 'Economic Scene', *New York Times*, 19 December 1986.

28. Beryl W. Sprinkel, 'Let's Not Torpedo the Growth of Jobs', *New York Times*, 5 June 1987.

29. Cited by Robert A. Bennet, *New York Times*, 20 June 1986.

30. Kessler-Harris, p. 231.

31. Berch, p. 5; Bureau of Labor Statistics, 'Employment and Earnings', vol. 34, no. 1 (1987).

32. OECD, *Historical Statistics*, (1983).

33. *Women at Work*, (Bureau of Labor Statistics, 1983) p. 22.

34. European Trade Union Confederation, *Women at Work: White Paper of Working Women in Europe* (Brussels: COODIFF, 1976) p. 29.

35. Berch, p. 9. The Census Bureau, The Bureau of Labor Statistics, and the House Committee on Children, Youth and Families, cited in *New York Times*, 25 November 1984 and 4 August 1985.
36. William Serrin, 'Experts Say Job Bias Against Women Persist', *New York Times*, 25 November 1984.
37. Berch, pp. 12–13.
38. US Bureau of the Census, The US Bureau of Labor Statistics, cited in *New York Times*, 25 November 1984 and 26 July 1987.
39. Quoted by William Serrin, *New York Times*, 25 November 1984.
40. US Bureau of the Census, US Bureau of Labor Statistics, *New York Times*, 4 August 1985.
41. Robert Pear, 'Women Reduce Lag in Earnings But Disparities With Men Remain', *New York Times*, 4 September 1987, citing September 1987 report of US Bureau of the Census.
42. Janet Norwood, *Monthly Labor Review* (December 1985) pp. 3–4; cited in Andrew Hacker, 'Women at Work', *New York Review of Books*, 14 August 1986, p. 29.
43. Cited by William Serrin, 'Shifts in Work Put White Men in the Minority', *New York Times*, 31 July 1984.
44. Bureau of Labour Statistics, July 1984, cited in W. Serrin, *New York Times*, 31 July 1984.

CHAPTER 3

1. For a discussion of human capital and its effects, see G. S. Becker, *Human Capital* (New York: National Bureau of Economic Research, 1964); P. England, 'The Failure of Human Capital Theory to Explain Occupational Sex Segregation', *Journal of Human Resources*, vol. 17 (1982) pp. 358–70; Martha Tienda, Shelley A. Smith and Vilma Ortiz, 'Industrial Restructuring, Gender Segregation, and Sex Differences in Earnings', *American Sociological Review* (April, 1987) pp. 195–209.
2. For a description of the social attitudes towards women in Brazil and elsewhere, past and present, see, Bernard C. Rosen, *The Industrial Connection: Achievement and the Family in Developing Societies* (New York: Aldine Publishing, 1982) Chapters 4 and 5; T. Lyn Smith, *Brazilian Society* (Albuquerque, New Mexico: University of New Mexico Press, 1974); Michelle Z. Rosaldo and Louise Lamphere, (eds) *Woman, Culture and Society* (Stanford: Stanford University Press, 1984); Amaury de Riencourt, *Sex and Power in History* (New York: Delta Publishing, 1974).
3. L. M. Terman and L. E. Tyler, 'Psychological Sex Differences', in L. Carmichael (ed.) *Manual of Child Psychology*, 2nd edn (New York): Wiley, 1954); A. Anastasi, *Differential Psychology*, 3rd edn (New York: Macmillan 1958).
4. E. E. Macoby, *The Development of Sex Differences* (Stanford: Stanford University Press, 1966); E. E. Maccoby and C. Jacklin, *The Pschology of Sex Differences* (Stanford: Stanford University Press, 1974).
5. Maccoby and Jacklin, p. 85.

6. Edward B. Fiske, 'American Students Score Average or Below in International Math Exams', *New York Times*, 23 September 1984, p. 20.

7. Debra R. Kaufman and Barbara L. Richardson, *Achievement and Women: Challenging the Assumptions* (New York: The Free Press, 1982) p. 7. For a review of research and theory on gender-related variables and academic performance, see Jacquelynne Eccles (Parsons), 'Expectancies, Values and Academic Behavior', in S. T. Spence (ed.) *Achievement and Achievement Motives* (San Franscisco: W. H. Freeman, 1983).

8. Cited in K. Patricia Cross, 'Women as New Students', in M. T. S. Mednick, S. S. Tangri and L. W. Hoffman, *Women and Achievement: Social and Motivational Analysis* (New York: Halsted Press, 1975) pp. 339–43.

9. Cross, p. 342.

10. Maccoby and Jacklin, p. 135. See also, Erkert Sumro, 'Exploring Sex Differences in Expectancy, Attribution and Academic Achievement', *Sex Roles*, vol. 6, nos. 2, (1983) pp. 217–31.

11. European Trade Union Confederation, *Women at Work* (Brussels: COODIFF, 1976); Alice H. Cook, Val R. Lorwins, and Arlene K. Daniels (eds) *Women and Trade Unions in Eleven Industrialized Countries* (Philadelphia: Temple University Press, 1984); OECD, Department of Economics and Statistics, Paris, 'Quarterly Labour Force Statistics', no. 2 (1987).

12. O. Duncan, D. Featherman, and B. Duncan, *Socioeconomic Background and Achievement* (New York: Seminar Press, 1972); W. Sewell, A. Haller and A. Portes, 'The Educational and Early Occupational Attainment Process', *American Sociological Review*, vol. 34 (1969) pp. 82–91.

13. We drew upon the following sources in developing a ranking system for occupational expectations. Peter M. Blau and Otis D. Duncan, *The American Occupational Structure* (New York: John Wiley and Sons 1967); John H. Goldthrope, *Social Mobility and Class Structure in Modern Britain* (Oxford: Clarendon Press, 1980); S. S. Acquaviva and Mario Santuccio, *Social Structures in Italy* (London: Martin Robertson, 1976).

14. For a discussion of women's movements in the United States, Britain, and Italy, see: B. Deckard, *The Women's Movement* (New York: Harper and Row, 1975); Ann Oakley, *Subject Women* (New York: Pantheon Books, 1981); Rosalba Spanoletti (ed.) *Movimento Feminista in Italia* (Rome: Savelli, 1978).

15. This comparison of American and British adolescents is taken from Christine M. Russell, 'Achievement and Socialisation of British and American Adolescents', PhD dissertation, Cornell University, 1983. See also L. Smith, 'Sexist and Female Delinquency', in B. Smart, *Women, Sexuality and Social Control* (London: George Allen and Unwin, 1980). For a study of achievement in British schools, see Olive Banks and Douglas Finlayson, *Success and Failure in the Secondary School* (London: Methuen 1973).

16. For an analysis of the Church's impact on Italian family life, see S., Acquaviva, C. Saraceno, E. Belotti, S. Rodota, E. Gorrieri, L. Cacrini, *Ritratto di Famiglia Negli Anni '80* (Roma: Editori Laterza, 1981).

CHAPTER 4

1. A concise review of sex role socialisation theories can be found in Shirley Weitz, *Sex Roles* (New York: Oxford University Press, 1977) Chapter 2; and in Irene H. Frieze, Jacquelynne E. Parsons, Paula B. Johnson, Diane N. Ruble, and Gail L. Zellman, *Women and Sex Roles* (New York: W. W. Norton 1978) Chapters 6 and 7. For a review of research on the relationship of sex role socialisation to occupational behaviour, see Jacquelynne S. Eccles and Lois Hoffmann, 'Sex Roles, Socialization, and Occupational Behavior', in H. W. Stevenson and A. E. Siegel (eds) *Research on Child Development and Social Policy*, vol. 1 (Chicago: University of Chicago Press, 1984), pp. 367–420.

2. Some of the material in this section draws upon my book, *The Industrial Connection* (New York: Aldine, 1982).

3. Walter G. Bennis and Philip E. Slater, *The Temporary Society* (New York: Harper and Row, 1968) p. 43.

4. Bennis and Slater, p. 37.

5. Eleanor E. Maccoby and Carol N. Jacklin, *The Psychology of Sex Differences* (Stanford: Stanford University Press, 1974); M. M. Marini, 'Sex Differences in the Determination of Adolescent Aspirations: A Review of Research', *Sex Roles*, vol. 4 (1978) pp. 723–53.

6. Janet H. Block, 'Issues, Problems, and Pitfalls in Assessing Sex Differences: A Critical Review of the Psychology of Sex Differences', *Merrill-Palmer Quarterly*, vol. 22 (1976) pp. 285–308; Althea C. Huston 'Sex Typing', in Paul H. Mussen (ed.) *Handbook of Child Psychology*, 4th edn, vol. IV entitled 'Socialisation, Personality, and Social Development', E. Mavis Heatherington (ed.) (New York: John Wiley 1985).

7. Margaret M. Marini and Mary C. Brinton, 'Sex Typing in Occupational Socialisation', in Barbara F. Reskin (ed.) *Sex Segregation in the Workplace* (Washington DC; National Academy Press 1984); Huston, 'Sex Typing'.

8. Sara Delamont, *The Sociology of Women* (London: Allen and Unwin, 1980) p. 78.

9. Delamont, pp. 38, 40. See also R. Deem, *Schooling for Women's Work* (Boston: Routledge and Kegan Paul, 1980).

10. J. Newson and E. Newson, *Seven Years Old in the Home Environment* (London: Allen and Unwin, 1976).

11. Rudolph Bell, *Fate and Honor, Family and Village* (Chicago: University of Chicago Press, 1979) p. 123; see also John Davis, *Land and Family in Pisticci* (London: Althone Press, 1973).

12. David P. Ausubel *et al.*, 'Perceived Parent Attitudes as Determinants of Children's Ego Structure', *Child Development* (September 1954) pp. 173–82.

13. A good summary of recent studies of the differential treatment by parents of sons and daughters can be found in Huston, pp. 429–32. See also J. H. Block, 'Another Look at Sex Differentiation in the Socialization Behaviour of Mothers and Fathers', in J. Sherman and F. L. Denmark (eds) *Psychology of Women: Future Directions of Research* (New York: Psychological Dimensions, 1979).

14. Lois W. Hoffmann, 'Effects on Child', in L. W. Hoffmann and F. I. Nye (eds) *Working Mothers* (San Franscisco: Josey-Bass, 1974) pp. 126–68; S. M. Miller,'Effects of Maternal Employment on Sex Role Perception, Interests and Self-Esteem in Kindergarten Girls', *Development Psychology*, vol. 11 (1975) pp. 405–6.

CHAPTER 5

1. The articulated antipathy of some men toward women antedates this comment by St Thomas Aquinas by many centuries. Thus Metellus Numidicus, The Roman censor, 'acknowledged to the Roman people in a public oration that had kind nature allowed us to exist without the help of women, we should be delivered from a very troublesome companion, and he would recommend matrimony only as the sacrifice of private pleasure to public duty', Edward Gibbon, *The Decline and Fall of the Roman Empire*, vol. 1 (New York: Modern Library, 1932) p. 130.
2. Will Durant, *The Story of Civilization: Part IV, The Age of Faith* (New York: Simon and Schuster, 1950) pp. 825–6.
3. Edward Shorter, *The Making of the Modern Family* (New York: Basic Books, 1975) p. 54.
4. Harry W. Hutchinson, *Village and Plantation Life in Northeastern Brazil* (Seattle, Washington: The University of Washington Press, 1957) p. 143.
5. Antonio Candido, 'A vida Familial do Caipira', *Sociologia*, vol. 16, no. 4 (October 1954) pp. 351–2.
6. Oscar Lewis, *Tepotzlan: Village Life in Mexico* (New York: Holt, Rinehart and Winston, 1960).
7. William N. Stephens, *The Family in Cross-Cultural Perspective* (New York: Holt, Rinehart and Winston, 1963).
8. Jean Lipmen-Blumen, *Gender Roles and Power* (Englewood Cliffs, New Jersey: Prentice-Hall, 1984) p. 76.
9. E. E. Maccoby and C. Jacklin, *The Psychology of Sex Differences* (Stanford: Stanford University Press, 1974).
10. Janet Block, 'Issues, Problems, and Pitfalls in Assessing Sex Differences: A Critical Review of *The Psychology of Sex Differences,*' *Merrill-Palmer Quarterly*, vol. 27 (1976) pp. 285–308.
11. Judith M. Bardwick, *Psychology of Women* (New York: Harper and Row, 1971) p. 155; Linda T. Stanford and Mary E. Donovan, *Women's Self-Esteem* (New York: Penguin Books, 1978).
12. Donald Pierson, *Cruz das Almas: A Brazilian Village*, Institute of Anthropology Publication No. 12 (Washington, DC: Smithsonian Institution 1948) pp. 135–6.
13. Pierson, p. 136.
14. Irene Frieze, *et al., Women and Sex Roles* (New York: W. W. Norton 1978) p. 59.
15. Frieze, *et al.,* p. 58.
16. Maccoby and Jacklin, pp. 152–3.
17. Pierson, pp. 135–6.

18. R. M. Oetzel, 'Annotated Bibliography and Classified Summary of Research in Sex Differences', in E. E. Maccoby (ed.) *The Development of Sex Differences* (Stanford: Stanford University Press 1966); Maccoby and Jacklin, *The Psychology of Sex Differences*; Block, 'Issues, Problems and Pitfalls in Assessing Sex Differences.'
19. Lipmen-Blumen, pp. 76–8.
20. Lipmen-Blumen, p. 57.
21. T. Tieger, 'On the Biological Basis of Sex Differences in Aggression', *Child Development*, vol. 51 (1980) pp. 943–63.
22. Diane Ruble, in Frieze, *et al., Women and Sex Roles*, p. 53.
23. Maccoby and Jacklin, p. 371.
24. Maccoby and Jacklin, p. 180.
25. Bernard C. Rosen, 'Social Class and the Child's Perception of the Parent', *Child Development* (December 1964) pp. 1147–53.

CHAPTER 6

1. Midge Decter, 'The Intelligent Woman's Guide to Feminism', *Policy Review* (Spring 1981) pp. 121–6.
2. Jean Lipmen-Blumen vividly describes these stereotypes (she calls them 'control myths') in her book, *Gender Roles and Power* (Englewood Cliffs, New Jersey: Prentice-Hall, 1984) Chapter 7.
3. Althea C. Huston, 'Sex-Typing', in H. Mussen (ed.) *Handbook of Child Psychology*, 4th edn, vol. IV entitled 'Socialization Personality and Social Development', E. Mavis Heatherington (ed.) (New York: John Wiley, 1985) p. 440.
4. Margaret M. Marini and Mary C. Brinton, 'Sex Typing in Occupational Socialization', in Barbara F. Reskin (ed.) *Sex Segregation in the Workplace* (Washington, DC: National Academy Press 1984) pp. 212–13.
5. For an analysis of the impact of the peer group on the adolescent's attitudes and behaviour, see Bernard C. Rosen, *Adolescence and Religion* (Cambridge: Schenkman Publishing, 1965).
6. Huston, 'Sex-Typing', p. 442.
7. This section draws upon the following sources: Bernard C. Rosen and Carol S. Aneshensel, 'The Chameleon Syndrome: A Social Psychological Dimension of the Female Sex Role', *Journal of Marriage and the Family* (November 1976) pp. 605–17; Christine M. Russell, 'Achievement and Socialization in British and American Adolescents', Cornell University doctoral dissertation, 1983.
8. US Census Reports, 27 May 1984, 30 March 1986. In 1987 the median age for first marriage for females was 23.6 years, as compared with 20.3 years in 1950. For men, the median age for the first marriage climbed to 25.8 years.
9. Judith Bardwick, *Psychology of Women: A Study of Pro-Cultural Conflicts* (New York: Harper and Row, 1971).
10. Inge K. Broverman, Susan R. Vogel, David M. Broverman, Frank E.

Clarkson, and Paul S. Rosenkrantz, 'Sex Role Stereotypes: A Current Appraisal', *Journal of Social Issues*, vol. 28 (1972) pp. 59–78.

11. J. H. Block, 'Conceptions of Sex Roles: Some Cross-Cultural and Longitudinal Perspectives', *American Psychologist*, vol. 28 (June 1973) pp. 512–26.

12. Lois W. Hoffmann, 'Early Childhood Experiences and Women's Achievement Motives', *Journal of Social Issues*, vol. 28 (1972) pp. 129–56.

13. J. Newson, and E. Newson, *Four Years Old in an Urban Community* (Harmondsworth: Pelican Books, 1968).

14. Ronald D. Lambert, *Sex Role Imagery in Children: Social Origins of Mind* (Ottawa: Studies of the Royal Commission of the Status of Women in Canada, 1971).

15. Clyde O. McDaniel, 'Dating Roles and Reasons for Dating', *Journal of Marriage and the Family* (February 1969) pp. 97–107.

CHAPTER 7

1. See, for example, K. L. Alexander and B. K. Alexander 'Sex Differences in the Educational Attainment Process', *American Sociological Review* (October 1974) pp. 668–82; W. H. Sewell and R. Hauser, *Education, Occupation, and Earnings: Achievement in Early Career* (New York: Academic Press, 1975); K. Alexander, B. Alexander, and L. Griffin, 'The Wisconsin Model of Socioeconomic Achievement: A Replication', *American Journal of Sociology* (September 1975) pp. 324–42.

2. A review of these studies can be found in M. M. Marini and M. C. Brinton, 'Sex Typing in Occupational Socialisation', in B. F. Reskin, (ed.) *Sex Segregation in the Workplace* (Washington, DC: National Academy Press, 1984) pp. 202–4.

3. Marini and Brinton, p. 200. See also Betina Berch, *The Endless Day: The Political Economy of Woman and Work* (New York: Harcourt Brace Jovanovich, 1982) Chapter 5.

4. Valarie Oppenheimer, 'The Sex Labeling of Jobs', *Industrial Relations* (May 1968) pp. 219–34.

5. M. Marini and E. Greenberger, 'Sex Differences in Occupational Aspirations and Expectations', *Sociology of Work and Occupations*, vol. 5 (1978) pp. 147–78.

6. L. B. Lueptow, 'Sex-typing and Change in the Occupational Choices of High School Seniors', *Sociology of Education*, vol. 54 (1981) pp. 16–24.

7. H. H. Garrison 'Gender Differences in the Career Aspirations of Recent Cohorts of High School Seniors', *Social Problems*, vol. 27, 1979, pp. 170–185.

8. A. R. Herzog, 'High School Seniors' Occupational Plans and Values: Trends in Sex Differences 1976 through 1980', *Sociology of Education*, vol. 55 (1982) pp. 1–13.

9. See, for example, W. H. Sewell and V. P. Shah, 'Socioeconomic Status, Intelligence and the Attainment of Higher Education', *Sociology of*

Education, vol. 40 (Winter), pp. 1–23; M. Hout and W. R. Morgan, 'Race and Sex Variations in the Causes of the Expected Attainments of High School Seniors', *American Journal of Sociology* (September 1975) pp. 364–94.

10. Christine E. Bose, *Jobs and Gender: Sex and Occupational Prestige* (Balimore: Center for Metropolitan Planning and Research, Johns Hopkins University, 1973).

11. D. J. Treiman and K. Terrell, 'Sex and the Process of Status Attainment: a Comparison of Working Men and Women', *American Sociological Review* (April 1975) pp. 174–200.

12. M. J. McClendon, 'The Occupational Status Attainment Process of Males and Females', *American Sociological Review*, February 1976, pp. 52–64; Alexander, Alexander and Griffin, 'The Wisconsin Model of Socioeconomic Achievement.'

13. The causal model and path analysis of the American data are drawn from a paper by Bernard C. Rosen and Carol Aneshensel, 'Sex Differences in the Educational–Occupational Expectation Process', *Social Forces* (September 1978) pp. 164–86. A path analysis of the Italian data appears in D. Capozza, A. M. Rattazzi, A. C. Tajoli, and B. C. Rosen, *Aspettative di Istruzione e Occupazione nei Grovani: Un analisi di adolescenti veneti* (Bologna: Quaderni di Psicologia, 12, Patron Editore, 1988).

14. See, for example, Otis D. Duncan, David L. Featherman, and Beverly Duncan, *Socioeconomic Background and Achievement* (New York: Seminar Press, 1972).

15. See Oppenheimer, 'The Sex Labeling of Jobs'.

CHAPTER 8

1. Donald Pierson, *Cruz das Almas: A Brazilian Village*, Institute of Anthropology Publication No. 12 (Washington, DC: Smithsonian Institution 1948) p. 79.

2. Margaret Mead, *Male and Female: A Study of the Sexes in a Changing World* (New York: William Morrow, 1949).

3. Pierson, p. 132.

4. Rudolph Bell, *Fate and Home, Family and Village* (Chicago: University of Chicago Press, 1979) p. 123.

5. John Davis, *Land and Family in Pisticci* (London: Althone Press, 1973) p. 52.

6. Davis, p. 43. Analyses of the Italian family appear in Laura Balbo, *Stato di Familiglia* (Estas Libri, 1976); and Chiara Saraceno, *Anatomia della Famiglia*, (de Donato, 1976).

7. Pierson, p. 131.

8. A relatively recent study of two-career couples found that domestic tasks continue to be divided in traditional ways. See *New York Times*, 27 June 1981. Even women who bring home more money than their husbands often end up doing the domestic chores. Thus a survey of women

executives in large American corporations reports that the wife assumes the primary responsibility for taking care of the children. See *Wall Street Journal*, 2 November 1982.

9. B. B. Polk and R. B. Stein, 'Is the Grass Greener on the Other Side?', in C. Safilios-Rothschild (ed.) *Toward a Sociology of Women* (Lexington, Massachusetts: Xerox, 1972) pp. 14–23. See also N. F. Russo, 'The Motherhood Mandate', *Journal of Social Issues*, vol. 32 (Summer 1976) pp. 143–54.

10. *New Yorker Magazine* 16 February 1987, p. 46.

11. This section draws upon a paper by Carol S. Aneshensel and Bernard C. Rosen, 'Domestic Roles and Sex Differences in Occupational Expectations', *Journal of Marriage and the Family* (February 1980) pp. 121–131.

12. C. R. Rao, *Linear Statistical Inference and its Applications*, 2nd edn (New York: Wiley, 1973); R. I. Jennrich, 'Stepwise Discriminant Analysis', in K. Enslein, A. Ralstan and H. F. Wiff (eds) *Statistical Methods for Digital Computers* (New York: Wiley, 1977).

Index

achievement, 2, 8, 14–15, 91, 211; and anger, 107; and the Chameleon Syndrome, 146; and educational–occupational expectations, 45–6; and human capital, 35–6; in industrial societies, 12–13, 85, 123, 211; and the IQ controversy, 37–9; and the mass media, 114; and mental ability, 175–6; non-academic, 47–8; and parental expectations, 176–7; and the perception of women, 10–11; in pre-industrial societies, 12; and self-esteem, 91–6, 163; sex differences in, 35, 51–6; and status attainment, 152; and stereotypes, 119

academic performance, and anger, 107; and parental expectation, 78–9; and self-assessment, 94, 178–9; sex differences in, 36–7, 43; and status attainment, 163, 175–6

achievement motivation, 86, 211

achiever, the, 12–13

aggressiveness, and the domestic role, 192; national differences in, 105–7; sex differences in, 86–8, 99, 210

Alexander, Lenora Cole, 32

Allen, Barry M., 30

Anastasi, A., 38

anger, and domestic roles, 192; national differences in, 105–7; sex differences in expression of, 99; uses of, 97–8

Ascot, 221

Ausubel, David, 65

Bardwick, Judith, 130

Bell, Daniel, 10, 29

Bell, Rudolph, 64

Binghamton, NY, 221

Block, Janet, 62, 63, 86, 99, 137

Brinton, Mary C., 63, 149

Bristol, 221

capitalism, 5, 10, 12, 159, 186

Caporotondo, 185

Chameleon Syndrome, and domestic orientation, 143–5; index of, 131–4; in marriage, 143; parental socialisation of, 136–9; and the peer group, 139–43; sex differences in, 134–6

child care centres, 189, 214–15

Common Market, (EEC), 29

Cruz das Almas, 89, 185

dating relationship, and the Chameleon Syndrome, 141–3; index of, 141

Davis, John, 185

Dector, Midge, 110

division of labour, 6, 10; in the home, 19–20, 187; in industrial societies, 182, 188, 190–1; in traditional societies, 183–4; in the workplace, 21–2, 185

divorce, 26–7

domestic orientation, 143; and the Chameleon Syndrome, 144–7; index of, 144; in traditional societies, 183–6

domestic roles; index of, 193; in the industrial system, 181–3; and occupational expectations, 191; and role conflict, 186–91; sex differences in, 194–5; in traditional societies, 183–6

domesticity, ideology of, 4

double standard, in role performance, 191

earnings gap, 33

educational expectations, 44; and anger, impact of grades on, 45–6; impact of mental ability on, 45–6; and independence, 94; index of, 153; and parental expectations, 78–80; and self-assessment, 94; sex differences in, 154–7; and sex role

socialisation, 76
Engles, Frederick, 5
equality, 10, 11, 109, 208, 211, 216;
  and domestic roles, 188, 192; in
  industrial societies, 117; as a
  value, 11, 211, 213
experiential chasm, between parent
  and child, 58–61

factory system, 21
family, and domestic roles, 181–2;
  cross-sex effects of, 172–4; and
  educational–occupational
  expectations, 163; and
  identification, 53; and sex roles,
  54–9; and sex role stereotypes,
  112; and status attainment, 170–1;
  structural changes in, 25–6
feminism, 23, 49, 208
Feminist Movement, 22–3
fertility, decline of, 26
Freedman, Audrey, 29
First World War, 49
Fromm, Erich, 14

Garrison, H. H., 152
Gilder, George, 29
Guilford's Test of Divergent
  Thinking, 39

Henley-on-Thames, 221
Herzog, A. R., 152
Hoffman, Lois, 72
Holcombe, Lee, 23
human capital theory, 35–6, 40
Huston, Althea, 62, 64

identification, and role modelling,
  71–3; theories of, 53
independence, 10, 85; and
  educational–occupational
  expectations, 80–1; and expression
  of anger, 106; index of, 67; and
  role conflict, 187; and self-
  assessment, 94–5; sex differences
  in, 118–19; training in, 66–70, 93,
  95, 106–7
individualism, 2, 10–11, 211

Industrial Revolution, 6–7, 11, 21,
  209
industrial value shift, 9–13
industrialisation, 2, 10; and domestic
  roles, 181–2, 187–8, 194; and
  educational–occupational
  expectations, 50–1; homogenising
  effects of, 126; impact on women,
  15–16, 24–7; and labour force
  participation, 209; negative effects
  and images of, 4–7; and
  personality, 16–17, 90; and sex
  roles, 197; and sex role
  socialisation, 55–7
intellectuals, hostility of to
  industrialisation, 5–6
Intelligence Quotient (IQ), effect on
  educational–occupational
  expectations, 45–6; measurement
  and controversy, 37–8; sex
  differences in, 39–41
isomorphism, 13; and the new
  women, 14–16

Jacklin, Carol, 38, 41, 62, 63, 86, 99,
  102
Jennrich, R. I., 206
Johnson City, 221

Karp, Walter, 27
Kessler-Harris, Alice, 21, 30

labour unions, 24
Lambert, Ronald D., 140
Langley, 221
Lewis, Oscar, 83
Leuptow, L. B., 152
Lipmen-Blumen, Jean, 85, 99, 100
London, 21
Lyon, 21

Maccoby, Eleanor, 38, 41, 62, 63,
  86, 99, 102
Maccoby, Michael, 14
McDaniel, Clyde O., 140
male dominance, 20–1, 83–4, 111–12
Manchester, 3
manufacturing, decline of, 28–9
Marrini, Margaret, 63, 149

marriage, attitudes toward, 131–2;
　　rates of, 131
Massachusetts, 3
mass media, and sex role
　　stereotypes, 115; as a socialisation
　　agency, 14, 85, 114, 211–12
mathematical skill, sex differences in,
　　39
mental ability, and educational
　　expectations, 176; measurement
　　of, 41–2; and self-assessment, 178;
　　sex differences in, 43–6
Metzger, Jack, 33
Milan, 3
Miller, S. M., 72
minority group, women as a, 109–10
Morris, Charles R., 9

National Women's Congress, Brazil,
　　11
new industrial family, 25–6
New York, 21
Newson, J. and E. Newson, 64, 137
Nissorini, 64
Norwood, Janet, 33
Nottingham, 64

occupational expectations, 44–5; and
　　anger, 106; and anticipated labour
　　force participation, 201–2;
　　congruence with occupational
　　attainment, 149; discriminant
　　analysis of, 204–6; impact of
　　grades on, 45–6; impact of mental
　　ability on, 45–6; and
　　independence, 95; and parental
　　expectations, 78–80, 176–8; and
　　self-assessment, 94; index of, 159;
　　sex differences in, 157–8, 201–2;
　　and sex roles, 160–2; and sex role
　　socialisation, 76; sex typing of,
　　149–51; of traditional females, 186
Oetzel, R. M., 99
Oxford, city of, 221; university of,
　　23

Padua, 222
parents, 14–15, 63; and the
　　Chameleon Syndrome, 136–9; and

educational–occupational
　　expectations, 163, 176–7; and
　　industrialisation, 55–7; and
　　grades, 78; mother–child
　　relationship, 62; perception of,
　　65–70; and role modelling, 71–6;
　　and personality development, 84;
　　and sex roles, 111–12, 212; and
　　status attainment, 170–1, 176–7
Parsons, Talcott, 14
peer group, 111, 175; and the
　　Chameleon Syndrome, 139; and
　　sex role stereotypes, 115; as a
　　socialisation agency, 85, 115–16
perception, index of, 77, 202; of
　　parental expectations, 78–80; of
　　parents, 65–70, 78–80; and
　　occupational choice, 205; of
　　opposite sex, 122–5; of sexism,
　　205
personality, and aggression, 86–8;
　　expression of anger, 99–107; and
　　the industrial system, 8–9, 16–17;
　　self-esteem, 89–96; sex differences
　　in, 82, 88; and sex role
　　stereotypes, 111; in traditional and
　　modern societies, 84–5, 210
Pierson, Donald, 185
pink ghetto, 2, 190
Pisticci, 185
Podhoretz, Norman, 6
prejudice, against women, 1, 109–10,
　　113
Project Talent, 41

questionnaire, 224–6

Randall, James R., 191
Rao, C. R., 206
Reading, 221
role conflict, 186–91
role modelling, and sex roles, 71–6;
　　and status expectations, 171–4;
　　and working mother's effect on
　　daughter, 174
Rome, 21
Ruble, Drane, 102

Sampling procedures, 223

school, and self-assessment, 178; as a
socialisation agency, 14, 85, 113–
15, 211–12
Scott, Joan W., 23
Second World War, 3, 4, 28, 31
self-assessment, and academic
ability, 178; and educational–
occupational expectations, 178–80;
sex differences in, 91–4
self-esteem, 88, 163; and academic
performance, 163; among
traditional women, 89–90; impact
of industrialisation on females,
111; in industrial societies, 95–6;
of modern women, 110; sex
differences in, 91–4, 163
service economy, appeal to women,
30–1, 186; and traditional women,
186–7
sex differences, in academic ability
and performance, 4, 36–7, 46; in
the Chameleon Syndrome, 134–6;
in domestic roles, 194–207; in
educational–occupational
expectations, 148–52, 154–64; in
the expression of anger, 99–108; in
IQ, 37–41; in non-academic
performance, 46–50; in perception
of opposite sex, 122–5; and role
modelling, 71–6; in self-esteem,
89–96; in sex role socialisation,
61–70; in sex role behaviour, 125–
8; in sex role stereotyping, 117–21;
in status attainment, 148–80
sex roles, 8–9, 11, 13, 51, 61, 87,
116, 150, 187; and behaviour,
125–8; changes in male, 215;
conformity to norms of, 112, 116;
and the division of labour, 52; and
domestic roles, 193–207; and
industrialisation, 197, 210–11; and
occupational expectations, 158,
191; and role modelling, 71–6; and
stereotypes, 113
sex role behaviour, and the
Chameleon Syndrome, 132–4; and
the service economy, 188; sex
differences in, 125–8
sex role socialisation, and

expectation levels, 76 81; and
independence training, 69–70; and
industrialisation, 55–7, 85;
parental part in, 57–61, 71–2; sex
differences in, 62–8; theories of,
52–3; through role modelling, 71–
6; in the traditional society, 54,
64, 68, 85, 101
sex role values, sex differences in,
198–9; index of, 195–6; and labour
force participation, 196–7
sex segregation, in social activities,
185–7; in the workplace, 184–5,
208, 211
Shorter, Edward, 20
Slough, 224
social norms, 14
social status, and the expression of
anger, 106; and self-assessment,
94; and status attainment, 165–70
socialism, 12–13, 187
Sprinkel, Beryl W., 30
Stanmore, 221
status attainment, and occupational
expectation level, 148; index of,
155; model of, 164–70; and mental
ability, 175–6; and parental
expectations, 177; relationship of
educational expectation to, 154,
156–7; and role modelling, 171–4;
and self-assessment, 178–9; and
sex, 157–63; and sex typing, 149–
52, 162, 190
Stephens, Williams, 20
Stereotypes, 109–111, 116, 158, 191;
and the Chameleon Syndrome,
140–3, 146; impact of
industrialisation upon, 113–14;
and labour force participation,
195; and the mass media, 115; and
modern adolescents, 116, 189–90;
and occupational expectations,
158; origins of, 112–13; sex
differences in, 117–21; and sex role
values, 197; and sex typing, 63
study design, 217–23
success, competition for, 13, 209

techno-service economy, 7, 209; rise

techno-service economy – *continued*
of, 27–9; and women, 31–3
technology, impact of on women,
23–5
Tepotzlan, 83
Terman, L. M., 38
Tilly, Louise A., 23
Tyler, L. E., 38

values, 8–9, 55; in industrial
societies, 12–13, 211; and sex
roles, 191; in traditional societies,
98
Verona, 22
Vestal, 221
victim, blaming the, 214

Welfare State, 7
women, changing status of, 208–9;
composition of in labour force,
32; discrimination against, 1, 2, 8,
35, 109, 179, 209; employed wives
with children, 32; enemies of, 82,
192; future jobs of, 33–4; and
human capital, 35–6; in industrial
societies, 181–2; in the labour
force, 3, 8, 10, 21–2, 24–7, 35, 162,
181; as objects of prejudice, 110–
11; in the service sector, 31, 186–7;
in traditional societies, 101, 151,
183–6
Women's Movement, 1, 3, 22–3, 208
working mothers, 9, 174